P9-CBQ-330

BIO CAMERON
Cameron, Julia.
Floor sample : a creative
memoir /

Floor Sample

Also by Julia Cameron

JEREMY P. TARCHER · PENGUIN
a member of Penguin Group (USA) Inc.
New York

Floor Sample

a creative memoir

Julia Cameron

JEREMY P. TARCHER/PENGUIN
Published by the Penguin Group
Penguin Group (USA) Inc., 375 Hudson Street, New York, New York 10014, USA •
Penguin Group (Canada), 90 Eglinton Avenue East, Suite 700, Toronto, Ontario M4P 2Y3,
Canada (a division of Pearson Penguin Canada Inc.) • Penguin Books Ltd, 80 Strand,
London WC2R 0RL, England • Penguin Ireland, 25 St Stephen's Green, Dublin 2, Ireland
(a division of Penguin Books Ltd) • Penguin Group (Australia), 250 Camberwell Road,
Camberwell, Victoria 3124, Australia (a division of Pearson Australia Group Pty Ltd) •
Penguin Books India Pvt Ltd, 11 Community Centre, Panchsheel Park, New Delhi–
110 017, India • Penguin Group (NZ), Cnr Airborne and Rosedale Roads, Albany,
Auckland 1310, New Zealand (a division of Pearson New Zealand Ltd) • Penguin Books
(South Africa) (Pty) Ltd, 24 Sturdee Avenue, Rosebank, Johannesburg 2196,
South Africa

Penguin Books Ltd, Registered Offices:
80 Strand, London WC2R 0RL, England

Most Tarcher/Penguin books are available at special quantity discounts for bulk purchase for
sales promotions, premiums, fund-raising, and educational needs. Special books or book ex-
cerpts also can be created to fit specific needs. For details, write Penguin Group (USA) Inc.
Special Markets, 375 Hudson Street, New York, NY 10014.

Library of Congress Cataloging-in-Publication Data

Cameron, Julia.
Floor sample : a creative memoir / by Julia Cameron.
p.   cm
ISBN 1-58542-494-3
1. Cameron, Julia.   2. Authors, American—20th century—Biography.   3. Creative
ability.   4. Creation (Literary, artistic, etc.).   I. Title.
PS3553.A4333Z466   2006
818'.5409—dc22   2005055965
[B]

Printed in the United States of America
1   3   5   7   9   10   8   6   4   2
This book is printed on acid-free paper. ∞

Book design by Claire Vaccaro

For those I have loved

Acknowledgements

I am deeply grateful to those who have shaped my life
and these pages.

WHY WE WRITE

There are many things which resist naming,
And that is why we write.
We write because language is slippery,
And the truth is.
We write because
The light we have to see by
Is always shifting

Never forget that writers are prophets.
We speak in tongues.
We testify.
We are for each other a believing mirror.
Our words make us visible.
Our listening makes us heard.

Never forget that writers are soldiers.
Our writing is the long march,
The walk into time.
Each word is a drum.
We sound it across great distances,
Reaching one another and ourselves.
Every poem is a day's march.
A celebration more necessary than water or wine.
Every poem is a drink of blood.

Never forget that writing is an act of courage—
Not on the days when it is simple and we discount it.
Not on the days when it is hard and we write like sand.
Our words are torches.
We pass them hand to hand
And mouth to mouth
Like a burning kiss.

Never forget to say thank you.
Every syllable is a grace.

J.C.

1.

The late afternoon sky is pewter. Wind whips through the Manhattan canyons. In Central Park, a single large gingko tree stands golden against the glowering clouds. Underfoot are the thickly fallen leaves of maple, oak, and ash. Gusts of wind send the leaves dancing. Dog owners like myself hurry their charges on their rounds. It is nearly Thanksgiving, and the dark comes early.

Perhaps because of all my school years, fall for me is a time of beginnings. The short, steep days send me tumbling into my past. I am fifty-seven years of age, neither old nor young. My life has swept me along on its tide, but now, at the midpoint, it is time to pick my way along the shoreline, to see what of value has been washed up, which mementos should be pocketed and which cast aside. Mine has been a turbulent life. But it did not start out that way.

I grew up in Libertyville, Illinois, in a large yellow house in the woods. An oversized, overstuffed English cottage, the house was made of fieldstone and wood. Cold pried at the windows. Dark gathered in the surrounding trees. As early as late September, fires were built in the three fireplaces to ward off the chill. Just outside the front door stood a large maple tree. When its leaves turned crimson, my mother would carefully press the best between sheets of waxed paper. These leaves were then tacked on our kitchen bulletin board amid vivid charcoal drawings of Halloween.

Fall was fierce, but my mother domesticated it. As the wind stripped the trees, my mother made simmering pots of vegetable soup. She baked shortbreads and berry pies. As early as October, she began her holiday baking, filling the downstairs freezer with a dozen different Christmas cookies, divinity, and fudge.

"Let's go to your house," my school friends would say. Of course they did. Homemade cookies and frosty milk were staple after-school fare. If we felt daring, we raided the freezer. Christmas cookies tasted best a month or two before their time. "Who's been after the Christmas cookies?" my mother would interrogate us, but she always seemed secretly pleased by the chance to bake some more.

When winter displaced fall, reading spots in front of the fireplaces were at a premium. The best locale was in our living room. There the reader could loll on thick café-au-lait carpeting. A mesh screen protected errant bookworms from flying sparks. Prodded by a wrought-iron poker, the fire could be built to a snapping roar, so hot that clothing singed. "Don't crawl in the fire," my mother would warn. Pajamas were the favored gear. What could be more idyllic than flannel pajamas and a new volume of Nancy Drew? Even better, the latest volume by Marguerite Henry, *Misty of Chincoteague, Sea Star, Brighty of the Grand Canyon,* or *King of the Wind.* Ours was a house filled with books.

Just off the kitchen, the den was a snug reading room with

floor-to-ceiling bookcases. Here were found the classics: *Crime and Punishment, A Tale of Two Cities, Oliver Twist, Gulliver's Travels,* and rows more. The books in this room were leather-bound and gleamed in the light of the brass lamp that hung suspended from the ceiling. An overstuffed sofa, ideal for sprawling, ran wall to wall, bookcase to window. The only other furniture was Mother's writing desk and a straight-backed chair.

It was in the den that I first discovered Lawrence of Arabia, striding through the pages of his memoirs. His hot Arabia was accompanied by cool jazz. Hidden behind a magic wooden panel, the stereo played Dave Brubeck for my father or, if my mother did the programming, "The Nutcracker Suite." I went through an obsessive phase when all I wanted to hear was Ravel's "Bolero." I choreographed my sisters and brothers dancing and dying. "Either change the music or change the ending," my mother pressed me. I went back to reading.

Upstairs, in the long hallway that ran between the bedrooms, there was another floor-to-ceiling bookcase—and this one not for classics. Here was the family cache of mysteries and big, popular potboilers like *Exodus, The Listener,* and *Dear and Glorious Physician.* Here was my brothers' stash of Hardy Boys and my older sister Connie's Nancy Drews. I do not know that I read every book, but I do know that I tried. I still remember the guilty exhilaration I felt racing through the Reader's Digest condensed books, three tales to a volume.

Augmenting the books we owned were the books we borrowed. Once weekly my mother would load us in the car, a navy blue Vista Cruiser station wagon, and drive us the two miles to Cook Memorial Library, where we were allowed to take out fourteen books apiece, two per day. The library was a mansion donated to the village. It rose snowy white and stately amid splendid rose gardens. Outside and in, it was a place of enchantment. The horse books were upstairs on the second floor, front. There, Walter Farley reigned supreme: *The Black Stallion, The Island Stallion, The Island Stallion Races* . . . I read them all.

I had a limitless appetite for horse books, and for books of all stripes, for that matter. As a precocious sixth-grader, I got in trouble with the vigilant checkout lady. She thought I was far too young to be reading *Auntie Mame*. I remember my shock and pride when my mother stood up for me. "Julie is allowed to read what she wants," my mother told the clearly disapproving matron behind the desk. And so I learned of the profligate Mame and her secretary, Agnes Gooch, pregnant out of wedlock.

Reading about pregnancy was one thing; seeing a movie about it was quite another. Books had the legitimacy of being books. Movies were more lurid. During my teen years, the Legion of Decency graded every movie that went into major release. As young Catholics, we were allowed to see the A films and strongly cautioned against the Bs. (The few notorious films that were C were completely beyond the realm of possibility.) Our village theater, the Liberty, prided itself on family entertainment. It showed only As. Catholics went to see As.

Protestants were allowed to see whatever films they chose—A through C. My closest girlfriend, Lynnie Lane, was a Protestant. To be specific, she was a Christian Scientist. I was fascinated by the difference in our religions. Hers seemed so much friendlier than mine. She didn't believe in hell and Satan. When I would tell her what the nuns were teaching us, she would laugh and dismiss it as scary hokum, "Catholic tales." For my part, I was torn between embracing Lynnie's viewpoint and believing the nuns—the nuns seemed so positive about what they believed.

I was in second grade when a nun briskly informed me that Lynnie could not go to heaven because she had never been baptized. For good measure, she added that animals had no souls and wouldn't be joining us in the afterlife either. "Sister, you're wrong!" I piped up. The class was flabbergasted. No one ever said, "Sister you are wrong!" But I knew she was wrong about heaven and Lynnie.

From my perspective, Lynnie herself was heaven. My mother worried that I was under her spell—a Protestant spell—and I was. She was a born storyteller, and to spend time with her was to enter the enchanted kingdom. She had a horse, Hotnote, a chestnut mare, and I had a small bay pony, Chico. Although barely that tall himself, Chico could jump well over four feet. So could Hotnote. We jumped our horses bareback and no-handed. We raced through twisting woodland trails—daredevil riders. In Lynnie's imagination our horses were Arabian chargers. We were exotic slaves. When we weren't being slaves, we ran off to join the circus, practicing riding bareback, no-handed, and even standing. No nun was powerful enough to disenchant me with Lynnie.

Together we formed a club called The Roughriders. To belong, you had to be a daredevil and a tomboy. Initiation involved swimming your horse across the Des Plaines River—home to water moccasins, we claimed—and sinking yourself neck deep in the muck of the swamp. In the years that we ran The Roughriders, no one ever made it past initiation and into the club itself. It was really just for me and Lynnie. We shared everything. Even boyfriends. I "gave" Lynnie Joe Thomas. She loaned me Skippy Creguire.

It was in Lynnie's musty hay-barn that I played spin the bottle and received my first real kiss from Skippy, Lynnie's official boyfriend. If Skippy wasn't exactly Prince Charming, he was close enough.

With a little embroidery from Lynnie's ever-present imagination, he did nicely. With just a pinch of imagination, everything did nicely.

Lynnie was six inches taller than I was and she had a mane of thick chestnut hair. She looked like a Thoroughbred, we would joke. I looked like an Arabian. She would toss that mane like a wild horse's as she sang anthems from Rodgers and Hammerstein, strumming enthusiastically away at her guitar. Lynnie was nothing if not fierce as she trumpeted, "Climb every mountain . . ." and "When you walk through a storm/Hold your head up high . . ."

I told Lynnie stories of saints, angels, and devils. There was St. Lucy, whose eyes got poked out. And St. Agnes, crucified upside down. Lynnie's Christian Scientist mother was horrified. From her perspective, mine was a primitive religion. She didn't want Lynnie getting contaminated. From my perspective, her religion was like no religion at all. Why, sin barely entered the picture. Kisses were kisses, not venial sins, and by the time Lynnie moved from Libertyville to Lake Forest at age twelve—a catastrophe in my world—mortal sins seemed hard to conjure as well.

I went to stay at Lynnie's nearly every weekend. Friday afternoons, we would rendezvous at Kraft Pharmacy, where they made delicious bacon, lettuce, and tomato sandwiches. More Fridays than I care to remember, I would forget that it was Friday, forget that meat was forbidden, and order a scrumptious triple-decker club. Yes, weekends at Lynnie's my Catholicism seemed far away.

The Deerpath Theater, in sophisticated Lake Forest, Lynnie's new town, featured more cosmopolitan movie fare than we had back in Libertyville. It was there, seated in the third row of the balcony amid the smells of popcorn and Eau Savage cologne, that I saw *A Summer Place*—a B movie in which Sandra Dee yields her virginity to Troy Donahue. Her resulting pregnancy was far more disturbing than that of Agnes Gooch. Gooch, after all, lived in New York, where anything, including pregnancy, could happen. Alarmingly Sandra Dee got pregnant in a small town not so different from our own.

In the movies, there were bad girls and good girls, and the same was true in real life. Bad girls flirted and "put out." Good girls flirted and did not put out. Cheerleaders were the only girls who seemed to straddle the line. They were good girls who pranced and preened like bad girls but to the approving applause of the crowds.

Clad in formfitting letter sweaters and satin-lined skirts, they flaunted what they had. Cartwheeling and doing splits, they were overtly sexual, but all in the name of "school spirit." Egging the team on to victory, they could kick like a cancan line and then finish their routine off with a pyramid and a casual back flip. You weren't supposed to notice that cheerleaders were sexy, but they were. They had charisma. Peggy Conroy, Joyce Bork, Debbie Hobson—these were names to conjure with. Forty-five years later, I can still remember that Joyce Bork was the first girl in our crowd to "need" a bra. Once Joyce got one, Peggy and Debbie quickly followed suit—and then the rest of us, lagging behind, not wanting to look too "fast."

We were anything but fast. There were eighty-five girls in the Carmel High School for Girls' first graduating class—and not a single unwanted pregnancy. We didn't drink, we didn't smoke, and our make-out sessions were limited to seniors-only parties with the parents right upstairs. Our knowledge of sex was largely theoretical: that B movie with Sandra Dee; the lingering shame down through the centuries of Mary Magdalene. At Carmel, where we had a boys' high school as well, devoted couples went steady and in doing so invited speculation. How long would Sue be able to hold out against Bill's advances? The fact was that the Carmelite priests held a tight rein on the Carmel high school boys. Bill was being watched, and he knew it. We all knew it.

If the boys were watched, and the girls were watched over, no one talked about the sexual subtext that existed between the girls and the young priests who were our confessors. Father Elliot, Father Bryan, Father Fintan, Father Chester—the priests were virile thirty-year-olds. We told them everything—impure thoughts and impure deeds. They gave us penance and went on their way, carrying our burdens. Did any one of us dare to say that the priests themselves were the objects of our desire? I doubt it. And yet Father Elliot was the recipient of heated attention. Tall, dark, long-lashed, and handsome, he had a sensitive nature that made him an ideal confessor for tremulous adolescent girls. He listened with such acuity and attention that it was hypnotic. Confession was an erotic rite of passage. The priests, self-contained and inviolate. The young girls, all whispers and yearning. Who could ignore the masculine appeal of the young priests? Far from solemn and repressed, they played basketball with the boys. They wore loose-fitting, coarse-woven habits belted low across the hips. A sinewy forearm would shoot out of the folds of cloth. Swoosh, the ball would fly through the net. The priests always scored.

By the time I was sixteen, I was reading Teilhard de Chardin and Paul Tillich. I was striving to find a God I could believe in, one concerned with more than the As, Bs, and Cs of the diocesan movie code. Surely God had larger concerns than that? Paul Tillich thought he did. He called God "the ground of being," and I craved a God that would give me a sense of grounding.

My junior year, the Carmelite priests supplied a retreat master who would answer all of our questions about faith. I remember sitting in the small auditorium, listening to him say, "And so, heaven, you see, would be like watching God on the silver screen seated next to your mother." I was horrified. I muttered my discontent to the other girls at break. "But he's so handsome," they breathed back, missing my point entirely. Handsome wasn't enough for me, I groused.

Word of my unrest reached Sister Mary Cecil, our principal. I was called into her office, a troublemaker. "You're so unhappy," she said. "There's no pleasing you, and now you're getting the other girls upset." Stoop-shouldered and kindly, she had only my best interests at heart. It was possible, she felt, that I needed the services of a psychiatrist. My God concept needed adjusting, and so, for my own good and the good of my immortal soul, I was sent to see Sister Marie Raymond, a one-hundred-forty-mile round trip to be made every Thursday afternoon after school. There was no question that I would do it.

Sister Marie Raymond, both a Sister of Charity and a psychiatrist, held a residency at St. Xavier's College, a campus on the far south side of Chicago. To get there, I drove the tristate toll road. There were seven toll booths each direction. I would drive through at perhaps thirty miles per hour and catch the toll basket with a well-flung quarter. I prided myself on my toss. I prided myself, too, on my honesty with Sister Marie Raymond. I told her of my disbelief in the cozy God I was being taught. Surely God was larger than the nuns and priests were letting on? Surely God must have some answers to supply, some balm for my tormented feelings of emptiness? Sister Marie Raymond wasn't shocked by my angst. She implied that it was part of the spiritual path.

"There's nothing really wrong with you." I remember Sister Marie Raymond's considered opinion. "You are just smart." Being "just smart" had made me into an agnostic. I couldn't believe in God as told to me by the nuns and priests. Surely there was something to their vocation that they were not telling us? Surely they believed in something more substantial than God on the silver screen? Every day in the school library, I read Paul Tillich and tried to fit his teachings to my life. Grappling with my spiritual turmoil, I looked for answers in the busy, seemingly happy lives of those all around me.

Sister Mary Elizabeth, who worked part-time for NASA, taught us calculus and seemed to believe in a God of higher mathematics. Sister Julia Clare, who taught us English, mentioned only her devotion to Shelley, Wordsworth, and Keats. God was implied in her classroom by a love of beauty. We studied poem after poem as if all the meaning of life could be found distilled in the beautiful lines. Was God a poet?

Forty years later, I am still in touch with Sister Julia Clare. Ninety-two and going strong, she has made a whole life out of the love of words and beauty. When I write well, I get an excited note from her. "How I wish I'd had this book of yours when I was thirty-five," she generously writes to me. Sister Julia Clare is kind—and determined to throw a wide enough net to catch us all.

The influence of Carmel is hard to shake. Take the ideal of modesty. Our uniforms were long plaid skirts and shapeless navy blue blazers worn over wide-collared white blouses. Four decades later, a best-selling author, I still go out to teach wearing ankle-length skirts in somber, subdued colors. I still wear shoes any nun would be proud of. My jackets diminish any curves. Make no mistake, my teaching persona is Mother Abbess incarnate. Sexuality has no place in the classroom. I learned this from the young nuns who taught us. Lesson learned, I pass it on.

"We learned about sexuality from women who gave all that up," jokes my friend Julianna McCarthy. She is not kidding. Catholicism lingers. Seated at the head of a boardroom table, surrounded by attractive men, I do not flirt. My attention is on the topic at hand. The nuns have taught me how to be focused.

The year I craved a personal God, our theology teacher, Sister Mary Benedicta, focused us instead on maps of the Holy Land. She drew arrows to indicate the migrations of the twelve tribes. To her, the parting of the Red Sea was no metaphor. She firmly taught and firmly believed the Bible was grounded in historical fact. But the facts seemed distant and far removed from any idea of a working faith. I needed a God I could talk to.

I wanted a God as intense and personal as my spiritual questioning. I wanted a God who just plain liked me. Running for student body president, I concocted a poster of Christ rising from the dead. On his billowing tunic he wore a campaign button that read "I like Julie." Under his ascending feet ran the logo "Continue a proud tradition. Vote for J.C."

I thought the poster was hilarious. I liked pointing out the fact that Christ and I shared the same initials. Sister Mary Benedicta thought my poster was sacrilegious. She wanted it torn down immediately. "I can't believe in a God who has no sense of humor," I protested. But clearly my own sense of humor was pushing the envelope. My posters were taken down. I lost the election to Marie Crovetti, who ran a far more conventional campaign.

"I'd always decide you were right about something later," one classmate told me. "But at the time that you first did something, I was always just plain scared by you. You were outrageous."

At Carmel High School for Girls, we were not supposed to be outrageous. We were being raised to be ladies, not women. We did not have sex drives or even urges. We learned the proper protocol for sexuality: arm's length. Once a year, on Sadie Hawkins Day, a Carmel girl might be forward enough to ask out the boy of her choosing. My senior year, I chose John Kane, a boy a year younger than I. This choice created a mini-scandal. Protocol decreed that the boy should be the same age or older. The fact that John Kane was brilliant and very funny, the fact that he knew all of the Beatles' lyrics, plus all of the Rolling Stones', and all of Bob Dylan's never quite offset the damning fact of his age. How did I dare ask him out?

How could I not?

Then, as now, I thought that sex appeal came down to brains. Smart was simply sexy and John Kane was very, very, very smart. When it came time for him to take his College Boards, he scored 800 on both math and verbal, an unheard-of feat. Equally dazzling, he wore a khaki-colored corduroy jacket with epaulets on the shoulders like Paul McCartney's. His wire-rimmed glasses and ready wit already lent him a passing resemblance to John Lennon. I noticed and appreciated all of this.

Sadie Hawkins Day led to a full-fledged romance between John and me. (I would date him all through college and beyond.) We would drive my father's MG roadster to Lake Michigan, park on the rocky beach, plunge into the icy waters, and declare ourselves "Free!" shouting at the top of our lungs. Free to read *The Catcher in the Rye* and *The Sun Also Rises.* Free to imagine the writer's life. Free to try our own hand at writing.

John Kane was my first experience of the muse. Knowing John, knowing his love of good writing, I resolved to become a better writer myself, to write something he would deem worthy. Of course, my notions of what good writing could be were limited to imitations of the "great" writers we had read and read about. And my notions of what the writer's life could be also mirrored my favorite authors. I thought real writers drank scotch neat and smoked unfiltered cigarettes. Like many others, I confused alcoholism with creativity. I read of Hemingway's suicide and I blamed it not on drinking but on writer's block. My notions of the literary life came straight out of F. Scott Fitzgerald's legendary battles with the bottle. I read Hemingway's *A Moveable Feast* and concluded that the feast moved bar to bar.

I desperately wanted to be a literary femme fatale. I longed to pattern myself after Lillian Hellman and Dorothy Parker. I wanted to be known for my wit and not my beauty. It all seemed possible. After all, John Kane was as dashing as Dashiell Hammett, wasn't he?

Side by side, John Kane and I worked on the student newspaper, *Crossroads*. Under the watchful eye of Sister Julia Clare, we honed our prose and our flirting skills. I remember John with a number-two pencil stuck behind one ear, his shirtsleeves rolled up, and his brow furrowed in concentration. He was a genius at layout. I marveled at his skills.

Together, tutored by books like Hellman's memoir, *Pentimento*, John and I practiced adult literary personas. We both read *The New Yorker* faithfully, keeping up-to-date on the literary goings-on in Manhattan. From our distant midwestern vantage point, we talked a big game and couldn't wait to be able to follow it up, to escape to adult life, meaning college in the East. John would escape to Yale. My parents told me I could go wherever I wanted as long as it was Jesuit. I applied to Georgetown University, hoping for a rejection so I could go to Radcliffe, but instead I was granted early admission.

With my college choice settled early on, I spent a restless senior year. I was a straight-A student, the class salutatorian, behind Sue Venn. Sue was a good girl, and I was a bad girl waiting to happen. Officially virtuous but actually curious, I caught the eye of one of the teachers, who plied me with bourbon and hashish one spring night. Both substances seemed exotic to me and a little dangerous, although not as dangerous as the teacher himself. His attention thrilled and rattled me. After a few drinks, I took myself to bed, alone but no longer such an innocent.

Early the next morning, hungover, I rear-ended a car on the way to school to take my College Boards. I scored well on them despite my misadventure. I do not remember what I told my parents about my accident. The possibility that I was drinking never came up. In our house drinking was something that adults did—and discreetly. My mother offered both of my brothers a thousand dollars apiece if they would refrain from drinking, but it never occurred to her to make the same offer to any of her five girls. We were, after all, young ladies, and "ladies" didn't drink.

In retrospect, it is easy to see that a few words of caution might have been timely. My beloved grandfather Daddy Howard was a drinker, and my mother well knew the pain that his drinking had caused. A virtual teetotaler herself, she kept a watchful eye on my father's drinking, but it was moderate, unlike his father's. Drugs were a second lecture that went ungiven. If my parents had known that my teacher had hashish, they would not have known what it was. In Libertyville, Illinois, the sixties were a rumbling upon the distant horizon. Hippies and Haight-Ashbury were things you could read about in magazines. Underage drinking was another remote possibility, something that happened in the big city, not in our small town. I was so sheltered, I didn't know I was sheltered. My sole risqué adventure was reading *Lady Chatterley's Lover*, given to me by the wayward teacher. I didn't find the book erotic. Erotic was kissing with John.

At eighteen years of age I went east to school. Georgetown, in Washington, D.C., was a drinker's paradise. The varsity sport in those days was polo. To attend a game, you carried a flask—or perhaps lugged along an entire cooler. Liquor to lips, there you were, the epitome of sophistication as the polo ponies harried back and forth mere feet from where you were standing. Drinking white wine spritzers, I had my first alcoholic blackout. A blackout is a period where although the drinker appears to be acting normally, his or her memory ceases to record. Blackouts are a symptom of alcoholism and may last moments or days. Of course, I didn't know any of this.

One moment I was sipping a chilled drink, waiting for the bus to arrive that would take us to the game; the next thing I knew I "came to" riding in the back of a school bus on the way home after the game and talking with a strange boy—also doubtless under the influence. He was assuring me that virginity was a renewable option, that "it grew back after five years." This same boy later went on to enter the priesthood, and I often joked that his level of misinformation was about "par for the course."

At Georgetown, where students were groomed to enter the diplomatic corps, we politely ignored the sixties. No tie-dye and dreadlocks for us. Not even any blue jeans. Instead, we wore cocktail clothes and learned how to make polite cocktail-party conversation. There was no such thing as small talk, only small minds. I was educated to talk to anyone about anything. Along with the conversation came the actual cocktails, and we quickly moved on from wine spritzers. My favorite drink was scotch: J&B on the rocks. The third one always hit like a spiritual experience, transfusing me with benevolence. Under the influence of J&B, the world became a friendly and interesting place. People became friendly and interesting too. They say that alcohol releases inhibitions, and so it does. Drinking, I happily surrendered my virginity to a tall, handsome actor. Drinking, I imagined myself the femme fatale I aspired to be. With a drink in my hand, I was a cosmopolitan citizen of the world. Sex was possible, even probable—no mean trick for a Catholic girl. The Pill was newly available. I got my first prescription with the help of a worldly Jesuit priest who accurately took my measure and decided that the Pill was preferable to pregnancy. Thank God for the Jesuit construct of "situation ethics"!

I belonged to the campus theater troupe, Mask and Bauble. We were a gang of misfits, reading Edward Albee and Harold Pinter. There, under the doting eye of Professor Donn Murphy, I danced center on the kick line in each year's original musical. Our costumes were skimpy and our lyrics often naughty. We were pushing the Jesuit envelope, staging productions of plays such as *Marat/Sade*. It was in Mask and Bauble that I first met director Jack Hofsiss, then a gangly schoolboy, destined to become a Tony Award winner for his legendary production of *The Elephant Man*. It was also in Mask and Bauble that I became the friend and confidante of Tray Mongue, who would later become very famous as the gay pornographer Christopher Rage.

"There's something you should know about me," Tray told me the very first day we met. "I am a homosexual."

"So?" I responded. I knew all about homosexuality from reading James Baldwin's novel *Giovanni's Room*.

"I remember you and Tray making a grand entrance into a party I was at," recalls Jack Hofsiss. "You were carrying a flask. It was all very racy. It turned out that the flask contained chocolate milk, but I was impressed."

Most evenings I drank something stronger than chocolate milk. Georgetown was surrounded with student bars, and many of the upperclassmen worked as bartenders. Apple Pie and Clyde's were two chic drinking establishments. I was a regular at both of them. To me, it was a point of pride that the bartender knew my drink of choice. While bars were sexual hunting grounds, I was there to drink, and drink I did. Bartenders knew enough to tell sexual predators that I was off-limits. Most of them enjoyed having a pretty girl mascot. I would sit at the bar or a small table for two and I would read or write. To me, writing and drinking went together. I would nurse my scotch and read *The New Yorker*. In a sense, I was isolated in the midst of company. Other than *The New Yorker*, I read Camus and Sartre, past masters both at spiritual malaise and alienation. Their darkness called to my own. I often read and wrote until last call.

Although I certainly didn't know it was a diagnostic symptom of alcoholism, I continued to experience the phenomenon of blacking out—after a certain number of drinks, never a predictable number, my memory simply stopped recording. We could have a wonderful conversation. We could enjoy a great connection. I could be witty and flirtatious and "yours"—and the next morning I would recall none of it.

"You really had blackouts?" marvels my college friend Gerard Hackett. "You never seemed drunk to me. You never got sloppy or maudlin or dramatic." Maybe not—not yet—but drunk I was. While Gerard would nurse one drink or perhaps two in an evening, I would order doubles and then double that. If Gerard drank one or two nights a week, I drank nightly. You would think that my grade point average would reflect this, but no. I continued to make the dean's list.

While the rest of the country quaked and shook with the political turmoil of the sixties, Georgetown largely remained frozen in the fifties. Sexual roles were rigid and rigorously enforced. Georgetown was reluctantly coed. There were still two codes of standards, one for the boys and one for the girls. As a girl, I had an early curfew and a dress code to contend with. Trousers—especially blue jeans—were not allowed. Also off-limits were certain coveted majors. I entered Georgetown as an Italian major but very quickly wanted to transfer to English. I was informed it was not possible.

"Boys become writers. Girls become wives," one Jesuit gravely told me. Listening to him, I decided to do what seemed appropriate and necessary, namely, transfer schools. One more time my choice was limited to Jesuit institutions. Not wanting to go home to Marquette in the Midwest, I chose Fordham. I would spend my junior year abroad in the Bronx—territory easily as foreign as Paris.

At Fordham, I did not live on campus. Instead, I rented a lonely room from a crabby landlady. The room had a large oak tree outside its window. If I left the window open, a rambunctious squirrel would cross the sill and scamper across my writing desk. Through the open window, I could always smell freshly baked bread from a nearby Italian bakery. My rooming house on Adee Avenue wasn't far from a train line to school, but most mornings I rode my bike, balancing my books carefully in the basket.

At Fordham they were serious about learning. Most students were first-generation collegiates, and they took to their classes with passion and intensity. They took to their drinking that way as well—at least the crowd I gravitated toward did. As at Georgetown, the campus was ringed with bars like the Pennywhistle Pub, but I quickly found that in the Bronx there were such things as "after hours" clubs, where the drinking continued until dawn. This suited me perfectly—particularly once I made the acquaintance of John Woodruff, a wild and handsome young Irishman who could, it seemed, match me drink for drink.

Like me, Woodruff was a young writer. Encouraged by him, I submitted poems to the college magazine, where they were promptly published. Now I had something to show for my troubles. Back at Georgetown, when I had approached the newspaper about writing for it, the young male editor had inquired, "Can you bake cookies?" I could bake cookies, but no one asked me to that year in the Bronx. I seemed to be accepted as a young writer, the identity I chose for myself.

Despite my drinking, I managed to achieve straight As both semesters at Fordham. With this as a bargaining card, I reapproached Georgetown. Were they certain that they wouldn't accept me back as an English major? "This is against my better judgment," said the Jesuit dean as he reluctantly relented and welcomed me back to the fold. A thankless girl and a born troublemaker, I repaid him for his kindness by promptly founding a feminist think tank that quickly leveled the charge of sexism at the Jesuits.

To say that my image was confused was to state the case mildly. "You were the campus wet dream," a friend of mine told me about twenty years after we graduated. Had I known, I could have enjoyed it.

"I thought I was Lillian Hellman," I protested.

"Hell, no. You were too pretty. Maybe Lillian Gish."

They say that what we don't know can't hurt us, and so my self-image in my college years was that of a fearless intellectual, not a beauty. "You'd make a first-rate theologian—except that you're a girl," one Jesuit advised me dolefully. And then, insult was added to injury: I was nominated for homecoming queen. This didn't mesh with my self-image at all. Lillian Hellman was not a pinup. I withdrew my name from the list.

I wanted to be a woman of letters. I longed for a literary life. Back home in Libertyville, for one interminable summer, I spent my stir-crazy evenings writing long, long handwritten letters back east to Nick Cariello, the smartest boy in my English class. Every day I filled page after page with my observations. What did Nick think of these daily missives? ("Oh, I liked them" is all he ever said.) Like John Kane before him, Nick was a muse for me, and words, all sorts of words, were the result.

I am not certain when I decided that I would be a writer. Rather than deciding, I think that I became one simply through the doing. I wrote daily to Nick and then I found I wrote daily, period. Burning the candle at both ends and in the middle, as my mother always joked, I read at all hours of the day and night and I wrote at all hours too. Encouraged by two inspirational professors, Roger Slakey and Roland Flint, I began to become serious about the craft of writing. High up in the stacks of the Georgetown library, I read the works of Theodore Roethke and James Wright, two poets with difficult lives and artful art. I wrote my senior thesis on Theodore Roethke. I wrote my own poems and fledgling short stories. They were dark and, I hoped, sophisticated. I aimed for *The New Yorker* but was very happy to publish in *The Yale Literary Magazine*, where John Kane was now an editor. Georgetown offered no such venue for my writing.

Intellectually and socially, my senior year soon proved bumpy.

To begin with, there was a certain boy named Bob O'Leary. A writer like myself, he was a dazzling black Irishman with a scalding sense of irony. Welcome where girls were not, he was a high-ranking contributor to both the school newspaper, *The Hoya*, and to the yearbook. To add to his attractiveness, he enjoyed a drink, and I enjoyed drinking with him—among other things. He had the sex appeal of a young Mel Gibson, and I found him irresistible. Drinking, he found me irresistible as well. Sober, he preferred a wholesome, sweet-tempered blonde named Lynn Burke. She was my polar opposite. The resultant triangle was the official cause of my considerable anguish.

Alcohol is a depressant, and I was certainly drinking enough to depress even the most buoyant of spirits. Drinking, and recovering from drinking, much of normal life passed me by. Alcohol was my priority. Everything else, however important, ranked a distant second. I did not, for example, march on the White House to protest the war, although I disapproved of it. (My antiwar activities consisted of one unpublished political cartoon.) Nor did I realize that two of my housemates were engaged in a lesbian liaison. I became aware of this fact only when one of the lovers leapt at me from behind the shower curtain, clutching at my throat, accusing me of trying to seduce her mate.

"I don't know what you are talking about!" I managed to gasp, choking for air. I fought off my attacker but was left with a bruised throat and a shaken sense of safety. The attempted strangulation shook me to the core. I responded to it by moving out of the house immediately, renting yet one more lonely room. This time there was no obstreperous squirrel to keep me company. There was no scent of freshly baked bread. I took to solitary daily drinking, cutting my classes and brooding over my troubles nightly in the bars. Preoccupied with their plans for graduation, my friends did not notice my troubles. Besides, they were used to having me "gone" up in the Bronx. I was quite "gone" right in their midst.

And then my troubles got compounded when Bob O'Leary chose to invite my nemesis Lynn to Senior Week. (He would later marry her.) Scotch and a razor blade seemed to me to be an appropriate response. I drank all night and sawed at my right wrist toward morning. Then I went running out into the street.

Hysterical with grief, as much for what I had done as for what had been done to me, I took myself to my neighbors Tom Horan and Nick Cariello, looking for someone to help me. Horan bandaged my wrist and insisted that I should go home. Instead, I called my older sister, Connie, and asked if I could come to stay with her. I was too frightened and ashamed to tell my parents what I had done. Then, too, my parents themselves were fragile. I didn't want to worry them. I arrived at my sister's with my arm bandaged. I had made what the doctor would call a suicidal gesture. My sister insisted that I level with at least my father and, reluctantly, I did.

"I slashed my wrist, Dad," I told him. We were eating lunch together in an exclusive dining club on the thirty-third floor of a Chicago skyscraper. I ordered lamb chops while my father considered what I said. Then he asked, "Would you like me to pay for a therapist?"

I accepted his offer and moved home to Chicago. It was the week of Kent State, and Georgetown was abruptly shut down until graduation, which I would not attend. A high school girlfriend of mine offered me a place in the Magnolia Avenue commune where she was living. I took it gratefully and dutifully took myself to therapy as well. I made no connection between my suicidal gesture and my drinking. Neither did my therapist. He focused on what he considered my grandiose career aspirations.

"So you want to be a writer," the therapist said. "Don't you think it might be more sensible to be a secretary?"

"No," I told him.

My older sister was an advertising copywriter, as was my father.

Both held high-powered jobs at prestigious firms. Clearly, I was too unstable to audition for their world. I found an assistant's job at a publishing house. At least there I was near the world of books. I still had ambitions of becoming a writer. I wrote John Kane of my lingering dreams.

"Treating yourself like a precious object will make you strong," John wrote back to me, quoting another of his writers.

This was radical advice. The nuns had always advised us on self-sacrifice as the means to attain our goals. But martyrdom was clearly not the route to a literary career. Writing involved a certain self-centeredness, a belief that the world as I saw it might prove interesting to others. And so, at age twenty-one, at John's urging, I set forth on the sea of my first novel.

Circumstances conspired to give me a long bolt of writing time and isolation. An abrupt phone call from my sister told me that our parents had suffered devastating simultaneous nervous breakdowns. "Come home," my sister said. "We need you."

And so I came home, back to the Libertyville house and my fragile family. My parents were hospitalized one after the other. At first my older sister was in charge of the household, but then one afternoon I looked out a window to see her running barefoot in circles in the snow. "Go back to the city," I told her. "I'll take care of the kids." And so, though only the second oldest, I was in charge of the household for the next year while my parents slowly recovered. Once a week I would drive to the hospital for a visit. Sometimes they knew me, sometimes not. Shock treatments were administered and seemed to help. Meanwhile I did the cooking, the cleaning, the laundry, and the child care for my five younger siblings. Amid all of this, I wrote.

I worked in an upstairs bedroom at a great green enamel desk on an old Olympia typewriter. I established for myself a daily diet of writing—three pages——augmented by J&B, apples, and cheddar cheese. The J&B was aimed at getting me past my fears—my fears of writing and my fears of what was happening with my parents. The apples and cheese were intended to deflect the J&B and keep me sober enough to actually write. Write I did. I wrote a dark, moody novella centering on a famous reclusive author and his smitten fan. When I finished the book, called *Morning*, I sent it off to John, who promptly sent it to Emily Hahn at *The New Yorker.* Aside from thinking the book was written by John himself under a pseudonym, she loved it. "Divide the number of roses and sunsets by two and publish!" she shot back.

I should have been encouraged. Instead, I was embarrassed. I felt like a hick—and a hack. Clearly, to Hahn's sophisticated eye I was a sentimentalist. How could I ever have put any roses or sunsets into the book? How juvenile! How saccharine! I put the novella in a bottom drawer, and no one, not even John, could persuade me to simply make the suggested cuts and get on with things.

When my parents were safely out of the hospital and stabilized, my father came to me with a problem. "Your mother feels you have usurped her role," he told me. "Perhaps you had better leave." And so with fifty dollars to my name—a laughably small nest egg—I went back to Washington, D.C., where Georgetown gave me a belated diploma.

Once there, I got a phone call from Bill Niederkorn, a high school friend of John's. "How would you like to work for *The Washington Post?*" Bill asked. An interview was arranged, and I went in to meet with Tom Kendricks, then the editor of Style, the arts section of the *Post.*

"I hope you don't think you are a writer," Kendricks grimly advised me. His eyes twinkled but his manner was curt.

"I am a writer. I hope you don't think I am a journalist," I archly fired back. I may have gone on to tell him that my aspirations were far higher than mere newspaper work. Amused or titillated, Kendricks hired me and I began my duties as a copy aide, sorting mail and answering phones. My salary was $67 a week, and my schedule consisted of five four-hour shifts at work and lots of free time to write. One night, as Kendricks went out for his dinner, he cast a glance in my direction. "You look awfully glum," he remarked.

"I've just typed tomorrow's section and it sucks," I told him, mincing no words.

"Well, if you think you can do any better—" He tossed the challenge over his shoulder and headed out the door.

I did think I could do better, and while Kendricks dined, I typed. I wrote a short and snappy piece about the impact of the movie *Cabaret* on Georgetown's nightlife. I cited plunging décolletage and green fingernail polish on Rosemary Welden, a chic bartender. I called Rosemary up and got a few pungent quotes. By the time Kendricks returned from dinner, I had the piece in hand.

"It seems I owe you an apology. I'd like to run this piece on Sunday," Kendricks told me, stopping by my desk with his good news. Bill Niederkorn and my fellow copy aides were flabbergasted. I took the news in stride. Of course I could do journalism. I was a writer, wasn't I?

For the next six months I enjoyed my newfound stature as a hot young writer. Nearly every Sunday, and some weekdays as well, my byline could be found in Style. I wrote on politics and I wrote on the arts. I wrote on drugs, sex, and rock and roll. I wrote so often that my byline became a regular attraction. I was still officially a copy aide, but to the world at large I appeared to be a staff writer.

Out club-hopping at night, I suddenly had cachet. Drinks were on the house. I was that new *Post* writer. The hip one. Why, I might write about anything or everything. Kendricks had created a monster. As my bylines accumulated, so did my cockiness. My copy aide's job was beneath me. Called on the carpet for sorting the mail wrong—who could be bothered?—I got into a tiff with Bill Niederkorn, so recently my benefactor. Kendricks intervened.

"I hear you told Bill Niederkorn to go to hell," he scolded me.

"I didn't tell him to go to hell. I told him to fuck himself."

"I see." Kendricks was not amused.

"He's just jealous," I sniped.

I probably had the diagnosis right, but Kendricks did not like my attitude. Writers at the *Post* behaved with more dignity, he chided me. He might have added, "And more gratitude."

"Then perhaps I don't belong at the *Post*." I spat out the words. "I am who I am."

"I think you need to mend your ways."

"I like my ways." To hear me tell it, it was a case of "to thine own self be true." Kendricks was asking me to compromise my values. Of course, I could not.

"Well, then . . ." And that was the end of my brilliant career at the *Post*.

I had a little money set aside. I used it to buy good stationery and write thank-you notes to my editors. "I am going to freelance," my cards cheekily announced. "Thank you for all of your help."

I must have sent a thank-you card to God, because what happened next was clearly an act of divine intervention. One afternoon, as I sat typing a new short story, my phone rang. The caller identified himself as Jonathan Walsh, an editor for *Rolling Stone* magazine. He had enjoyed reading my pieces in the *Post*, he said, but now he wondered, would I be interested in writing a Watergate piece for *Rolling Stone*? They wanted a piece on E. Howard Hunt's children. Could I do it? I could.

Borrowing a yellow Volkswagen bug from Joe McClellan, a *Post* writer, I drove out to suburban Maryland, where I simply pulled into the Hunts' sumac-overgrown driveway and introduced myself. I was from *Rolling Stone*, I said. Would they care to talk to me? Hunts' children conferred. Self-declared children of the counter-culture, they trusted the name *Rolling Stone*. They decided to talk. And so I was welcomed into their household and made privy to their many secrets. It wasn't easy having a Watergate conspirator for a father.

"Life Without Father," *Rolling Stone* dubbed the piece, and ran it as a cover story. Writing well was the best revenge, and I had scooped the *Post*. It was the first time that a Watergate family had opened up to the press. Godfather to the children, William F. Buckley phoned me to say he thought that what I had done was terrible, an invasion of privacy. *Time* magazine, on the other hand, wrote an article on *Rolling Stone*, citing its new and serious reporto-rial direction. (Mine.) One more time, I had a hot career.

It seemed that the *Rolling Stone* piece opened doors as well as windows. I was invited to write for *The Village Voice*, *New York*, and *New West*. In between my short stories and the articles I gladly under-took, I was a full-time writer earning my living by my craft. I sought to play the part. Mine was a hard-drinking and hard-writing crowd. We would gather nightly at a journalism bar called The Class Re-union. There it was a mark of honor that the bartender knew your drink and ran you a tab. After work, drinks became drinks with dinner and then after-dinner drinks. Most nights, we closed the bar.

By day I began to use my writing to try to control my drinking. "Don't start drinking when you have an interview," ran one rule I made for myself. "Don't drink and write unless you have drugs to keep yourself lucid," ran another rule. It was easy to get speed— still not a class-A drug—and speed allowed you to drink without blacking out. The combination of wine and speed was a good writing elixir.

The *Rolling Stone* staff was known for its substance abuse. As a *Rolling Stone* writer, I had a reputation to live up to. And I tried. When he came to Washington to cover politics, I became drinking buddies with Hunter Thompson, who made an entire literary persona out of his drug and alcohol abuse. Long-legged and boyish, Hunter was a capricious man, frequently tender and then inexplicably cruel.

We would settle in at a place called The Guest Quarters with a bottle of Southern Comfort or Wild Turkey. Then another. Then another. It was Thompson who first told me I might do well to quit drinking. "Five nights out of six, you are the best date in town," he told me. "But on that sixth night . . ."

My talent as a writer attracted wide attention and well-meaning advice. "You know, kid," director John Cassavetes told me, "you really don't need to drink the way that you do."

But I did need to drink the way that I did. From my very first drink, I craved alcohol. It was like oxygen to me—necessary and taken for granted. Looking back, I can see that I was what might be called a "cup of soup" alcoholic. Simply add alcohol to my system and I was an instant alcoholic. There were no long years of drinking waiting to cross the "invisible line." I crossed it with my very first drink. Then and ever after, my first drink made me drunk, and that drink took the second drink, the third, the fourth, and so on. Like many writers, I confused my drinking identity and my writing identity. I thought they went together. In my crowd they certainly did. I thought I had to drink in order to write—not that the drinking was in fact getting in the way of my writing, as it already was.

Drinking, my unmanageable life seemed manageable. I was dating a man who lived in Boston, the writer Paul Monette. Every Friday Joe McClellan and I would pile into his Volkswagen and make the long drive north. Joe spent the weekends visiting with his children. I spent mine with Monette, who had not yet settled on his eventual—and highly public—gay identity.

To me, Paul was gay in a different sense. Tall, handsome, and lethally charming, he was very good company, a born storyteller, and quite a seductive companion. He thought he "might" have some issues with sexual identity but not identifiably in our bed. Drinking blurred the edges, but I remember bed as a happy place. One of the few people I knew who actually was a lark, Paul woke daily in high good spirits, sometimes even singing, "I can see clearly now the rain is gone/I can see all obstacles in my way." What we couldn't see, or chose not to, was that a long-distance relationship, limited to weekends, was not quite enough for either of us. Commuting became more and more difficult. Eventually, as gracefully as we could, we moved on. Paul moved on to other companions. I moved on to more serious and solitary drinking.

I lived in an apartment behind the Washington Zoo. I wrote at a large desk near an open window. Through the window came the roars of wild animals. My writing life had an exotic sound track. It also had a distinctive flavor. Striving for control, I had replaced hard alcohol with wine, and my favorite was something called Bull's Blood, a brackish dark Hungarian red. My apartment was tiny and dark, but with the addition of alcohol, it lit up like a lantern. Suddenly I was a citizen of the world. I drank as I wrote, trying not to let the drinking get ahead of the words. While lions roared and hyenas bayed, I hammered out short stories and journalism assignments. I wrote daily and I drank daily. It was unthinkable that I skip either one. During my long, boozy bouts at the typewriter, I was beginning to hatch a plan. On the heels of my successful Watergate piece, *Rolling Stone* had asked me to write about the movies. I did long on-location stories. In doing so, I found I loved the movies. What I should really do, I decided, was take a few more East Coast assignments and then move to Hollywood. There I could write for the movies and have a typewriter in the sun.

My writing brought me to the attention of *Playboy* and *Oui*, magazines that prided themselves on their serious content despite their fleshly allure. *Playboy* paid very well and wanted me to write for them. Thinking of the nest egg I needed to go west, I quickly set aside any feminist scruples and suggested that I go to Italy to write about Robert De Niro, a rising star.

"Why De Niro?" *Playboy* wanted to know.

"Trust me. He will be famous."

"Go to New York and write about Martin Scorsese instead."

I knew nothing about Martin Scorsese. I was disappointed not to be going to Italy, where I could have used my vestigial Georgetown language skills. Still, the pay was good and I needed the work, so I took the Scorsese assignment. Getting ready to write about him, I boned up on his background. He was a young director, critically hot after directing *Mean Streets*, an autobiographical film of life on the edges of the Mob in Little Italy. He had since directed *Alice Doesn't Live Here Anymore*, a feminist movie starring Ellen Burstyn. He was now set to direct something called *Taxi Driver*, which promised to star none other than Robert De Niro. *Taxi Driver* was to be shot in New York. I could meet Scorsese there.

Operating on a shoestring and the goodwill of friends, I called an ex-boyfriend and asked him if I could stay with him while I wrote the piece. I was set to meet Scorsese in the King Cole Bar of the St. Regis Hotel on Wednesday. I would take the train north from Washington to New York, arriving late Tuesday afternoon.

My plan was simple, but my drinking soon complicated it. I got to New York and my ex-boyfriend's. We opened a bottle of wine. With the benefit of a few drinks in my system, I could not clearly remember just why I had broken up with the former boyfriend. He was so appealing, so tall and noble looking, such a fine actor, so sensitive and smart. How could I have let him slip away? Well, volunteered the boyfriend, there was more to it than that.

Although our sex life had been "pretty spectacular," he now wondered whether or not he was gay. In fact, since his arrival in New York, he had been living a gay lifestyle, and he frankly enjoyed all of the attention he was getting. While I was welcome to stay with him, he wasn't sure it was such a great idea that we go to bed together again. Exactly how long did I need his hospitality? I told him the Scorsese interview was set for the next day, surely we could get through until then? But that's when the phone rang. It was Marion Billings, Scorsese's publicist, wondering if the interview could be postponed for just one day. . . . It was to be a "nice lunch," surely I didn't mind waiting in New York for just one day? Publicists can be very persuasive.

Feeling I had little choice in the matter, I agreed to the delay. I rescheduled the interview for one day later. All I needed until then was to stay safe and sound—easier said than done. Wanting to be modern and with it, I agreed to share an apartment—and a platonic bed—with my former boyfriend. If he gave me a roof over my head, the least I could do was respect his new sexual persuasion.

What was I thinking of? Our mutual attraction was undeniable—and a really bad idea given his new lifestyle. "I always felt so awkward with women," he told me. (Now he tells me!) "With men it is just so easy." He had discovered he was quite a catch.

We were drinking during this conversation. One complicated thing led to another, as it often does when there's drinking. Maybe it wasn't such a terrible idea to celebrate the good old days with each other. Maybe he wasn't so very convinced he was gay after all. . . . The phone rang. My ex answered it.

"It's for you. Someone named Martin Scorsese."

"Hello," I answered the phone. "Mr. Scorsese? Don't say you want to postpone the interview again, because I am staying with my ex-boyfriend and I have been here one day too long already."

"Ah, actually, I was just confirming."

"Oh, that's great. I'll see you tomorrow. Thanks for calling."

I returned to the boozy conversation with my ex-boyfriend. Further drinking made sleeping together seem like a good idea—at least to me. To his credit, my ex-boyfriend was drinking less than I. Our proposed fling gave him second thoughts.

"I think we could just split the bed," he offered. "I mean, I am sure it would be great to sleep together, but it would only confuse me. And you have to work tomorrow."

And so it was decided that we would table any sexual attraction between us so that I would be alert and well rested for my important interview. This was a fine theory, but it proved difficult in practice. It is, to say the least, tempting to share a bed with a former lover, especially one whom you now cannot have.

32

My ex-boyfriend had never seemed so desirable as he did that night. As one long leg or leanly muscled arm would stray across the Great Divide, I would have to repeat to myself, "Julia. He's gay now. This doesn't mean a thing." Then I would scoot out of reach until he reached out again. Again I'd repeat, "Julia. He's gay now. This doesn't mean a thing." This continued all night. By morning I was curled into a tight little ball. My former lover was sprawled in splendor across the rest of the bed. After a miserable night of temptation and rejection, I was ready to go meet Martin Scorsese.

The King Cole Bar of the St. Regis Hotel featured stunning murals by Maxfield Parrish and an atmosphere of elegant revelry. I arrived at our pink-clothed table before Martin Scorsese and ordered black coffee and a double scotch on the rocks. Although I had a rule about not drinking while I worked, my miserable night had left me shaky and hungover. I needed a hair from the dog that had bit me.

I downed my black coffee. My head cleared. I sipped at my scotch and I waited. Clearly, punctuality was not one of Scorsese's long suits. Ten minutes ticked past, then fifteen, then twenty. I was hungry and I was crabby. Who was this Scorsese, and why couldn't he play by the rules? I ordered another drink. If he could break the rules, so could I. While I was waiting for my second round, Scorsese arrived. He took his place across from me. I had exactly enough time to register this thought: "Oh, my God. I have met the man I am going to marry."

2.

Scorsese made himself comfortable—or as comfortable as an uncomfortable man could. He hunched over the table. He rearranged the silverware. He noticed my drink and the tape recorder and notebook at the ready. I picked up a pen.

"Shouldn't we eat?" he asked. He was a small, dark, and handsome man with lively eyes, a close-trimmed beard, and a mustache. He spoke in staccato bursts. But he was so immediately playful, he reminded me of an otter—or perhaps his namesake, a "marten." He did not say "Will you marry me?" but he might as well have. I did not say yes, but I would have. His energy was intent, alert, and humorous. "Shouldn't we eat?" he repeated. I agreed that we should eat and that questions could perhaps wait.

"Now, what was that on the phone about an ex-boyfriend?" Scorsese wanted to know. Clearly his idea of what we should eat began with the devouring of information. He was instantly more mischievous fun than any man I'd ever met.

"So marry me," I thought. "We could have so much fun."

I had never planned a trousseau or browsed through bridal magazines. I had never daydreamed about my future husband and what life might be like as a wife. When I planned the future, I thought solely in terms of writing. Marriage was not my goal. I wasn't looking for Mr. Right. And now, completely unexpectedly, I had found him. What's more, it was my job to get to know him.

Lunch stretched from one hour into two. I picked at the chicken Cobb salad. I sipped at the second scotch. Somewhere around dessert, it was agreed that I would go upstairs to Scorsese's suite and we would continue the interview there. Despite the minutes ticking past, we had barely begun. Our conversation had zoomed wildly from our childhoods to whom we were dating. I was single and unattached. Scorsese was in the throes of ending a long-term relationship.

"I'll meet you upstairs," I told Scorsese as he signed for the check. "I need to make a phone call."

"Not to that ex-boyfriend?" Scorsese joked, but he wasn't kidding.

"That's for me to know . . ."

When Scorsese went upstairs to the suite, I made my phone call. It was not to my ex-boyfriend. It was to my mother. As adult, soignée, and sophisticated as I tried to be, there were still times when this girl needed her mother. This was such a time. "Mom? Mom, I have met the man I am going to marry," I squeaked to my mother.

"You have?"

"Yes. I have. His name is Martin Scorsese."

"Does he know you're going to marry him?"

"He knows something. I can't talk now. I just wanted to tell you the news."

"Good luck, dear."

After I spoke with my mother, I placed a second call. This one was to the novelist George V. Higgins, a friend and confidant. "George?" I asked. "I've met the man I am going to marry and I need to borrow enough money to stay in New York for the summer. Could you stake me?"

By the time Martin and I rendezvoused back in his suite, I had my mother's blessing and my summer's money. Now all he had to do was realize that he should marry me.

Martin's suite for the duration of the shoot was the Cecil Beaton Suite, a brightly colored affair designed by Beaton himself. It was on the eighteenth floor and featured a large, distinctive round window looking north up Fifth Avenue. Through that window, taxis poured south like so many koi swimming in a stream.

Sprawled out on the living room floor, I scribbled notes and went through tape after tape. I asked Martin about his childhood, his education, his family, his friends. He talked about religion, sharing his once-upon-a-time yearning to go into the priesthood. I told him of my own difficulties with Catholic school, of my explorations into Tillich and Teilhard de Chardin.

I have the first six hours of our relationship on tape. We can be heard rushing through preliminaries, impatient with small talk. He talked about his displacement in Los Angeles, his crippling asthma, for which he used an inhaler and pills. "Marty Pills," his childhood friends had dubbed him. He shrugged ruefully. Through the round window, the evening taxis now poured south in a brightly lit stream. Sometime during the afternoon, I switched from scotch to Courvoisier. My questions became more and more personal. Martin took off his shoes. "You have beautiful feet," I told him. I have the tipsy compliment and his startled response on tape.

We had more than run through the allotted time for the interview. I nursed my final drink, reluctant for the interview to end. Signaling me to stay, Martin fielded several phone calls. He had a meeting slated with Michael Phillips, his producer, and he was eager to talk with Paul Schrader, the writer. We were not nearly done talking with each other, but Martin could either talk about making movies or actually make one. Handing me a copy of the shooting script, he ushered me reluctantly to the door and suggested we meet again after I had had the chance to read it. The door clicked shut behind me and I stood in the hotel hallway. I was heady in a way that did not come from alcohol.

"How did it go?" my ex-boyfriend greeted me as I came through the door to his apartment. "You were there forever." He cocked an eyebrow.

"Actually, I think it went fine," I said. "I'm just a little shaken up." I set the script on a table. I took a chair.

"Shaken up? Why's that? You're an old hand at interviews by now, aren't you?" He winked at me, pouring us both a glass of wine. He had always teased me.

"The thing is," I announced solemnly, "I think I am going to marry him."

"Ah."

To his credit, my ex-boyfriend did not make fun of me or of my unlikely marital conviction. He offered a toast as if it were the most normal thing in the world to meet a man and hours later announce your intention to marry him. For my part, I still felt the implacable certainty that I had when I called my mother. I drank the toast.

The script for *Taxi Driver* was a good, fast read with a few rough patches where it sounded politically naive. I was friends with Richard Goodwin, John F. Kennedy's speechwriter, and I knew that politicians did not speak in quite the formal way Martin and Schrader had them speaking in their off-hours. Thinking nothing of it, I took a pen in hand and scribbled some suggested revisions. All in all, I tinkered with a half dozen scenes. My experience as a journalist and a short-story writer made writing on a screenplay feel easy.

When I met with Martin a day later, I said, "There were a few places in the script that didn't work, but I fixed them." As always, where my writing was concerned, I had cheeky confidence. Martin read the changes and liked them. What was even more evident was that he liked me. Our interview now seemed like the greatest excuse for continued intimacy. We shared a long, winey dinner at a small, romantic French restaurant. We went from the restaurant straight to bed. I should have been thinking, "Oh, my God, my story!" Instead, I was thinking, "This is the man I am going to marry."

Journalistic ethics went out the window when love flew in. I moved from my ex-boyfriend's place over to Martin's hotel. Without so much as a word of discussion, we began living together. Our days took on an easy pattern. I would write all day. He would go to the set to shoot his movie, and at night we would rendezvous at the hotel for dinner and bed. I had brought with me clothes enough for one week's stay in New York, but this was quickly remedied when it turned out that Martin's blue jeans fit me perfectly, as did his black T-shirts. Now we looked like the Bobbsey twins, his-and-her filmmaker dolls. Martin wore a khaki safari jacket and soon I had one too.

"I've met the man I am going to marry," I told my baffled Washington friends, who were shocked and disturbed by my sudden departure. My mother began telling me that if I were "used goods," Martin might not be eager to marry me. "Oh, Mom!" I exclaimed. "He doesn't think like that." Just what he did think like was still the object of my fascinated scrutiny. I should have called my editor and confessed my romantic involvement. Instead, I set for myself the impossible task of writing an objective piece.

I found if I stayed in the hotel suite all day, I got stir-crazy. I was delighted when *Playboy* offered me a free office to write in. Martin would go to location each day and I would go to my office. I opened my story with a description of the Cecil Beaton Suite and Martin's blue-jeaned presence there in its very posh midst.

The shooting schedule for *Taxi Driver* was lean and mean. The time quickly came for me to observe Martin at work. Early in the morning, I would go to set with Martin and his driver. In our enchantment with each other, we were anything but discreet. We were in love and love showed. It showed up in the columns as well, where our romance became an item. If my editor read the trades, he never let on to me.

On set, I quickly learned that Martin's directorial style was nearly as intimate as anything he had ever said to me. When an actor needed an adjustment, he would cross to his side, crouch down, and whisper. In this way, the actor-director exchanges remained confidential. When Martin spoke to the crew, he did so in a low-pitched voice. It was a little like the fabled Jacqueline Onassis trick of always whispering so a man had to pay close attention. Like Mrs. Onassis, Martin was wonderfully seductive. I used to tease him, comparing him to a highly adrenalized Cary Grant. His crews were crazy about him. His actors adored him. Of course, based on my own feelings, I thought such reactions were appropriate.

The climax of *Taxi Driver* is a bloody shootout that unreels for several gory moments. Martin well knew that it would be a difficult day for both the crew and actors—so much blood, such an unrelenting assault on the senses. "We'll go again." "Let's get another." "One more time, please." Martin worked his crew quickly but never frantically. His filmmaking was meticulous despite the pressures of the scene. Watching him, I thought that young as he was, he was already masterful. I decided that I would write that he was brilliant and let objectivity be damned. Besides, I thought, if I were able to be objective, I would think the same thing.

Taxi Driver shot all during a long, hot Manhattan summer. As the shoot drew to a close, Martin and I faced imminent separation. He was due to go to Europe for a film festival and I faced a return to the life I had abandoned down in Washington. "Come with me," Martin abruptly invited me one day. I had no passport, no ticket, and mere days to get them in order before we left. In the passport photo taken for the trip, my hair is wildly disheveled. I look like a terrorist. Young love did not promote serenity.

We flew first to Scotland for the Edinburgh Film Festival. After the luxury of the St. Regis, our Edinburgh hotel seemed positively chaste—white walls, white bedspread, an aura of pin-neat cleanliness. It didn't take us long to put the virginal bed to use. Equally exciting, Martin's films played to rapt audiences. Still profiling him in my head, I made a note to myself to remember to write that he was an international, not merely American, artist.

Edinburgh was a small, dour city, chock-full of history. We went to formal dinners in gloomy castles. We went to screenings tucked down medieval alleyways. On a tiny, twisted street, Martin led me into a cramped shop and bought me a kilt, velvet jacket, and silk blouse in my family tartan, Cameron of Lochiel.

Now our time together was really drawing to a close and we were numb with grief. We traveled by train south to London, where we had lodgings at the Cadogan Hotel. The rooms were large, square, and airy. They featured elaborately tiled baths. One of my favorite memories is a travel-worn Martin soaking up to his neck in an outsize Roman tub. "This is the man I am going to marry," I continued to think.

The time had come for us to separate. Martin stayed on to do business in London. I flew back to the States. I was greeted upon my arrival with a copy of a magazine. It featured an article on Martin written by one of my colleagues. The article opened with a scene in the Cecil Beaton Suite—my scene from the Cecil Beaton Suite. I read on in horror. I had been plagiarized.

I phoned my colleague. "How could you?" I demanded.

"Well, I thought . . . under the circumstances . . ."

"What circumstances?"

"I mean, you and Scorsese are an item, aren't you?"

"That doesn't mean you can just steal what I wrote."

"Yes, it does." My colleague laughed.

I realized he was right. I didn't have a leg to stand on. I couldn't have both my relationship with Martin and my brilliant career. I had chosen the first moment I met him, and now the choice was simply coming home to roost.

As I always did when I felt overwhelmed, I called my mother. I told her what had happened to me, that my work had been stolen and published under another writer's name. I told her how the writer had explained that he felt I was fair game.

"Well, you can't really have it both ways, can you?" my mother asked.

"Help! You are supposed to be on my side."

"I am on your side. But you did say that you were going to marry this man. That hardly makes you an objective observer."

"Don't lecture me."

"So how are things going?"

"What do you mean? They're going." I didn't need to hear my mother's doubts about my being used goods.

"You left him in London?"

"I left him in London, but then he's on his way back to Los Angeles and I am going to join him there. He's going to send for me."

"You wouldn't like to come home for a while?"

"Mother. He is going to send for me."

"Yes, dear. But I thought you might like to come home while you waited."

My mother was being both kindhearted and shrewd. She wanted to give me a safety net although I professed to not need one. Her invitation was enticing. How much better to be home with my family than alone in my Washington apartment, waiting for the phone to ring?

"I guess I could come home for a little while," I relented.

"Why, that would be lovely."

"Just until he calls."

"Yes, dear. Just until he calls."

And so I went home to Libertyville, Illinois, to the big yellow house in the woods. I didn't want to admit to myself that I had effectively blown up my journalism career by getting involved with a subject. No, rather than concentrate on the wreckage of my career, I tried to concentrate on my dreams for the future. I had met the man I was going to marry. Now I was just waiting for him to call for me.

I took a typewriter down to the basement and began working on a short story. I tried to lose myself in the plot, but my real life kept intruding. What if my mother were right and Martin considered me damaged goods? That was a plot twist more dramatic than any fiction I could undertake. A day went by with no reassuring phone call. Then another day passed and another. By then I was having trouble sleeping and eating. I tried to remember how right things had felt between us but found that my memories seemed slippery and will-o'-the-wisp. "Remember your certainty," I lectured myself. "Count on that." Meanwhile, my mother treated me with grave pity.

"Going to try to write again?" she would query.

"Yes. I thought I would."

"I'll let you know if the phone is for you."

"Thanks, Mom. Don't worry. He'll call."

Ten days home and counting, he finally called. He missed me. He was sorry it had taken him so long, but now the coast was clear. When could I fly out? Twenty-four hours later I was on my way to Los Angeles. Martin met me at LAX wearing his signature blue jeans and black T-shirt, driving a maroon Lotus Elan. The car looked like an oversize shoe. We barely shoehorned my baggage into it, driving "home" through the hills to the strains of David Bowie's "Ziggy Stardust."

Home was a Spanish-style house perched on Mulholland Drive, overlooking the San Fernando Valley. Outside, there was a small and pretty courtyard, a neat and trim backyard. The house itself had glass sliding doors, the better to make you feel you were living right amid the cacti. Downstairs, there was a large living room, a dining room, a rec room, and a kitchen with a screening room just beyond. Upstairs, there were three large bedrooms. The master bedroom featured a hand-painted mural of a sunset, its technicolored hues taken straight from *Alice Doesn't Live Here Anymore.* I liked the house. I would add rose gardens to the courtyard and brightly colored cutting beds to the perimeter of the yard.

Taxi Driver was shot in New York, but it was being cut and assembled in Burbank. Martin would get up in the mornings and go to the studio for long days in the editing room. I would stay home to write, staring out the glass doors at the view of the valley. I had no car of my own, and Martin's extra car was a vintage Corvette, which was very hard to handle. I was afraid to drive the Corvette and so I was effectively stranded. I had nothing to do but write.

"Julia, it is just going to take some getting used to," I lectured myself, and the long days in the empty house did take getting used to. I was also running up against something unexpected. Martin didn't like it when I saw my old friends—many of them men. As it happened, I didn't have very many friends in Los Angeles, and those whom I did have were men, chiefly fellow *Rolling Stone* writers— a lot of bad boys, I had to admit. When I would go to lunch with these cohorts, I would inevitably drink the afternoon away. Martin didn't like my drinking. It worried him. When we were still in New York, he had sought to limit my drinking to one drink with dinner. I found one drink left me craving more. I would sometimes sneak drinks, going down to dinner early and quickly downing a drink or two before Martin arrived and then having my official drink.

I felt both guilty and rebellious about cheating on my quota. One glass of white wine was a minuscule amount—and who was Martin to tell me I shouldn't drink? I was drinking when he met me. No one was using the word "alcoholic" to describe me, but later Martin would tell me that seeing *The Razor's Edge* made him fear my drinking. For the character in the movie, drinking proved fatal. I still thought of my drinking as something casual, a part of a writing lifestyle. I smoked, drank, and swore. It was all part of my tough-girl persona. Lillian Hellman had drunk. So had Dorothy Parker. Why, a little drinking had never hurt anyone—but that was a little drinking, and I was drinking a little more than that.

What I needed, Martin decided, were a few trustworthy girl-friends. With that in mind, he introduced me to Dita Sullivan, an astrologer. Dita quickly cast some charts to augur Martin's and my compatability. We were made for each other, she declared. Our aspects were overwhelmingly favorable. With such optimism to recommend her, Dita quickly became a close friend. Unlike me, she was not a drinker, and her presence tended to moderate my behavior—at least for a while. From Dita's astrological perspective, my move to Los Angeles and my involvement with Martin all made sense in terms of my "Saturn's return." It was right in the stars. Everything was being made anew.

In addition to Dita, I made another new girlfriend, superagent Sue Mengers. With a client list that included Barbra Streisand and a number of A-list directors, Mengers was at the epicenter of Hollywood. A short, round blonde with scarlet fingernails and a fondness for caftans, she liked me because I was bright and opinionated. I liked her for the same reasons. She had a shark's reputation, but I found I trusted her. As she once remarked to me, "I thought Martin had gotten himself a little brown wren, but then you opened your mouth."

It was at Sue's house that I was kissed hello by David Geffen, an encounter that left me thinking, "No matter how good he is at business, he certainly can kiss." Parties at Sue's house ran toward a crowd and the crowd ran toward notables. Gore Vidal might attend. Or François Truffaut. There was no telling who you might run into. The crowds were mix and match, some from the movie world, some from the music world, some from the literary world. Many faces were known, but others, like my own, belonged to newcomers. Sue did not believe in parties with the same old crowd, however distinguished. She liked to mix it up.

It was at Sue's that I stayed up to the small hours talking with Gore Vidal. I liked Sue's parties because there was a great deal of conversation fueled by icy white wine. Martin thought I liked the parties a little too much, which I did. They were a welcome antidote to my daily loneliness. They made me feel like I had moved somewhere, not just to an empty house with a view.

In Washington I was used to being at the center of things. In Los Angeles there didn't seem to be a center of things unless it was at Sue's. I wrote most days, and despite Martin's disapproval, I took the time for long, winey lunches with old friends.

"Are you doing okay?" my *Playboy* editor Arthur Kretchmer wanted to know. He did not think I was flourishing in my isolation. "You can tell me," he urged.

"Maybe you should take a few assignments," Chris Hodenfield, a *Rolling Stone* confrere, advised me. "You need some real work."

They were right. I did need some real work, but not much of it was forthcoming. Falling in love with Martin, I had mixed business with pleasure. Editors were no longer sure that I could be objective. Martin had too strong a hold on me, they felt. I might just write his opinions instead of my own.

"If you want to write for us again, get divorced," one famous editor advised me. I wasn't married yet so I couldn't take the advice.

If they were advising me to dump Martin, their counsel fell on deaf ears. I was madly in love, and the madly part was very real. I was willing to spend long days at home writing. I was willing to try out long and elaborate Italian recipes.

"I've lost you," wailed my best Washington girlfriend, Judy Bachrach. "You've fallen in with them." She never clarified who "them" was, but I knew she meant "Hollywood people."

If Martin noticed my growing unhappiness, it was something he could not afford to think about. All of his energies were focused on editing *Taxi Driver*. He correctly sensed that it would be his breakthrough film, and nothing, certainly not his personal life, could come before it. It was up to me to make myself happy.

"You're a writer. Write, goddammit," I lectured myself. The long, empty days were perfect for starting a novel again or a screenplay. Daily, I tried to face down the blank page and/or the intricacies of eggplant parmigiana. Daily, Martin worked on his film. If he knew I was unhappy, he didn't say so.

"What you need are some real California blue jeans," his editor, Marcia Lucas, decided. Dutifully she took me out and bought me some skintight denim. "There, now you look like you belong here," she pronounced. But I wasn't fitting in. I could find no "in" to fit into. I soldiered on, increasingly sad and determined not to show it. But I did show it. Martin knew something was wrong, and he thought he knew how to fix it.

"I think you should marry me," Martin abruptly proposed to me one night. "I think we should get married."

"Do you know what you are getting us into?" I asked him back. Hardly the most romantic response.

"Will you marry me?"

"Yes. I will."

The phone rang then and the caller was movie critic Pauline Kael. Martin promptly announced to her our wedding plans. She had once uncharitably described me as a "pornographic Victorian valentine, like a young Angela Lansbury." She was no sweeter about our news. "Don't marry her for tax reasons," she told Martin waspishly. After a little movie small talk, they got off the phone.

"Let's call our parents," I suggested. I meant that I wanted to call my mother, who had been so certain that Martin wouldn't marry me. I would show her and Judy and my editors and anyone else who cared to doubt. Martin would marry me and everything would soon be much, much better than it was. I was determined to write a happy ending.

When Martin got on the phone with my father, Dad dryly suggested we set the date according to what year Martin wanted his tax break. We settled on December 30 in Libertyville, Illinois. The big yellow house in the woods was a fine place for a wedding. My mother had six weeks to organize it and I had six weeks of jitters. With Dita Sullivan's help, I found a lovely old-fashioned wedding dress, cream and lace. I would wear my long red hair on top of my head, interwoven with poinsettias. My older sister would be my maid of honor. Martin's best men would be movie director Brian De Palma and movie critic Jay Cocks. Mr. and Mrs. Scorsese would travel from New York to Libertyville for the wedding. I had met them only twice, interviewing them for my ill-fated article about Martin. I had asked them for a drink before I began my questions. Although they didn't say so, they had questions of their own.

I had a question of my own to ask, and I asked it during a medical checkup before we left Los Angeles. "Why aren't I pregnant?" I wanted to know. In a fit of romantic commitment, Martin and I had pitched out all of our birth control gear at the St. Regis. That was months ago. Shouldn't I be pregnant by now?

"It can take a while," the doctor said reassuringly. If I weren't pregnant by June, then I could start to worry. In the meantime, I should stop trying to rush things. My health was fine and I should enjoy getting married.

Martin was too busy editing the fine cut of *Taxi Driver* to be properly terrified about getting married. My nerves were mine to deal with and I prescribed sherry. Sherry seemed much more classy to me than Valium. I didn't really like it but I liked its effect: numb and a little bit dim, like a well-bred Victorian lady might be.

We flew from Los Angeles to Chicago and landed in a great snowstorm. There was a foot of snow on the ground and more in the air. Flakes swirled like petticoats, clinging to Martin's beard and mustache. More than ever, he reminded me of a character from "The Nutcracker Suite"—music that would be played as a bridal processional.

Fires were crackling in all three fireplaces as we entered the Libertyville house. The banisters were garlanded in pine and poinsettias. A large and elaborate tree dominated the living room. We would get married right in front of it. For now, though, the tree was a beauty to behold, with hundreds of handpicked ornaments and carefully hung tinsel, cranberry popcorn chains, and a large lace star on the very top. We sipped hot chocolate, hot mulled cider, and glogg. My parents' sense of decorum demanded that Martin, his parents, and his male friends would stay at the nearby Deerpath Inn. I was to have a last night's sleep in my girlhood room.

"I'll see you tomorrow," I told Martin. "You look mythological in the snow."

"I feel like I'm in a Bing Crosby movie. *White Christmas.*"

"I just hope your parents are comfortable."

"Comfortable!" Martin laughed. "This is a foreign country for them. It's not New York."

And so I went upstairs and crawled into bed under the gabled roof. Outside my bedroom window, caught in the beam of a floodlight, snowflakes dipped and danced. Feeling a little tipsy from the sherry, I snuggled into sleep.

Our wedding day dawned bright and crystalline. A foot and a half of snow lay on the ground. Spontaneous snowball fights broke out among the guests. You didn't see snow like this in southern California. We were dressing for the ceremony upstairs in my sister Connie's room. There was makeup to do and hair to be looped up just so. Someone brought me my first sherry of the day and then my second. By the time Mrs. Scorsese arrived, hours before the ceremony, I was woozy and had to lie down. I have a Polaroid snapshot of the two of us, Martin's mother and me. I am in full bridal regalia, stretched out on a twin bed. She sits near the head of the bed, worriedly holding my hand. The Libertyville house featured staircases at both ends, and all day long people dashed up and down the stairs offering homemade cookies, sandwiches, and more sherry.

Downstairs in the living room, tables were arranged. Each table had place cards plainly visible. Martin's Hollywood crowd was to be scattered in amid my Irish aunts and uncles and cousins. Everyone could get to know each other, the theory ran—but it was soon aborted by the shenanigans of one of Martin's Hollywood friends. Moving table to table, he gathered up the Hollywood names and placed all of them together so they could enjoy familiar company. "He's moving the name tags!" one of my sisters rushed upstairs to report. Fortunately my mother decided to let him move the name tags. The important thing was the wedding, after all, and it was finally time for the ceremony.

The strains of "The Nutcracker Suite" resounded through the house. It was Christmastime and the processional was festive. My sister Connie led the way, and then I made my way carefully down the spiral staircase and across the living room to Martin's side. He looked wonderfully handsome in a new suit that had cost more than my wedding dress. Faces turned to us expectantly. The room glowed with candles and with love. Our vows were short and very direct. We would love and honor each other. Yes. We would. Martin took me in his arms. The room applauded.

Outside the window, snow began to fall again. The day was perfectly romantic. Champagne toasts began to flow. Already fortified by sherry, I faced the toasts with hidden alarm. I well knew that for me a few more drinks would be a few drinks too many. I didn't want my wedding night to be just one more drunken party. As glass after glass was raised, I struggled to focus on Martin and the joy between us. Fortunately, the food soon arrived and it was delicious. Rock Cornish game hen went a long way toward reestablishing my sobriety. Happily Martin and I mixed and mingled. While snowflakes flew, the party took on wings of its own. It was only many hours later, driving back to the Deerpath Inn, that one of the Hollywood guests drove his rental car straight into a deep, snow-filled ditch. What did we care about such minor emergencies? We were married.

The plan was very simple. We would spend the night at the Deerpath Inn, Mr. and Mrs. Scorsese now, and the next day we would fly back to Los Angeles and work. There was no time for a proper honeymoon. *Taxi Driver* was nearly ready for its release. We would see about the movie, then see about an extended vacation. But first we would fall asleep beneath the eaves of the charming Deerpath Inn, and before we would fall asleep, we would conceive our daughter, Domenica, a wedding-night baby. For both Martin and myself, Catholicism lingered.

Although I didn't know it at the time, I was flying from my wedding straight into trouble. Upon our arrival back into Los Angeles, we were invited to a huge party at Sam Spiegel's house. He was a legendary producer, and it was a coup to be invited. Everybody who was anybody would be there, and we felt lucky to be included in la dolce vita. Donning our evening finery, we drove to Spiegel's house, where lanterns marked the way and the valet parkers took gentle care of Martin's Lotus. Making our way toward the house, we didn't know to vow to take gentle care of ourselves as well. No, this was to be a full-blown Hollywood party, swirling on until the dawn. In order to make it through the wee hours, more than mere champagne was needed. As the clock struck midnight, one of the partygoers slipped me a small vial of cocaine. It was a small glass bottle with a spoon attached to its lid.

I did not recoil in horror. I did not recoil at all. I knew very little about cocaine except that it was glamorous and illegal, appealing to my bad-girl side. This was 1976, years before the introduction of crack cocaine. Cocaine was still rare, an exotic, little-known drug that was not thought to be addictive. For me it was immediately attractive because, as a stimulant, it would allow me to drink without blacking out. With a line or two of cocaine in my system, I could actually drink safely. Is it any wonder that I saw cocaine not as a problem but as a solution?

It was dawn before the party wore down and we drove home through the Hollywood Hills. How innocent it all seemed. How seductive. That first night of using cocaine had merely rendered me a little more alert, a little more talkative, a little less drunk as the evening wore on. Yes, if you asked me, I would use the drug again. Using it, it seemed I could control and enjoy my drinking.

When a career lifts off, there is a sudden acceleration in velocity. Martin's career lifted off with *Taxi Driver* and our world speeded up to match it. First, there was the whirlwind of publicity. Marion Billings, Martin's publicist, was an old pro at handling star careers. As Martin got "hot," she scheduled interview after interview. It seemed the movie was news everywhere. As a new celebrity, Martin had to adjust to the many invitations and privileges that now came his way. Suddenly he was sought after by people like Andy Warhol, for whom life seemed to be one ongoing party.

We went to New York for *Taxi Driver's* opening, and the trip was a high-powered combination of publicity and parties. Martin seemed to be Andy Warhol's new favorite, and there were nightly invitations to drinks, dinner, and more. Warhol was a celebrity-loving celebrity, and he sought out people like Roger Moore, who was also in town on a film. Night after night Martin and I dined and wined with the Warhol set. Warhol himself was charming, capable of making the smallest of small talk with anyone. Despite his hospitality, it was easy to lose one's bearings. Just what were we doing, night after night, having intimate dinners with strangers united only by fame, the one thing they all had in common?

The *Taxi Driver* trip was a baptism by fire. We returned to a Los Angeles that was lonely no longer, where we were suddenly A-list party guests, in constant and instant demand. There is nothing hotter in Hollywood than a hot new director. Sudden fame gives instant access. It gave Martin the chance to meet many of his heroes—George Cukor, Billy Wilder, Gregory Peck. For me, my borrowed celebrity gave me a ringside seat. As Mrs. Scorsese, I was that spoiled and cosseted something, a Hollywood wife.

It was as Mrs. Scorsese that I first met Liza Minnelli, slated to star with Robert De Niro in Martin's next movie, *New York, New York*. It was a Sunday afternoon and Liza came by the house as a friendly gesture. She was dressed casually and her manner was warm and engaging. Far from aloof, she seemed eager to be liked.

"This is my wife, Julia," Martin said.

I reached out a hand toward Liza, and as we touched, my flesh ran cold. "My marriage is over," I caught myself thinking, and then, "Julia. Don't be ridiculous. Just say hello."

I was determined not to be a jealous wife or an insecure one. Movie stars came with Martin's territory, and I was determined to take them in stride. As movie stars went, Liza was an easygoing one. She favored a casual good cheer. "We're all in this together," her manner seemed to announce. I wasn't "merely" the wife. I was a writer in my own right and Liza's manner acknowledged that. Under any other circumstances, I might have liked her. She didn't seem predatory. Martin was to be her director, a relationship perhaps best categorized as "Daddy." That made me Mommy and Liza our doting daughter. She acted the part for the three hours of her stay.

"So?" Martin asked me when Liza left.

"She's okay. She's nice." I didn't want to go into it. What was I to say to him, "Are you going to leave me for her?" It sounded paranoid and it was paranoid. Which didn't mean that it was wrong. I kept such thoughts to myself.

With *Taxi Driver* safely and successfully in release, it was time for our delayed honeymoon. I said I would go anywhere we could ride horses. Martin selected the Hana Ranch on the back side of

Maui. Packing his clothes, he took with him a copy of *The Last Temptation of Christ.* I took a notebook to write in.

"Feeling queasy," my first entry might have read.

It took two flights to reach Maui, and as the second plane, a tiny island hopper, landed, my stomach flipped over. I blamed it on a bumpy landing. When my stomach stayed on edge for the next two weeks, I blamed it on heights. Maui's cliffs towered above its beaches.

The Hana Ranch was a half day's drive from the airport along a high road that twisted along atop cliffs offering staggering views of the Pacific. I am nothing if not a trooper, and so I fought down my nausea without a word to Martin. This was our honeymoon, after all. I wanted to be romantic. I wanted to be spunky. I wanted to be a good-sport heroine, like the ones found in the Howard Hawks films Martin so enjoyed. I had on California blue jeans and a khaki safari jacket. Except for an exceptional pallor, I looked the part.

Early our first morning at the ranch, Martin and I rose for a buffet breakfast to be followed by a long morning ride. Moving down the buffet line, I found myself drawn to two items, and only two items: Cream of Wheat and fresh sliced pineapple.

"That's what you're eating?" Martin looked at my plate doubtfully.

There was bacon, sausage, ham and biscuits, poached eggs, scrambled eggs, hash browns, and papaya. The buffet was a feast and I was picking a beggar's portion. No matter. It was our honeymoon and anything went. I inhaled my Cream of Wheat and pineapple and got back in the line for seconds.

I have a photograph of Martin on that morning's ride. He is astride a golden palomino, a good hero's horse, and he sits in the saddle, tall, easy, and proud, just the way all the heroes sit in all the Westerns he had devoured since childhood.

"I don't know how to ride," Martin later confessed, but his bluff that day was very convincing. I had been riding since before I could walk, so for me, ease on a horse was natural. I simply expected as much from my groom.

What I did not expect was the fact that whenever we stopped moving, my stomach kept right on going. No question about it, I had nausea. I could no longer blame it on the high-rising cliffs. I couldn't be suffering vertigo from the back of my handy quarter-horse. No, something else was afoot.

"Are you sure you're okay?" Martin asked me the next morning as I made my way, avid as a homing pigeon, to the pineapple slices and Cream of Wheat.

"It's delicious, really," I assured him. "It's what I want."

What I really wanted was for the nausea to stop, and I found it did so only when I was eating pineapple or actually riding a horse. Martin wanted to lie by the pool and read. I wanted to ride cross-country. Normally compatible, we were suddenly at cross purposes with each other. I would come back from a morning's ride and crave an afternoon's nap. This was when Martin would be ready to hop in the car and go exploring. We had not been in paradise two days before it began to be too much for us.

"Are you okay?" Martin would ask me, usually as he eyed my choices in the buffet line.

"Are you okay?" I would ask him back. He had his nose in *The Last Temptation of Christ.*

"It's a good book."

"I had a great horse yesterday."

"You're sure you're okay?"

"Yeah. I'm okay."

But I was beginning to wonder what was wrong with me. Could

I have contracted some tropical bug? Alcohol tasted wretched to me. Was my fatigue a very bad case of the flu? Why did Martin's reading make me feel locked out? Exactly how insecure was I? I took to my journal and wrote. Two weeks in paradise began to feel like hard time. We had to relax. For two solid weeks we worked at relaxing. By then Martin was suntanned. I was freckled and subtly rounder—all that Cream of Wheat.

When we flew back to Los Angeles, I took myself directly to my Beverly Hills doctor. There had to be a good explanation for my condition. As it turned out, there was an excellent explanation: I was pregnant. My nausea was nothing more than acute morning sickness. I called Martin at the studio and told him our news.

"A wedding-night baby," I told him excitedly. "The doctor counted back the days."

I called my mother to tell her the news. Over the long-distance wire, she took a long, deep breath. "Let's just hope the baby doesn't come early," she finally said. I didn't speak to her for several months after that call.

To be fair, my mother wasn't the only one I was estranged from. I was on the outs with my editors and I was on the outs with my friend Judy Bachrach too. "You left Washington a writer and now you're a wife," Judy wailed. My pregnancy was proof of my betrayal. I was turning into one of "them."

I actually was turning into one of "them," meaning a movie person.

Unlike the script for *Taxi Driver*, which was taut and well crafted, the script for *New York, New York* needed work. Martin decided that I should work on it along with his friend Mardik Martin and the script's original writer, Earl Mac Rausch. I was glad, even thrilled, to have a writing job again. If editors no longer wanted me to write about the movies, I could solve that problem by writing for the movies.

Now there were two of us heading off to the studio in the morning. As we had been during *Taxi Driver*, Martin and I were one more time enchanted by each other's company and ideas. It was difficult for me to work with Mardik Martin, and it was difficult for Mardik to have to work with me. For one thing, I wasn't drinking during the early months of my pregnancy. I wasn't smoking either. For that matter, I wasn't drinking caffeine. I was doing everything I was told would help to ensure a healthy baby. Our producers, the Irwin Winklers, threw a baby shower for me. In the photos I have a distinct glow. Pregnancy suited me. Hollywood suited me. Working with Martin on his movie, I was very happy. It was working with the others that seemed difficult to me. Without a drink in my system, I was high-strung and paranoid. I didn't think they liked me, and perhaps they did not.

"Just do your job, Julia," I lectured myself. My job was to make the script ring true. *New York, New York* was a love story between two musicians, a jazz player and pop singer, played by Robert De Niro and Liza Minnelli. Theirs was to be a passionate, highly competitive relationship. De Niro was to have a wandering eye. It wasn't the happiest material for a newly married woman to be writing.

It didn't take Earl Mac Rausch very long to realize that his script was going in darker directions than he had intended. He withdrew from the scene. That left Mardik Martin and me, and we had a hard time agreeing on anything.

"I don't think she would do that, Mardik," I would complain.

"Well, she certainly wouldn't do what you are having her do."

In my version of reality, true love could conquer all. De Niro's Jimmy Doyle and Minnelli's Francine Evans could see their way clear to understanding each other and surviving infidelity. I wrote a draft of the film that ended with them resuming an affair years after their marriage had dissolved. In my scenario, what was right with them outweighed what was wrong. I was an optimist. All around me, a different scenario was unfolding.

After my initial fear of her, I came to see Liza Minnelli through much the same lens that she saw herself. She was a waif, I thought, a woman whose life had been very traumatic. She needed all the help and support she could get, everything from writing her good scenes to reassuring her at day's end that she had, in fact, played them well. Liza and I became inseparable. In the film Francine Evans becomes pregnant. In real life I was pregnant, and Liza claimed I taught her how to act the part. On film Liza played the vulnerable, abandoned wife. In life the role was mine to play. Martin and Liza drew closer and closer. They began to work late, then later still. There began to be rumors of their romantic involvement.

"Julia, don't be paranoid," I told myself. "Martin needs the freedom to work. Give it to him. He loves you." Night after night Martin stayed at the studio to work. I came home early and waited in the empty house, sometimes phoning the studio gate to see if his car had left yet. I was frightened to be pregnant and alone. Our house was situated only about a mile from the house where director Roman Polanski's pregnant wife, Sharon Tate, was murdered.

Soon we were fighting. Fights blew in out of nowhere and left us confused and exhausted. What was there to fight about? We were young and in love. And yet we fought. We disagreed about the ending of the film. Martin wanted a harsh ending and I feared it. If Jimmy Doyle and Francine Evans could divorce, where did that leave us?

"We're making a ten-million-dollar home movie," Martin began to say. I hated this remark. I didn't think I bore much resemblance to Francine Evans. I didn't think Martin was Jimmy Doyle. In the end, it didn't matter very much what I thought. The movie's reality overcame our own. The story he was telling captured Martin's imagination. He began to live it out. Despite Dita's predictions to the contrary, Martin and I were now star-crossed lovers.

Now very pregnant, I came to the set daily, watching Martin shoot scenes that were increasingly dark. Clearly the fictional Jimmy Doyle felt trapped in his relationship with Francine Evans. He cheated on her with a singer. Did Martin feel trapped with me? Was he cheating on me with Liza? "Julia, don't even think it," I scolded myself. Meanwhile, the columns began to have "items."

On Labor Day 1976, our one day off in a twenty-two-week-long schedule, Martin's and my daughter, Domenica, was born. I was determined to be "no trouble" and so I went into labor perfectly coiffed and made up, wearing an exquisite Chinese dressing gown. In between labor pains, I sent out for Chinese food and inaugurated a pool, betting on exactly when the baby would arrive. My guess was off by one minute, the closest anyone had ever come, according to our doctor. Martin was in the delivery room with me. Quick as a cat, he counted Domenica's fingers and toes. Ten. She was perfect. Maybe the bad dream was over? But no, Martin had plans to meet Liza and celebrate the baby's birth. Did I need anything, other than him? He was spoken for.

"I'd like some champagne and cocaine," I requested, trying to wrap myself in bad-girl allure. "And I'd like to get out of here as soon as I can." There was no getting out of the hospital, but soon I had my requested provisions. I thought that they would work to keep me company, but nothing could offset Martin's absence—and Liza's undeniable presence.

When it was time for me to come home from the hospital, Martin was at the studio shooting, and so, when the limousine came to fetch me, I asked the driver to take me not home but straight to the soundstage where he was filming. I see this now as a desperate action, but at the time I tried to tell myself it was normal. Of course I wanted to show off the baby. He would be glad to see me—to see us—and we would not be interrupting his work.

Looking back now, it is easy and painful to see how adrift I was. My whole identity was wrapped up in working, and now my work was motherhood—and that meant long stay-at-home days. The day before I went into labor, I had struck upon the final major rewrite necessary to the script. "Now can I have the other baby?" I had joked, sitting in the studio commissary. With both babies delivered, there was no real need for me on set. My writing was done and now the movie was something Martin could make without me. But who was I without it and him?

I had avoided alcohol and drugs during the term of my pregnancy. Returning to their use, I found myself instantly out of control. My brakes were gone. The very first drink led to many more. The first line of cocaine led to the next, and the next, until there was no more cocaine left to consume and I was on the phone to a dealer.

"Missus, are you okay?" our nanny repeatedly asked me. We had hired her carefully. She was nurturing by nature. She saw it as her job to care not only for Domenica but for me as well. My behavior alarmed her. No matter how she tried to tempt me, I preferred wine to food. Drinking, I would call my worried East Coast friends, who didn't know what to do for me.

"Are you writing?" they knew to ask. Writing had always been the anchor of my world.

"I am trying," I answered—and I did try to write.

With cocaine in my system, I did not black out and so I could stay at the typewriter for long work sessions. But if cocaine kept me at the keys, it did not keep me coherent. It is an obsessive drug and my writing became snagged on repetitions. I would say something one way and then another. Then I would try it a third way and a fourth way. There were simply too many choices for me to make among them. I would fly forward, then screech to a halt. The writing was uneven and unproductive.

"Missus? Are you okay?" The question came again on an afternoon when I had collapsed, exhausted. "I think you need doctor."

And so, when Domenica was merely weeks old, I did go see the doctor, who diagnosed me as suffering from exhaustion. I told him nothing of my alcohol and cocaine abuse. He told me in no uncertain terms that I needed to go home to bed "and stop worrying so much." I wondered how he knew that I was worrying. Reluctantly I went to bed.

Once in bed, I could neither sleep nor rest. Martin was coming home later and later. My long and empty days began to include long and empty nights. "He's just working, Julia," I told myself, but I was beginning to dream terrible dreams.

I dreamed there was a cobra coiled in a corner of our bedroom. "Martin, a snake!" I exclaimed. As I said this, the snake turned its head slowly in our direction. "That's no snake," Martin said. To my horror, I saw the snake had Liza's face.

I dreamed that Liza was a cutout figure, like a large paper doll. She wore fancy clothes that covered her in the front but left her nude in the back. In my dream Martin saw her only from the front, only as glamorous. She had no flaws. She was never naked like the rest of us.

"They're only working," I chided myself about my imaginings. Liza was married, happily it seemed, to writer-producer Jack Haley. If he wasn't worrying, why should I? Martin had always overworked more than worked. His late nights at the studio were simply part of his character. I had married him for better or for worse. This was just a patch of "for worse," and surely I could get through it.

The problem was how I tried to get through it. I was stymied in my writing and stymied in my personal affairs. I was privately frightened by my alcohol and drug use, but among my companions, there were always people whose substance abuse was worse than my own. I would make a lunch date to talk with an old friend and I would end up at lunch plastered. I wouldn't remember getting home. Without cocaine I blacked out after only a few drinks. With cocaine I wanted to drink far more than just a few drinks. I could drink the ocean.

The dealer used to tease me, "You have a little tiny wife's habit. That's all."

I didn't want to be "a little tiny wife." I wanted to be myself again, the self I knew as a writer. I decided to rent an office. Martin could go to the studio to work. I would go to my office. Surely an empty room and an empty page would call forth the muse. I found an office in Beverly Hills that looked exactly right to me, like something out of Raymond Chandler. I settled in to write. I drank instead.

Telling myself that a glass of wine would get me past my fears, I would drink the first drink of the day. That drink would drink the second drink. By the third, I was in trouble. Without cocaine to forestall blackouts, drinking was dangerous. With cocaine my writing tangled up, and while I might spend a full day at the typewriter, I would have little to show for it. The office wasn't solving anything. To the contrary. It simply gave me a safe and secret place in which to binge. On more than one occasion I drank until I passed out, coming to on the office floor, late in the day. I was frightened.

"I think I am in trouble," I told Arthur Kretchmer, my *Playboy* editor. He had come to town for one day and we met near my office for lunch. I drank through lunch.

"I think you are in trouble," Arthur replied. "Why didn't you tell me sooner? You could have, you know." But I didn't know what to do with Arthur's pity and concern. I wanted to be tough enough to take it—"it" being whatever fate dished out.

Martin was now working on three separate projects: *New York, New York,* a music documentary film with Robbie Robertson called *The Last Waltz,* and a musical stage play with Liza called *The Act.* His career was in overdrive and he wanted to take every opportunity that came his way. Like so many newly famous, he was acting and feeling larger than life. Fame was an aphrodisiac. As he has said, the reality of a wife and a newborn baby did not deter him.

From our house on Mulholland Drive to Robbie Robertson's house in the Malibu Colony was about a forty-five-minute drive. I made it often. I liked Robbie's wife, Dominique, and felt she was a kindred spirit. She, like myself, had met her future husband on a writing assignment. She, like myself, had an identity as a writer. Spending time with her, I felt my spirits revive—this despite the fact that Malibu was laced with drugs, most notably cocaine. Spending more and more time out at the Colony, I began to score larger and larger amounts. My "tiny little wife's habit" was spiraling out of control.

Oddly, life in the Malibu Colony gave me a comforting feeling of normalcy. Drug habits were common among rock-and-roll wives. So were once-upon-a-time careers. No one was shocked by my behavior. They had seen addiction before. In the Colony, talk of what you could have and should have been was a tried-and-true topic. I fit right in.

The Last Waltz was to be a documentary filled with rock-and-roll notables from Bob Dylan to Neal Young to Joni Mitchell to Howlin' Wolf. It would be filmed in San Francisco and then additional footage would be shot on a Los Angeles soundstage. It was to be a lavish shoot with multiple 35-millimeter cameras. For Martin, the film was an act of love. He had served as chief editor on *Woodstock* and rock and roll was in his blood. For me as a journalist, the film presented many fine opportunities for interviews. I hoped that Martin would let me work.

Increasingly I lived a life of "would Martin let me." Without my writing to anchor me, I was fragile and storm-tossed. In a town that names credits before the arrest, my sole credit was being Martin's wife. I spiraled further and further into alcoholism and drug addiction, alone in the house on the hill. Meanwhile Martin's celebrity increased and the rumors of his involvement with Liza only increased it further. An on-set romance. What could be more common tabloid fodder? We were all stock players in a drama that Hollywood had seen played out many times before.

"You can't keep going the way you are going," Martin told me one night when he had arrived home earlier than usual to find me drunker than usual.

"What do you mean?" I didn't like being cornered.

"You know what I mean. I mean the drinking."

"You could come home."

"What's that got to do with it? You don't drink because of me. You drink because you drink."

Martin was right about that. I did drink because I drank. I didn't need reasons to drink or even excuses. I was simply a drinker, and drinkers drank. If anything, Martin's absence made drinking convenient. Self-pity was the rim of the glass: "Poor me. Poor me. Pour me a drink."

A friend of mine from the East Coast was visiting Los Angeles that week. Martin spoke to her about my drinking. She, too, agreed I needed to stop. He told me about their conversation. I didn't want to hear it. Life was difficult enough. Drinking was my solution, not my problem. I thought they were both crazy and also hypocritical. Let them clean up their own lives before pointing fingers at me. It never occurred to me that their motivation might be genuine concern and not moral superiority. If I had once believed that Martin loved me, I didn't believe it anymore. Alcohol was now my lover and my friend. Alcohol was my constant, understanding companion. Don't let anyone try to take it away. Not anyone.

I have a telling photo from those days. It was taken on the old MGM lot where we were working. *King Kong* was being remade, and Kong inhabited a soundstage near our own. Martin was invited to visit the great creature, and he took me with him. In the photo Martin and I are standing in Kong's palm. When I look at the photo now, I see it as emblematic of the trouble we were in. Like Kong, our trouble held us in its fist. Like Kong, it could crush us at any moment. Martin and I smile for the camera, but our smiles are death-row grins. It is easy in cozy retrospect to see the irony of the photograph. We smile triumphantly, oblivious of our danger. We were so young and in so desperately over our heads— clichés in the maw of Hollywood. Our messy lives made the papers.

Martin and Liza. Liza and Martin. The tabloids couldn't get enough. Then, as now, the tabloids were full of broken hearts and broken lives, this time ours. Sudden fame is a tsunami that sweeps into a life. On its tide it carries new people and opportunities. In its wake it savages sweet relationships. Martin's sudden fame had swept into our lives. We were spinning out of control. Martin saw it for me. I saw it for him. But we couldn't listen to each other's warnings.

One night I dreamed that he and Liza were out at sea in a small skiff. A storm was threatening to sweep them away. Martin tried to pilot the skiff but it could not be steered. For one thing, Liza would not listen to his instructions. They were in danger of capsizing. "Be careful!" I tried to warn him. He would not listen to me. Suddenly another figure appeared in the dream. This strange man took over the prow of the skiff. Under his hand, it steadied. Liza obeyed his directions, but Martin was swept overboard. I watched in horror as he managed to cling to a passing spar, barely surviving with his life.

"You're in trouble," I tried to warn Martin. Real life was now imitating my dream. His production of the musical *The Act* was spinning out of control. There was talk of bringing in a second director, Gower Champion. There was talk, period.

Martin took *The Act* to San Francisco to work on it. I followed him there, hoping that my writing skills might somehow save the day. Going to the theater to work, Martin left me with the scenes that didn't play. Locked in our hotel room, I tried to solve them—and I drank. Room service brought me bottles. The scotch did not bring me clarity. The scenes remained unsolved. *The Act* had a perfectly good writer, George Firth. My "help" was unnecessary and unwanted. Why couldn't I just go home? My presence embarrassed everyone. More than ever, the tabloids were filled with stories. I read those stories and I drank. Drunk, I had a violent fight with Martin. Drunk, I drank some more and packed for home.

But where was home? Martin and *The Act* were heading for Chicago, where my family lived. Was that home? It didn't feel that way. And Los Angeles without Martin seemed foreign as well. Nothing felt right until an East Coast editor called wanting me to come back east and work on a story. This I understood. Work was home to me. I flew to New York.

My plan was simple. I would check into the Sherry-Netherland Hotel, I would locate some cocaine to keep from blacking out, and I would settle in to write. I had done good work many times alone in a hotel room. I would do good work again, and that would serve to put things right. I belonged in New York, not in Hollywood, and I belonged writing my own material, not trying to help Martin with his. Sanity lay in autonomy. Baby Domenica was safe in the care of a trusted nanny. If I could just focus on writing, everything would be okay.

My room was on the twenty-second floor. It featured a stunning view of Central Park. I set up my writing table and phoned room service for supplies. I ordered J&B, my old standby. When it arrived, I quickly downed a double. It had been a long flight. I probably needed to eat something, I realized, but the arrival of my cocaine made any thoughts of nutrition disappear. It was early evening as I settled in to write. Predictably my drinking outpaced my literary production. And then the lights went out.

From my window, cabs still were visible pouring south along Fifth Avenue. But the familiar lights of Manhattan's West Side were no longer visible across the park. The West Side was dark and so was Midtown. No matter how far I strained to see out my window, all that met my eyes was darkness. I tried the phone. It still worked. I dialed the number for Martin's parents. Yes, they were all right, but what was I doing in New York without Martin? "Working," I told them. "I am here on assignment."

There was no leaving my hotel room. The elevators were not running and the hallways were dark. Alone with the phone and my bottle, I tried Martin's number in Chicago. He didn't answer. He would not answer his phone all night.

As long as I had enough cocaine, I could drink without blacking out, but I did not have enough cocaine. Just as darkness had seized the city, darkness now seized my mind. I could continue to act, but my mind would no longer record my actions. I do not know how many hours I sat awake and drinking, dialing the phone to hear it ring in an empty hotel room halfway across the country. Eventually I slept.

When I woke, the city was still in blackout. I was still unable to leave my hotel room. I had a third of a bottle of scotch left—not enough to get really drunk, too much to drink and remain truly sober. There was still no answer in Martin's Chicago hotel suite. He had either left very early or not come home. I drank my first drink of the day. As it burned its way into my system, so did the certainty that my marriage was over. I drank the second scotch of the day and then the third. The bottle was now empty and I was now halfway drunk. I would go to Chicago, I decided.

When the blackout ended, I made my way by cab to LaGuardia, where I flew to O'Hare Airport. The flight from New York was uneventful—but not for me. I sat next to a kindly stranger and I told him what I so newly knew: "My marriage is over." The stranger was sympathetic and polite. My drunken confession was received with kindness.

At Martin's hotel I got a key from the front desk and let myself into the suite. I opened the closet to unpack my clothes—and found myself staring at Liza's clothes instead. Neat as soldiers, her silk shirts marched across "my" half of the closet. I could hear the excuse: "The valet made a mistake," but I no longer had to believe it. I felt myself begin to shake apart.

For much of my childhood, my parents had suffered nervous breakdowns. When they came apart, we would drive them to Forest Hospital in Des Plaines. Now that I felt myself beginning to come apart, I placed a call to Forest. I got my parents' doctor on the phone and explained that I needed his help. He said he would see me as soon as I could get there. The friend who had worried about my drinking in Los Angeles happened to be in Chicago that week, and she volunteered to drive me. En route to the hospital, we had a car accident that sent me flying against the windshield. I arrived at the hospital streaming blood from a cut on my scalp.

"You need a real hospital for that cut," said the nurse in admissions.

"It will be okay," I told her.

"I don't really want to admit you, Julie," the doctor said when he greeted me. He knew me from my parents' many admissions. "Why don't you tell me what is going on?"

I told him that my marriage was blowing apart. I added, "And I think I am an alcoholic."

"You're a sensitive young woman and you have just gone through a traumatic marriage," he told me. "That's why you are drinking. It's situational." At my insistence, the doctor did admit me, although he was careful to tell me he didn't feel I was having "difficulties like my parents."

The doctor's plan was simple. He would test me to see if my

dreams were grandiose or realistic. Locked away safely in the hospital, I could survey my life. Now rendered genuinely sober, if only for a few days, I could study the wreckage of my marriage. Martin was informed of my hospitalization and responded by sending two dozen red roses. My daughter, Domenica, flown in from Los Angeles, was tucked away at my parents' house now. I have a photograph of me holding her on my lap on the hospital swing. The breeze lifts her bangs. She smiles happily. I look fragile and very sad.

"Your tests show you're very gifted," the doctor told me. "In all my years of testing, I have never encountered scores like these. You are right to have large dreams. You have large abilities."

"My marriage is over."

"Yes. It would seem so."

"I need a divorce."

"I think that might be wise."

And so, from the mental hospital, I contacted Martin and told him I would not be coming back. His red roses were still glorious when I made the call.

My parents were worried about me. They had no experience with divorce. Typically marriages in our family were long-lived and happy. How would I raise my daughter alone? they worried. I worried the same thing.

Where is home? I still asked myself. Was it in Chicago with my parents? Was it back in Washington or New York, where I had been a hard-drinking single? No, it seemed that home would have to be Los Angeles. Before Martin, I had planned on a life in the movies. If I wanted that life still, I had to go west to get it. And so, after five days in the hospital, with a newly initiated divorce on my hands, I boarded a plane to fly west. As the stewardess circulated to take drink orders, I reassured myself that the doctor did not think I was an alcoholic. Since I wasn't an alcoholic, I might as well have a drink. That drink was the first of many.

Back in Los Angeles I retrieved my typewriter from the house I shared with Martin. His house was his house, I decided, and moved myself into the Sunset Marquis, a hotel favored by visiting journalists. I set up my typewriter and called it home.

"You need a house. You can't live here. Not with the baby," pronounced Dita Sullivan, Domenica's godmother. She and her boyfriend, screenwriter Alex Jacobs, took me in hand. They would help me to find a house. In fact, there was a wonderful house where Alex had lived while he wrote *Point Blank.* That house used to belong to Dennis Hopper and would surely be good luck for a writer. It now belonged to veteran actor Max Showalter. He lived next door, in the old Gable and Lombard house, and he might be happy to rent to a young mother. The house was fully furnished and featured a glorious half-acre garden that Max fussed over daily. In the back of the garden was a log cabin playhouse. Domenica would love it.

Max Showalter had a golden heart. As Alex outlined the situation, Max quickly took it in. I stood before him fragile and shaky, trying to appear calm. I loved the house. It was snug and charming. There was room in it for me, Domenica, and a nanny. Max already knew from the papers of my divorce and stood ready to help. Domenica and I could move in immediately. We could rent for a year and see where it went from there.

And so I moved into 7959 Hollywood Boulevard. My mother flew out with Domenica and I placed an ad looking for help with child care. (Domenica's previous nanny had been fired for stealing.) I settled on a fresh-faced young woman named Kate. She could have the apartment over the garage. I would put Domenica in the bedroom near mine.

"I am a writer," I explained to Kate. "I need to get back to work or there won't be any money. If you can give me my days free to work—" Kate said she could.

"I hate to go home and leave you out here alone," my mother told me.

"I'll be okay. Kate will be good."

"You're so far away."

"Oh, Mom. I'll call. We can write each other."

"I just want you to know I am very proud of you and I think you are setting up a surprisingly workable household." With that said, my mother left for her plane.

It was true, as my mother said, that I had the rudiments of a workable household. It was also true that I had a drinking problem. Max had kindly told me about a package store that delivered, Almor Liquor. I opened an account and placed what was to be a daily order. In fact, it was to be a twice-daily order. In the morning, full of high resolve to control my drinking, I would order several bottles of white wine. By midafternoon, defeated again, I would order hard liquor, scotch or vodka or cognac. If the liquor delivery man ever judged me, he never let on. He would set the bottles on my kitchen table, accept my tip, and say, "Thank you, ma'am." I would add the receipt to a basket of receipts—precious few of them for food.

I set my typewriter on my dining room table and every morning I would take myself to the page. "This is a movie about love and friendship, treachery and revenge," I wrote on page one: "In short, 'the works.'" The trick was to write while I was still sober enough to write, to write while the liquor was working for me instead of against me.

"No cocaine," I lectured myself, even though with cocaine I could write far longer. "Coke is dangerous and illegal and you can't have it around the baby," I decided.

Casting about for something to blame for my failed marriage, I had settled on my cocaine use. Hadn't that accelerated my drinking? Hadn't that made me into a person I didn't recognize? Coked up and drunk, I was a handful. "Take her home," Martin would tell Mardik Martin, who did—although he didn't want a volatile drunk in his new Cadillac. What I now wanted to be was responsible. If I couldn't quit drinking, and I could not, I could at least try to quit cocaine.

And I did try—

Every morning I settled in to write with a bottle of white wine and the coffee cup I drank it from. My script was dark and vengeful. At first I would fly along. I would drink as I wrote and the drinking would give me fluidity—until it gave me something else, a blackout. Now I was in danger. I might keep writing or I might get on the phone. I might decide to visit Almor Liquor in person and lay in more booze for the afternoon's drinking. It was on one such trip to Almor Liquor that I met a neighbor, Nathan. He was a friendly bachelor who happened to sell cocaine and heroin.

"I am trying to stop," I told him.

"We're all trying to stop," he replied.

"Maybe just a gram," I relented.

Armed with cocaine, I attacked my script with renewed resolve. The only trick was to stay in my seat and keep writing. The drug made me paranoid, and that paranoia belonged on the page, not pacing window to window, staring out into the garden, looking for the intruders I thought I heard.

"Are you okay?" Kate took to asking me. Clearly I was not okay.

By day I would write and drink. By night I would try to be sober enough to spend time with my daughter—but Kate was understandably reluctant to leave me with her alone. There was the time when I simply passed out, locking us both in a bathroom while I slept it off. No, Kate did not think I was okay and she did not think I could be trusted. She was right. Every day became a test. I argued with myself and always lost.

"Cocaine will help you write."

"Cocaine will make me crazy."

"Cocaine will help you write."

"I can't afford cocaine."

"You can't afford not to write."

And so I would call Nathan and he would bring over the drug—except when he brought over heroin instead. I was afraid of heroin but I tried it. I was ready to try anything that might work—anything except quitting drinking.

In the wake of Martin's and my separation, I had begun to see a Beverly Hills psychiatrist. Like the doctor back in Chicago, he believed my drinking was situational.

"You're very smart," he said. "You will figure this out."

As close as I came to figuring it out was when I read an article in *Vogue*, "How I Stopped Drinking, Lost Ten Pounds, and Wrote a Novel." The article was by a Los Angeles–based writer, Eve Babitz. I would call Eve up and tell her how well she wrote, I decided. Every writer likes a compliment. . . .

The first Babitz that I located was Eve's grandmother. After ascertaining that I sounded harmless enough, she gave me Eve's unlisted number and I called. I must have done a persuasive job of sounding interesting. After some initial coolness, Eve agreed to pay me a visit. I planned for her to drop by early in the afternoon. My only job was to stay sober enough to receive her. I didn't manage the job.

"What you need to do is stop drinking," Eve told me as her afternoon's visit became a diagnostic one.

"Don't you think that's a little melodramatic?" I was trying for a tough-girl persona, but Eve's had mine totally beat.

"I think you called me because you want to stop drinking," Eve ventured.

"Oh, I don't think that's why I called you. I think I just wanted to meet another good writer." Maybe flattery would get me off the hook, but no.

"Think what you want. It wouldn't hurt to give stopping a try."

Eve left me with a few things to think about. Chief among them, drinking and writing didn't mix. I had to admit that my own dashes onto the page were becoming shorter and shorter. Cocaine made me lucid but repetitive. White wine made me muddy, and hard alcohol led to rapid blackouts. Maybe Eve was right, I found myself thinking. Maybe I should stop drinking. I no sooner had the thought than it multiplied and surrounded me.

"You should try not drinking," a newly made friend, songwriter Jupiter Rey, told me. "That's why your hands shake. That's why you're sick all the time. Just quit for a week."

A week sounded easy enough. Surely I could quit for a week. I told Jupiter I would give it a try. And I did. I was proud of my fresh resolve, proud of my several clearheaded days of writing. But on day three I called Almor's. I couldn't be an alcoholic if I could quit, could I?

In the midst of my personal chaos, my journalism career was heating up again. I once more had assignments to write for *New York* and *New West*. My editors were true to their word that if Martin and I would just divorce, I would again be employable. Juggling white wine and cocaine, I managed to write three pieces. Fan letters fluttered in, one of them from an old college friend. "Are you the same Julia Cameron I knew at Georgetown?" a letter wondered. It was signed Ed Towle, a name I knew very well. There was a number to call if I desired contact.

Tall, blond, dazzlingly smart, and attractive, Ed Towle was the Robert Redford of my college class. Of course I remembered him. I called the number on the letter and suggested that we meet for dinner. Ed suggested a chic restaurant in Venice Beach. I dressed with care.

"A drink?" Ed asked, not knowing the trouble he was buying. I ordered a margarita. Then a second. Then a third. Dinner became a boozy affair with me waxing maudlin about our college days together. At dinner's end Ed didn't think I could safely drive home.

"Stay at my place," he offered. "On the couch."

He did not say, "Drunk as you are, I wouldn't touch you with a ten-foot pole," but he might as well have. The rebuff was clear and so was the concern about my safety. We made it back to Ed's place, where I slept on the couch. I say "slept," but my night was fitful. I passed out initially and then came to—alone and awake in a strange house. I was still drunk, but not so drunk that I didn't want to keep drinking. Ed was sleeping peacefully upstairs. I crept up the stairs. "Ed," I said. No, he didn't want me to join him. Sober enough, I said I would drive home.

When I got home, Kate was feeding the baby breakfast. This was a first. I had stayed out all night.

"I don't know if you remember it, but you have a songwriting date at ten," she informed me. I opened a bottle of white wine and sipped at "breakfast."

At ten A.M. Jerry Frankel arrived to write with me. He was a tall, sparkling Yalie who thought I had lyrical talents. We sat down to write and then suddenly I slipped into a blackout. My carefully sipped white wine was no protection. Not when mixed with the pills my psychiatrist had given me. No, Elavil and wine were a deadly combination. With drinking to compete with, songwriting quickly went out the window. Thinking me talented "but wild, a handful," Jerry left before noon.

Now it was noon on a Saturday and the weekend stretched before me. I was drunk and drinking more. I might do anything. For the first time, Martin was back in Los Angeles and due to have visitation rights with Domenica. I knew through the grapevine that my dream of him in the skiff had proved prophetic. Director Gower Champion had taken over the helm of his show with Liza. According to rumor, Champion had taken over with Liza as well. With Liza out of the picture, Martin and I might reconcile. There might still be love between us, or so I thought as I drank my way through a long afternoon, poring over our wedding albums.

"Martin is here," Kate said. She stepped aside and he entered the room.

Martin was there and I was in no shape to receive him. He hated my drunks and that is what I was having. I begged him to please look at the albums with me. We looked so beautiful and so happy—but I didn't look beautiful or happy any longer.

"I think I should go," Martin said. "I don't think this is a good idea."

"We were so happy."

"I think I need to go, Julia."

And with that, he did leave. I watched from my living room window as he slipped into the driver's seat of the Lotus and pulled away from the curb. "My God, I have truly lost him," I thought. Mercifully a blackout seized my mind.

I cannot account for the next twenty-four hours. I do not know if I continued to drink or if the alcohol in my system was already enough to keep me drunk. What I do know is that when I came to, it was early Monday morning. A brown gram bottle of either cocaine or heroin sat on my bedside table. I had a cut at the corner of my right eye and a black eye was settling in. Had I fallen? Had someone hit me? Who had brought me the drugs and perhaps shared them or my bed? I didn't know the answer to these questions.

I made my way from my bedroom, past the room where Domenica lay sleeping, to the steep staircase that led downstairs. Carefully and cautiously, although it was too late for either care or caution, I made my way down. It was a clear winter's day. The sun rising in the east was chiseling its way through the shutters that kept the living room in semidarkness. I collapsed into a large white chair and watched the pattern the sun made as it walked its way in stripes across the floor. As they had for months, my hands were shaking and a film of cold sweat covered my brow. "I need a drink," I caught myself thinking. "I have to have a drink."

The bottle of scotch next to my bed had been empty. I had probably drunk my way through the night, passing out, coming to, and drinking again until the bottle was gone and I was awake despite myself. As far as I knew, I had not called the police to investigate intruders—the sounds I kept hearing from the garden. For months the police had come repeatedly and always assured me that no one was there. But I had heard and seen things, things inaudible and invisible to anyone else.

"I need a drink," I thought again, while still taking inventory of my situation. Was this night so much worse than others before it? Wasn't a blackout preferable to my occasional hallucinations? Blacked out, I had not had a visit from the tall, spectral man, dressed all in black, who would sit at the end of my bed or stand in the darkened corner. "The vampire priest" I called this nocturnal visitor—and this time he had not come.

"I have about twenty minutes before I have to drink," I caught myself thinking. "If I don't drink, I'll be very sick." This thought was a new one for me. I had always maintained that I chose to drink, not that I *needed* to. I felt a mounting panic. The glare from the window hurt my eyes. Suddenly, like a slot machine lining up a row of lemons, the events of my life clicked into place: I didn't drink for any of the reasons I told myself. I drank because I drank. I was a drinker, a drunk. Martin's warnings, the concerns of my friends— their accusations were all accurate. What was I going to do?

It was barely six A.M. The liquor store wouldn't open for another hour. Without a drink I needed some relief from my consciousness. If only I had someone to talk to. I reached for the phone. Who could I call at this hour? A trusted East Coast friend, I decided. I dialed the phone.

"Hello. Who is it?" My friend sounded groggy. It wasn't the first time I had called her when drinking. Her father was an alcoholic, and she was long trained at listening to a drunk.

"It's Julia," I managed to say. "I don't know what I am going to do."

"Julia? Just a minute. I'll call you back." My friend got off the phone. Maybe it was a mistake to call her, I thought. Maybe even her patience had been stretched too thin. I was just about to give up, when the phone shrilled.

"Hello?"

"Julia, I have a number for you. I think you should talk to another alcoholic."

"You really think I am an alcoholic?"

"Well . . ." My friend's voice trailed off. She wasn't willing to accuse me directly.

"Don't worry. I'll call." I had already diagnosed myself.

3.

I do not remember dialing the number. I do not know what I said. I might have said something like, "My name is Julia. I am a writer and I might be an alcoholic." I still had them intertwined, the writing and the drinking. I still thought they had something to do with each other, but the alcoholic on the phone had no such illusions. To her, I was an alcoholic, period. The solution to my alcoholism was very simple: don't drink. Total abstinence was the answer, she explained. And total abstinence meant exactly that.

I knew in my bones that she was right. The alcoholic stranger on the telephone clearly had my number. She intuitively understood the number of ways I had contrived to control and enjoy my drinking—all failures. What was more, she knew someone who could talk to me. Was I willing to listen? Could I stay sober just until help arrived? I said I thought I could. "Help" was another alcoholic willing to share his experience, strength, and hope with me. If I could accept myself as an alcoholic, there was a way out.

When I look at my life from the vantage point of today, twenty-seven years and half a lifetime later, I see that everything changed on the day I committed myself to staying sober. "Just don't drink," I was told. "It's the first drink that gets you drunk." It had never occurred to me that it was the very first drink that led me into trouble. I was astounded by this truthful simplicity. For years I had juggled my drinking and my behaviors, always thinking it was the third drink or perhaps the fifth that was the problem. Staying away from the very first drink seemed simple enough. There was great logic and simplicity to statements like "If you don't drink, you can't get drunk." After years of complicated living and complicated lying, my life needed such simplicity.

"Just don't drink," I told myself in the days that followed. "And don't use any mind-altering drugs either," my newfound friends added. Sobriety was defined as being both sober and clean. For me, this meant no more cocaine. Alcoholism was an addiction, I was told. I had a disease. It was fatal and progressive but could be arrested by total abstinence. My abstinence could be built one day at a time. In fact, all of my life could benefit from a one-day-at-a-time regime. Such a life would require faith, faith in some power greater than myself.

To Dr. Carl Jung, the formula was simple: Spiritus contra spiriti. (Spirit versus spirits.) I was told to pick a God of my own understanding. I was told to ask that God for help with my sobriety. Just what kind of God could I believe in? That question had troubled me since I was young. Surely there had to be something? If not Paul Tillich's "ground of being," something else? I found myself thinking of a line from Dylan Thomas: "The force that through the green fuse drives the flower." I could believe in a benevolent creative energy, I decided. That energy would be my higher power—and I would need a higher power.

"Jules," Nathan phoned me to say, "I have a scotch in one hand and a syringe in the other."

"I've quit drinking," I told him. "If you want to talk to some people . . . ?"

To my astonishment, Nathan was open-minded, and he, too, began the struggle to get sober.

Sobriety was foreign territory for me. I was accustomed to being drunk and single, then drunk and married. Now I was sober, unmarried, and a single mother. My daughter was fourteen months old and she needed my time and attention. Drunk, I could hand her off to Kate's care, telling myself she was better off, certainly safer. Sober, I wanted to care for her myself. Sensing this sea change, Kate abruptly quit. That left just the two of us. I might not be the ideal mother, but I was the mother that Domenica had gotten. I set up her playpen in the dining room near my writing station. One morning I cued up the Rolling Stones, and as their hit "Brown Sugar" pulsed through the room, Domenica and I danced to its beat.

"I am your mommy. This is what your mommy's like," I told her.

"Mommee!" Domenica exclaimed in return.

With Kate gone, Domenica and I were inseparable. From the moment she woke in the morning until I put her to sleep at night, we were a team. "On my hip," I would tell her, holding her by the hand to cross a wide Los Angeles street. Sober, I was a vigilant, even hypervigilant, mother. I took Domenica with me everywhere. She crawled under my feet as I wrote.

"How do I write sober?" was the big question that sobriety raised. I told the alcoholics who were helping me, "If it comes down to choice between my creativity and my sobriety, I don't know that I will choose sobriety."

"There is no choice," they promptly answered me. "Keep on drinking and there will be no more creativity."

I knew that they were right. I had to find a way to work that would not require alcohol or drugs. If I were honest with myself, my methods had not really been working for some time.

"Stop trying to be a great writer," they advised me next. "That's your ego. Get your ego out of your writing. You should be writing from a spirit of service. You are just the vehicle, the channel. Let God write through you."

"What if he doesn't want to?"

"Just try it and see." I was not at all sure that God would want to write through me. And wasn't it only normal to want to be a great writer?

"In order to write sober, you have to let God take care of the quality," my mentors sternly told me. "Your job is to take care of the quantity."

It was suggested that I post a sign in my writing area, "Okay, God, you take care of the quality. I will take care of the quantity." Then it was suggested that I set a manageable quota of daily work: three pages.

If it took all day to write three pages, I was to remain at my desk working until my quota was complete. More likely, the three pages would get accomplished quickly. When they were finished, I was done for the day. I was not to write more than three pages.

The idea that writing could be something that didn't require my whole day was a revelation to me—and a threat. My identity was bound up with being a writer. If writing was just one of the things I did, who was I, then? I was used to the self-importance of being a writer. I had bought into the notion that artists were tormented and that their every waking thought needed to be given to their art. My new friends were suggesting that such a stance was really just an ego trip. God was the Great Creator, they pointed out. I was, after all, one of God's creations myself.

I posted the little sign. I settled Domenica in her playpen and I started to write. My head started in, "This isn't any good. This is terrible. You can do better. Start again." I was used to such self-loathing diatribes while I wrote. I was used to writing and rewriting, striving for perfection. Then I remembered, "I am not supposed to be judging. I am just supposed to be writing." Quality was up to God. I was in charge only of quantity.

Now when my head started in with its vitriol, I had an answer for it. "Good, bad, or indifferent—it's not mine to judge."

Imagine my surprise when my writing began to respond to this new and far more charitable agenda. Now that I was no longer judging and condemning my sentences, my prose seemed to relax a little and to straighten out. If God were indeed writing through me, God had an easier and more accessible prose style than I did. Less self-consciously clever and ego-driven, my new prose was more likable. I even liked it myself.

"There is such a thing as a rough draft," my writing mentors advised me. "Try to simply get things on the page. They can be fixed later—if they need to be fixed, that is."

I was dubious about writing with such ease. Wasn't I supposed to suffer? Wasn't writing supposed to take everything I had? If it didn't, was it real writing?

To my surprise, the pages that I was accumulating seemed to have coherence and even flair. I began to like the three-pages-a-day quota. "Just give me a few more minutes," I would say to

Domenica when she fussed—and I would mean it. Writing seemed to happen now with insulting speed. I was still working on my movie script, *The Works,* and scenes and dialogue came to me readily. My characters fairly seemed to chatter. I wasn't so much writing as I was eavesdropping. I wasn't so much thinking something up as taking something down.

The sense of direction seemed to be important. I began to experience myself as dropping down a sort of well, coming into contact with a source of creativity that flowed of its own accord, something I tapped into rather than something I generated. Creativity is a constant, I ruefully realized. When I was writing out of my ego, I was the one who was fickle. The stream of ideas was always there, ready and available. I had been too high-strung, too self-centered to be able to avail myself of it. All of this was changing, and changing rapidly with sobriety. It began to seem natural to create, not some superhuman trait for which I should be applauded. I began to have the idea that the Great Creator enjoyed my own creativity.

Rather than facing my writing day with dread, I began to look forward to it. It began to be a process of discovery. I was curious to see what would unfold next. I found myself losing my sense of myself as an "author" and gaining a sense of myself as a conduit. I found I wrote best when I felt empty of ego, curious, and receptive rather than full of ideas.

There were days when I cheated and wrote more than three pages: "I'm doing so well, I can't stop now!" I found that as soon as I did so, my ego woke up, "proud" of what "I" had "accomplished." The reemergence of ego was distinctly uncomfortable. I began to see the wisdom that lay in a small, modest quota, nothing to get all worked up about.

When I was tempted to binge on my work, my advisers would

caution me, "Easy does it." At first I heard this as a bromide. I thought they were telling me something like "Oh, calm down." My ego hated the phrase "Easy does it." My ego still wanted binges of writing, the drama of trying to write flat-out.

All too soon I learned that binges invited an equal and opposite reaction. I would binge one day and feel "dry" and "empty" the next. Instead of steady production, I would experience spurts. My progress would zoom ahead, then skid to a halt.

"Easy does it," I was told again, and this time with a bit more explanation. "Easy does it means 'easy accomplishes it,'" I was told. "If you are willing to go along 'slowly,' you will be amazed how quickly pages accumulate. Three pages a day is ninety pages a month. That's a lot of prose."

"Try to make your habits nonnegotiable," I was advised. "Simply make it an unbreakable rule that you write three pages a day."

And so I settled in, writing three pages a day, writing them often very fast and with a great deal of ease.

"This stuff can't be any good," my ego would protest, but I soon observed that there was very little connection between how hard my writing was to accomplish and the caliber of the work in the end.

"I am not a writer. I am a word processor," I complained to my coaches.

"You're writing, aren't you?"

"Yes, I am."

"And it's pretty good, isn't it?"

"Yes, I think it is."

"Well then, who cares if you are a word processor?"

"Oh."

Working by the "easy does it" method, I completed the entire screenplay in my first three months of sobriety. To my surprise, the script read well and the fixes required to move from first to second draft were easy to see.

"How do you write with a baby underfoot?" people asked me.

"Oh, I write quickly," I joked, but I wasn't kidding. With my ego in check, pages did come to me quickly—so quickly that other people began to notice.

"I wish I could be as productive as you are," a fellow writer groused to me. He was stymied, blocked between novels. "I want to write another book, but I just don't feel ready," he told me.

"Ready?"

"You know. In the mood. I mean, it's such hard work."

"What if I told you writing could be easy?" I asked. "Would you be interested?"

"Of course I would."

"Interested enough to try a little experiment?"

"Well, sure. I mean, I guess so."

I told the blocked writer about the little sign in the writing area, the daily quota of three pages. He listened with skepticism. "This is really how you are writing these days?"

"It really is."

"I'm supposed to let something write through me?"

"That's the idea."

"What if nothing does?"

"Well, try it. Maybe the 'something' likes writing through you."

I thought perhaps calling the "something" "God" would be too much for the writer to swallow. I thought he would find the little sign hokey. I underestimated his desperation to get unblocked.

Obediently he made the little sign about God taking care of the quality and his taking care of the quantity. Then he began to write. At first he wrote longhand on legal paper, then he switched to little speckled-covered books. Like me, he found that a day's work could be accomplished with insulting speed. Like me, he found that if he binged, the work suffered. Following my lead, he began to work the "easy does it" approach.

"Hey, I am really racking up pages," he told me.

"I'll bet you are. I am glad."

About this time I got a phone call from my sister Libby, a fine artist. She, too, had noticed my productivity, as well as the way I seemed to have stopped whining so much about my writer's lot.

"I wish I could paint as freely as you write," she complained.

"Maybe you can," I told her. "Would you like to try an experiment?"

"Maybe."

"It's kind of hokey."

"Well, hokey or not, it seems to be working for you."

"So you want to try it?"

"Okay. I guess so. Yes."

And so I shared with my sister the basic principle that there was a larger creative something that would work through us as artists if we would just step aside and let it.

"You really posted a sign about quality and quantity?" my sister asked me.

"I really did."

"That would be such a relief."

"So try it."

"I will."

And so my sister posted the little sign that warned her that God was in charge of her paintings' aesthetics. Freed from constant judgment and self-scrutiny, she began to paint more freely. As the tempo of her work increased, so did her confidence. "If it's good enough for God, perhaps it should be good enough for me," she caught herself thinking. She was no longer criticizing and revising every moment that she painted. Her paintings seemed to take on a life of their own, as if enjoying their new freedom. Portraits began to seem less posed and more natural. She began to include the odd detail that previously she might have edited out. Almost without her noticing it, her career began to take off. When she reported this to me, I thought, "Maybe there really is something to this God stuff."

"Of course there's something to this God stuff," my sober alcoholic friends snorted at my skepticism. Reliance on a higher power had worked to win them sobriety. I was learning that it worked on other things as well. In fact, there seemed to be no area in which the "God stuff" didn't work.

"I need an idea for a new screenplay."

"Pray for one."

"What if God doesn't have any screenplay ideas?"

"Where else do you think ideas come from?"

"I don't know."

I was told to consider God my new employer. I was told that if I took care of his business—which meant staying sober and helping others to get sober—God would take care of mine. Such spiritual reliance seemed heretical and naive to me. Certainly God couldn't run the movie business. But was I so sure about that?

I wasn't really very sure about anything. Sober, the world looked very different to me. The oddest things seemed to be affected by sobriety. Take my color sense. Drinking, I was fond of black. Sober, I had a disconcerting affinity for pastels. White began to appeal to me. Even more disorienting, there was the little matter of humor. Drinking, I had favored caustic skepticism. My humor was acidic and laced with vitriol. Sober, I began to have a fondness for the merely silly. I laughed a lot more and I seemed to have a new-found capacity to laugh at myself. Everything wasn't the end of the world. And if it felt like it was, I needed to check myself for "an attitude of gratitude." In other words, there was nothing so bad that a drink wasn't going to make a whole lot worse.

Take the little matter of money. My only job experience was in writing, and if no one wanted to pay me to write, I had only the sketchiest of waitressing skills to fall back on. The month I got sober, I had three paying articles, but in the months that followed I had only one paying article for *Rolling Stone*—and that article met with my first professional rejection. The "kill fee" I received to-taled a couple of hundred dollars. I couldn't support Domenica and myself on that. No, I needed Martin's alimony and child support—but he temporarily had no money with which to pay it. The high life had bankrupted his coffers. He was burned-out and so were his finances. I couldn't afford to pay my rent. For food, Domenica and I were dependent on the good credit I had established with Al-mor Liquors. Their limited dry goods became our sustenance. I made box after box of macaroni and cheese.

"What are we going to do?" I asked my mentors. I meant, "Domenica and I are going to hell in a handbasket. We'll end up on the street."

"Do you have food today?" they would answer me.

"Yes. But what about my rent?"

"Go talk to your landlord. Tell him you will pay him as soon as you can. Tell him you're good for it."

And so I went to Max Showalter and told him we had been

stricken broke. Max told me to pay him when I could and to try not to worry. But worry seemed to give me something to do besides drink. Where once I had drunk at all hours of the day or night, now I worried.

"Turn it over," I was repeatedly advised, sobriety slang for "let go and let God." This seemed far easier said than done. I didn't know if I believed that God would take a personal interest in my affairs.

"What are we going to do?" I would ask again. I meant, "We're okay for right now, but what about tomorrow?"

"It's one day at a time," my sober mentors advised me. "Today you have a roof over your head. Today you have food."

When I wasn't worrying, I was writing. I put three pages of prose a day into the world.

The day I turned six months sober, my screenplay *The Works* was suddenly picked up. My agent Jeff Berg sold it to Paramount and I was rewarded with my very own office on the Paramount lot. Finally I was a "real" Hollywood writer. I could now go to "the lot" and act the way real writers acted. This meant enrolling Domenica in the Montessori preschool. It meant no more writing on my dining room table. I was thrilled—thrilled until I tried it.

Although my neighbor at the office was a kind and funny screenwriter named David Freeman, I found myself feeling trapped by the office itself. I had a big wooden desk and a single window. My office was a twelve-by-twelve square. No matter how I tried, I simply couldn't conjure enough writerly romance to soften the feeling that I was in jail doing time. I missed Domenica. I missed writing in my new, casual, three-pages-a-day fashion. I missed being dressed in my pajamas, scribbling at the dining room table. The office gave me a bad case of writer's block. It all boiled down to productivity. What did I want to do? Act like a writer or actually be one?

"I am afraid I have to give you your office back," I told a startled Jeffrey Katzenberg. "I've got a little daughter and I think I do better writing at home. Thank you very much though. I'll get you my rewrites fast."

With that, I handed over my office keys and with them a great deal of prestige and glamour. Am I crazy? I wondered. Until I had one, I always thought I would kill for an office on the lot.

"You're a writer and writers write and it is the writing that makes you a writer," my sober mentors assured me. It wasn't lunch in the commissary. It wasn't my own parking space. It wasn't even the office itself and my name on the door.

"Writing makes me a writer," I tried out the simple truth. I was relieved to be back home. I was delighted to be writing one more time with Domenica underfoot. Although I didn't put it that way, I was betting on the idea that God ran the movie business after all. Maybe I didn't need to hang out at the studio and play politics. Maybe I just needed to write. It was possible that God had made me both a writer and a mother and I didn't need to choose between the two roles.

With the Paramount script sale, I was able to clear my rent with Max. I was able to clean up my credit at Almor Liquor as well. "You're still not drinking?" the Almor clerk said as I paid my balance. I told him I was still not drinking and that sobriety was surprisingly livable. What I should have told him was that sobriety was a revelation.

With my writer's identity shrunk to the manageable size of three pages a day, I suddenly had time on my hands for other pursuits. Rather than sit at my desk obsessing over words, words,

words, I found myself lacing on walking shoes and taking to the Hollywood Hills. I lived not far from the base of two canyons, Nichols and Laurel, and I found that there was something tonic about setting off daily for a good steep climb. I preferred Nichols Canyon to Laurel and would often walk a strenuous six-mile loop, up the canyon to Mulholland Drive and then back down again. Walking, I discovered, was good for me as a writer. A footfall at a time, I came to clarity about plot and character. Sometimes I would rush home, eager to get to the page. Other times I would dawdle, admiring a bottle brush or a jacaranda, thinking, often, that the flora and fauna of Los Angeles were what qualified it to be called the City of Angels.

A footfall at a time, I also learned to pray. I would climb, and as my muscles stretched, so did my spiritual perspective. My sober mentors told me to pray for God's will for me and the power to carry it out. I tried doing that on my daily walks. "What is your will for me?" I would ask. Then I would listen. Often, I would walk my way into an answer. Often the answer I sought was very simple, so simple I would have tended to botch it by being too complex. For example, praying for God's will, I would get the notion "Just keep writing" or the notion "Take Domenica to the zoo."

These were homely, doable things, and I began to get the revolutionary idea that life was made not by thinking but by doing. By my actions I could craft a life. This was news to me. I had somehow felt that life was a mental construction. Now I was learning that life came out of living, that well-constructed days yielded well-constructed and fruitful periods. Domenica began to thrive.

On weekends I would take Domenica to the pony rides at Griffith Park. Clad in jodhpurs and riding boots, I would teach her the rudiments of riding. "Hold your reins low. Don't jiggle the bit.

Keep your legs quiet." I have pictures of toddler Domenica on ponyback. She smiles for the camera and I smile beside her. We are having a great adventure together: exploring the world of HORSE. It is a running joke in my family that our picture albums contain more pictures of pets than of people. I have photos of my own early riding days. I am the blond baby waving to the camera from atop a pinto pony. In teaching Domenica to ride, I was passing on a family tradition. The Cameron girls are all riders. Domenica, a rider, was a full-fledged Cameron girl.

My mother and I wrote and telephoned often. She wrote me in her elegant hand, "I am so proud of you and how you are doing." She didn't use the word "sobriety" just as she had never used the word "drunk," but what she meant was that she was glad I had stopped drinking. My father, too, was pleased that I was sober. He said, "I am glad to see you are making something of yourself." But I was not so sure that I was what was doing the making. Praying daily and then trying to act on my prayers, I was turning into a number of things that left to my own devices I couldn't quite manage. I was a better mother. A better sibling. A better friend. Although I tried not to think about my brilliant career, it seemed I was turning into a better writer. A second and third Paramount deal followed the first. Far from being a bar to creativity, sobriety seemed to be a benefit. Like Domenica, I started to flourish.

Struck open-minded by my daily walks, I found myself striving to listen. It seemed to me there was a higher octave that I could hear if I paid enough attention. I could sense something and that something seemed to be guiding me. I just needed to listen.

"Clean house and help other alcoholics," I was advised by my mentors. Obedient, I began trying to help another alcoholic named Jocelyn. Every time I would learn something, some new sober "trick," I would call her up and pass it on. Jocelyn was an actress, and a single mother like myself. Both of us were willing to do anything to stay sober. We would have painted ourselves blue if that had been the directive.

"We are supposed to write out our fears, our angers, and our resentments," I told Jocelyn. She came over to my house and we sat writing together at my kitchen table. A line at a time, a page at a time, the fears and poisons of our drinking pasts were poured onto the page. I missed Martin but saw in my written inventory how hard it must have been for him to live with my drinking.

"People tried to tell me," I told Jocelyn. "I couldn't hear what they were saying."

"I think you'll just have to accept that as one of the things you cannot change," Jocelyn advised me back. On my daily walks I asked to make peace with my past. A footfall at a time, I fought with regret.

"Change the things you can," Jocelyn would tell me or I would tell her. We were both learning from our mentors and what we learned was saving our lives. I was given a chart of alcoholic symptoms. There were forty-three symptoms. I had experienced forty-one. The two remaining were "wet brain" and "death." Abstinence was literally a matter of life and death.

Nine months into my sobriety and counting, the tabloids were again filled with news of Martin and Liza. Their musical *The Act* opened in New York and *People* magazine ran pictures of them dancing together on opening night. I would look at the photographs and think to myself, "Just don't drink." Sometimes I would open my mail only to find that it contained a clipping, some news of Martin and Liza that a well-meaning friend hadn't wanted me to miss.

I found myself filled with self-pity: "Poor me, poor me, pour me a drink." But miraculously I didn't drink. Instead, I tried to listen to what my sober advisers were telling me: "You have so much to be grateful for. You have your health. You have your child. You have a career. That's a lot."

Perhaps it was a lot, but without Martin it did not feel like enough. Although I officially knew better, although I strove daily to be sober and grateful, I was privately carrying a torch for the man who had gotten away. One morning the doorbell rang, and when I answered it, I found a reporter from the *National Enquirer*. Did I want to talk to them about Martin and Liza? the reporter asked. Did I want to tell my side of the story? "No. What is there to say?" I closed the door in his face.

Next I got a phone call from *Esquire*, wondering if I would be interested in writing my story for them. I had always wanted to write for *Esquire*, but I wasn't willing to write about what they asked. It was bad enough being the jilted wife. Did I want to be cuckolded in print? Instead, I called my sober friends, who advised me to steer clear of my old drunken life. I knew they were right, but it was hard doing as they suggested. In the pictures that life still looked glamorous. My new life felt tame by comparison. Despite myself, I missed glamour. I missed the high life—a very apt phrase. Looking at the tabloid revelry, it seemed as though the party had gone on without me. I was divided. Half of me was gratefully sober and half of me was still emotionally drunk. In the tabloids Martin's life seemed desirable. "You know what the glamour was really like," I was told.

I did know. Old bad memories flooded back. I was at the opening of *New York, New York*. Dressed to the nines but tipsy and fragile, I clung to Andy Warhol's chivalrous arm. (Later that night he would record in his diary that I was a "lush," an accurate if painful diagnosis.) I remembered cocaine nosebleeds, mysterious bruises, and the struggle to appear more sober than I was. No, it had not been glamorous.

"Try to live in the now," my sober friends advised me.

In the now my life was positive but not dramatic. I cared for Domenica. I wrote my three pages. I went for my walks. At the request of legendary editor James Bellows, I began to write a column for the *Los Angeles Herald-Examiner.* A day at a time, my identity as a working writer was being restored to me. Thanks to Jeff Berg and a new agent, Joel Dean, I had a movie-writing career independent of my work with Martin. Soon I was asked to write a television movie about Elvis Presley's drug addiction. I took the assignment joyfully, secretly glad to have a use for my own tawdry past.

And yet it was hard to remember that the past was tawdry. It was hard to detox from life in the fast lane. I began to think of fame as a drug in and of itself. I was detoxing from fame as much as from alcohol and drugs. I began to notice which of my friends called me Cameron and which still used my short-lived Scorsese. I told my lawyer that I wanted my own name back. Talking with my mother on the phone, I wanted to be one of her "Cameron girls."

"Domenica is good," I would tell my mother. "She loves to dance."

"Oh, how I wish I could see her."

"I'll send pictures."

And I did try to give my mother a picture of my new life. I sent letters and photos of Domenica. She was the first grandchild, and I knew that my mother longed to hold her on her lap.

"You're so far away," my mother would say on the phone.

"We'll be home for Christmas," I promised.

"Wonderful," my mother sighed.

It was several weeks before Christmas that I got the phone call in which my mother told me she had cancer. "They are giving me about four months," she said. "It will be good to see you."

My mother had had a stiff shoulder. The doctor had diagnosed the problem as bursitis, like tennis elbow. He prescribed steroids, but the course of treatment did not help. The stiffness spread upward, first to her neck and then to her head. X rays and CAT scans were called for. This is when they discovered the cancer. It was brain cancer. It was inoperable and my mother had four months to live.

Domenica and I flew home to Illinois for Christmas. The beauty of the fir trees and snow could not offset the sorrow. While my mother strove for courage, the rest of the family fought with their disbelief. She couldn't be dying! She seemed so vital. I have a photograph of my mother joyously holding Domenica aloft. They are seated on the couch in the living room. The Christmas tree glitters nearby.

"Oh, Julie. This is it," my mother said to me when we were alone. "This is all there is." I was her confidante, the person with whom she did not mince words. With the rest of the family she pretended to think there was some hope of cure or recovery. With me she acknowledged her condition as fatal. She had regrets for the parts of her life that were yet unlived—a long-postponed trip to Switzerland that would now never happen.

"Oh, Julie," she went on. "I told God it would be enough if he just let me live long enough to get the little ones raised. Why did I say that?"

She wasn't ready to die, although she told the family that it was by far the best that she die before my father. "I couldn't stand it without him," she said. As for my father, his grief was quiet but inconsolable. My mother was not only his lover and mate, she was also his best friend. As he had once advised me, "The trick is to find someone you genuinely like and then fall in love with them." That is what he had done with my mother.

Although there was faint hope, the doctor told my mother she could try both radiation and chemotherapy. She elected to try both. My father drove her to the hospital for her treatments. When her hair began to fall out, she bought a wig. As so often happens, the treatments prescribed to help my mother made her very ill. She fought back nausea and dizziness. She was exhausted all the time and had a hard time following the thread of a conversation.

"It's brain cancer," my mother would sometimes emphasize to me. A clever, verbal woman, she would reach for a word, say, "table," and another word, "flat," would come out. To her great distress, her speech was becoming scrambled. She could understand but she could not participate.

"Oh, Jimmy," she would say softly. "Oh, Jimmy." She would call my father by her nickname for him. He would respond by giving her hand a small and tender squeeze.

Christmas came and went and then New Year's. It was time for me to go back to Los Angeles. Before boarding the plane, I wrote my mother a long letter, trying to cite all that she had done for me, my gratitude for her love and caring. My letter was a farewell and my mother and I both knew it. Between the two of us there were never any illusions that there would be a miracle cure. Back in Los Angeles I mourned my mother. I wrote to her often—short, newsy letters filled with Domenica's learning curve. On my long walks I thought about my mother and the love she had for what she called Mother Nature. As the purple jacaranda trees began to bloom, I thought of how much she would have loved the pastel clouds they made.

On the phone with my father I tried to make sense of my mother's passage. Try as he did, my father could not really grapple with the fact that she was dying. His was a sturdy, loving denial. She was simply too important to lose. He could not believe it was happening.

But it was happening. The prognosis had given my mother four months to live and those four months were ticking past. In early April I flew home. I found my mother tiny and ravaged. My father had done all he could, but now it was time for a hospital bed and round-the-clock nurses. We put the bed in the den, the small book-lined room where mother kept her writing desk. With her head propped on pillows, my mother could gaze out the window at the bird feeder, where cardinals, her favorites, came to feed.

But soon there was no gazing out the window. My mother's eyes drifted shut and she began to float on an inner sea. After a day of flickering consciousness she sank deeper into a coma. The nurse said the coma could last days or perhaps weeks. She did not predict that my mother would return to consciousness.

I went to my mother's bedside, choosing to believe that she could still hear me and register my words. "I love you, Mommy," I told her. "Thank you for everything you have done for me, but I am going to go back to Los Angeles now to take care of Domenica. She loves you too." With that, I left my mother resting peacefully.

I was back in Los Angeles for four days before the call came. I got the news in early evening and set out for a prayerful walk under a full moon. "I love you, Mommy," I breathed out into the starlit night. The silent silver moon slid higher in the sky. "Oh, I will miss you," I sighed. Hours later, as I lay sleeping, the room suddenly filled with a fresh wind. I woke to the sound and feel of the wind and one more time said my good-byes.

In the years since my mother's early passing, there has been so much she would have enjoyed. As a toddler, Domenica was bright-tempered and lively, entertaining herself and me with words, words, words. Like her grandmother, Domenica loved beauty in all forms. "Oh, Mommy, look!" she would say. It could be the full moon or a cactus flower nudging into bloom. It could be the antics of a kitten or puppy. Max had a black-and-white Boston terrier that she adored. Nothing escaped Domenica's notice, just as nothing had escaped my mother's. "You're a good mommy," little Domenica would sometimes announce to me, summoning an authority that seemed to speak from beyond the grave.

I clung to all connections to my mother. I used her recipes. I imitated her housekeeping. She had run an immaculate house. I tried to at least run a clean one. My mother had swept her kitchen every morning. I kept mine swept as well. On my daily walks, when I would pray for knowledge of God's will for me, I often got nudged back to Domenica. I needed to spend more time with her, my guidance told me. I needed to be more playful with her. I needed to read her stories. I tried to do as I was guided.

In the wake of my mother's death, I felt shaky and insecure. Except for my alcoholism, I questioned everything about my identity. Nothing seemed securely in place—particularly my sexuality. "Maybe I am really gay," I found myself thinking, "and I just haven't been honest enough to admit it." If I were gay, that would explain a shattered marriage.

"Now, Julia," my sober mentors advised me, "don't jump to any conclusions after your mother's death. One day you will just know what your sexual orientation is and until then there's no use trying to figure it out. Let go and let God."

Easier said than done, I found. Instead of listening to them, I embarked on a short-lived and catastrophically painful affair. My partner was a lovely young woman, newly sober like myself. Her parents quickly fell in love with Domenica, the grandchild they never had. Everything went swimmingly except for just one fact: in the midst of my new gay identity, I met a man I was attracted to, the first man since Martin who captured my attention. So I wasn't gay after all! Feeling brutal, I extricated myself from my brief alliance. To my relief, my partner moved on quickly to another lover. As for the newfound grandparents, they stayed in place, becoming permanent figures in Domenica's life. Just how they got to be that way was always an awkward puzzle to try to explain.

"Julia, you need to learn how to give time time," my mentors said. "You can't keep on trying to force solutions. You have to let life unfold instead of trying to force it."

What they said was Greek to me. I was impatient—restless, irritable, and discontent. A day at a time, life did unfold. I raised Domenica. I took myself to the page. I took myself on long walks up the canyons. The Los Angeles days passed identically, one after the other. A day at a time, I grieved my mother. I wrote my column. I worked at staying sober and helping others to achieve sobriety. This was a lot, but it wasn't enough for me.

Domenica and I were now living on Huntley Drive, near the Los Angeles Design Center, the great "blue whale." We had an airy balcony jutting into the fronds of a palm tree. From the balcony we looked across the street and down to where a wall was entirely covered with vivid blue morning glories. The neighborhood featured some spectacular feral cats and flocks of sparrows they were always hunting. The apartment was sunny and tranquil—so unlike myself.

I was coming up on three years of sobriety. Sobriety implied tranquility and gratitude, but not for me. I was told to count my blessings, but I found this hard to do. Sobriety was painful. There was the not-so-little matter of Martin, whom I continued to miss. We had divorced quickly and he had rapidly followed our marriage with another one, this time to Isabella Rossellini, then a supermodel. This union, too, was short-lived. Burned-out on Los Angeles, Martin relocated back to New York, where he has lived ever since. With Martin gone from Los Angeles, the city seemed empty to me. I longed to rewind the clock and be back in New York in our courtship.

If I had spent three years preoccupied with getting sober and trying to stay that way, Martin had spent the same three years trying to recoup his career after the disappointment of *New York, New York*. Back in Manhattan, he had returned to his filmmaking roots, crafting a remarkable film called *Raging Bull*, the story of the boxer Jake La Motta. I went to see the film in Westwood on a bright and sunny Los Angeles afternoon. I found the film brilliant, and it made me miss Martin all the more.

Maybe we had never really stood a chance against the tsunami of sudden fame. Maybe now that I was sober and Martin was used to his stature, we would find ourselves compatible again. As far as infidelity went, I could forgive, if not forget. I blamed myself for my own drinking. Surely that had contributed as much to the marriage failing as anything that Martin had done. I sought a gesture of goodwill and found it in a small spiritual etching. I sent the etching to Martin with a note saying that I admired the film.

There is a section of downtown Los Angeles that for a few blocks resembles Manhattan. I found myself driving down there afternoon after afternoon. I would sip an espresso and pretend I was in New York. On my walks, Manhattan began to call to me. I would walk up a glorious Los Angeles canyon and picture myself in the concrete canyons of New York. I would pray, and as I did so the desire to go to New York would get stronger and stronger. My wishful thinking was becoming an obsession.

"I think you're out to sabotage your success," an older writer advised me. "You're a columnist. You have a screenwriting career. What's in New York?"

I did not say "Martin." I was not confessing to anyone that Martin had a place in my dreams.

"I keep getting, 'Go to New York,'" I told my sober mentors. I expected them to resist me.

"Well, then go to New York," they advised me.

And so I went to New York. I was going only for a few days, I told myself, just to get a little taste of what it was I was missing. There was no craving that a few days in Manhattan couldn't satisfy. I would get a slice or two of great pizza. I would go to the Village and drink espresso at the Caffe Reggio. The trip would be short but satisfying, I promised myself. I was as surprised as anyone when I returned to Los Angeles having rented a New York apartment, set for occupancy in one month. All that remained was for me to quit my columnist's job and pack my belongings.

"We're going home," I told Domenica. "You'll see Daddy and Grandma and Grandpa. We'll eat pizza and go to the park. You'll love it. I promise you. You'll love it."

The apartment that I had rented was on Seventy-first and Columbus. It was right next door to a coffeehouse, La Fortuna, which featured good espresso and great cannoli. Great pizza was a few steps farther.

"You will love it," I promised Domenica and myself as the plane sped eastward. We landed in New York only to discover that John Lennon had been killed while we were in flight, two blocks from our new apartment.

The first thing for me upon arriving in New York was to try to set up a sober support system. I was spoiled by my years of Los Angeles sobriety. I had been well and carefully mentored there. In New York I needed to make contact with other alcoholics. I needed to put sobriety first, before any rapprochement with Martin, before my brilliant career. "Just don't drink," I told myself, because New York seemed chock-full of glamorous bars and restaurants. "You're still an alcoholic even if you are no longer in Los Angeles at the scene of the crime," I lectured myself. Courvoisier, Rémy Martin, Martell—the brand names seemed to whisper to me in particular. "Surely you can drink, now. . . ."

Someone told me that one out of two alcoholics drank over a large geographic move. I did not know if the figure was accurate, but the mere threat of it was enough to scare me. All that Domenica needed was for me to start drinking. For that matter, what about me? I liked sobriety, even if I was not what you might call serene. Threatened with drinking, I set about making phone calls and meeting sober alcoholics for coffee. To my relief and delight, I found out that Manhattan's Upper West Side was liberally studded with sober alcoholic artists. To their credit—and my gratitude— they quickly made me welcome.

Determined to move to New York, I had chosen to not think that I was hurting my career. Now I was in Manhattan and I had no outer proof that I had a career. I was a Hollywood screenwriter, and Hollywood was the place I had just left behind. I was a columnist, but I'd resigned from that position too. What I needed, I told myself, was a little faith and a little windfall. Manhattan was the epicenter of the magazine publishing business. Perhaps I could write for magazines. I photocopied clippings of my column and from my days at the *Post*. Surely there must be some editor open-minded enough to take a chance on me? It turned out that there were two, Leo Lehrman from *Vogue* and Kitty Ball Ross from *Mademoiselle*.

Magazine writing is not lucrative, but it is steady, and when a relationship with an editor is good enough, there is some degree of writing freedom. "We're going to be fine," I announced to Domenica, directing it really to myself. Sure enough, I settled into a happy pattern of writing for *Mademoiselle*. I was able to produce a piece a month, which gave me the equivalent of a regular paycheck. I was thirty-four years old, perhaps ten years older than most of their readers, and I was full of ideas that those readers should think about. Sometimes Kitty would say, "Julia, write about X," but more often she was open to the pieces I was eager to explore. A day at a time, a rent check at a time, I was making my way in Manhattan.

Growing up back in Libertyville, Illinois, Manhattan had seemed to me to be the epitome of sophistication. I would lie in our front hallway, tummy down on the heating vent, and read my mother's copy of *Vogue*. Hemlines, shoulder lines, the right bag, and the current color of nail polish—all these facts were known to me. By age twelve I could tell you the major designers and knew what their signature pieces looked like. The New York that *Vogue* pictured was filled with treasures—and I was determined to find that New York and inhabit it.

Every Monday afternoon I would take Domenica to Seventy-second and Madison. From there we would walk north to Ninetieth Street, our faces pressed to the windows. One window might sport Italian gloves. Another window might display paperweights. Window by window, Domenica and I would browse our way north. We divided what we saw into three categories: yes, no, and almost.

"What do you think of that?" I would ask, riveted by an elegant evening gown.

"I think it's a yes!" Domenica might vote. Or, "Sorry, Mom. I think it's an almost."

Shop by shop, block by block, we would make our way up Madison Avenue. At Ninetieth Street, we would repair to a sidewalk café and order hamburgers. Our conversation would be full of what we had seen.

"I liked that pair of globes. They were magnificent. So magical."

"I liked the paperweight with the tiger lily in it."

If you had asked me, I might have told you that I was teaching my daughter discernment. We certainly couldn't afford to buy what we saw, but buying wasn't the point, appreciation was. It was beauty, not consumerism, that was at focus.

I have often felt very lucky that the child I had to mother was Domenica. She was lively, brave, and adventurous. I remember no tantrums, just a precocious intelligence. She was always game for whatever adventure I set for us. We would ride the subway downtown to Greenwich Village. There was a world of antique shops to browse through there. Our favorite find was an antique globe, although we had a fondness, too, for stained glass. In the Village there was a toy store that seemed to specialize in hobby horses. We would pick one out for Domenica as carefully as if we were choosing a live pony—and live ponies weren't missing either.

Claremont Riding Academy was tucked into a brownstone on West Eighty-ninth Street. At four years old Domenica was just a little young for lessons, but because of her experience back in Los Angeles, pony riding at Griffith Park on Sundays, she was accepted. I stood ringside with the other mothers and watched as our progeny learned to walk and then to gently post. The children's mounts had reassuring names like Sugar, Pickwick, and Spot.

One day when I was out on a solo walk through Central Park, I spotted a rider up bareback—my favorite way to ride. Furthermore, her horse was wearing a Western bridle. I waved hello. The rider, a beautiful blonde named Tracy Jamar, proved to be hospitable. She boarded her horse, Arrow, right at Claremont. She would be glad to go out riding with me anytime I wanted to—the trick was finding "somebody" I could ride. I liked a spirited horse, not the gentle hacks I had seen in Domenica's lessons. "Maybe Headliner," Tracy suggested.

Headliner was an Appaloosa who stood about sixteen hands. They were having difficulty with him in the hack line. He had thrown several riders on their sorties to the park. The stable was just about ready to get rid of him, when I suggested that I'd like to give him a try. Tracy and I took Arrow and Headliner out to the northernmost trails in the park. Headliner proved to have wonderful gaits and a very good mouth. He was naughty but nothing I couldn't handle. I was used to sitting crowhops. I had grown up riding bareback.

I might have liked Headliner, but no one else did. The stable was ready to sell him. In fact, they had set a date to haul him off to auction. Before I knew quite what I was doing, I owned Headliner. He cost fifteen hundred dollars and I cleaned out my savings to buy him. Once I had him, I bought him Western tack, as he was clearly far more used to being a cow pony than a lesson horse. Once I got him to settle down a little, I took Domenica up with me double. She was just old enough for her little round legs to barely curve downward around his barrel. Many mornings when the sun was just clearing the buildings on the East Side, Tracy, Domenica, and I circled the reservoir. Many afternoons after I retrieved Domenica from her Montessori school, we spent long hours grooming and polishing Headliner. I renamed him Camouflage because he was secretly a nice horse, particularly sweet to Domenica, carefully lowering his head so that she could run a comb through his skimpy mane.

While I was settling into the cozy Upper West Side, learning the bookstores and the bridle trails, Martin inhabited the other side of the park. He had moved back from Los Angeles to a glamorous high-rise apartment building, The Galleria, on Fifty-seventh Street. It was just walking distance across the park. Sunday afternoon, by foot or by cab, Domenica and I would set out for Daddy's house.

Because our marriage had ended so abruptly, there had been very little of what the therapists call closure. I was still in love with Martin and still thought of him as my husband. This boded well for Domenica, because she did not have to choose between us. Taking her cue from me, she could find it perfectly normal to love her daddy. He certainly loved her.

Food is love in an Italian household, and Martin's life, even his bachelor life, was no exception. His mother would cook for him in her apartment on Elizabeth Street, and somehow the food would get from Little Italy to his swank digs in Midtown. When Domenica made her weekly pilgrimage to Daddy, she would be treated to whatever goodies his mother had sent. One week it would be pizza. The next week it would be lemon and garlic chicken. Along with the selection of food, Martin would have picked a film for them to watch together. One week it would be *The Thief of Baghdad* and the next week *Fantasia*. It didn't seem to me that it was my imagination that Domenica always came home from her father gesticulating a little more expressively. It was as if each weekly visit was a renewal of the Italian side of her genetics.

As a sober alcoholic I was taught to pray for acceptance of the things I could not change. Slowly and painfully it began to be clear to me that my divorce from Martin was one of those things. Despite my fantasies and my wishes, we were not going to be reconciled as husband and wife. Martin loved Domenica and wanted regular contact with her, but to him I fell into the category of exwife, with an emphasis on the ex. This was heartbreaking for me. During our brief exchanges over Domenica, we would laugh at the same jokes and I would always feel a flaring up of affection—that, and desire. Tantalizingly close yet out of reach, Martin remained attractive to me. If anything, he was more attractive to me sober than when I was drinking.

"I still love him," I would tell my sober mentors. They were sympathetic but firm. "You need to accept the relationship in its current form," they would tell me. "You need to get on with your life." By getting on with my life, they meant dating. I wasn't ready for that. For one thing, I had been raised Catholic, and Catholics married for life. Divorced, "modern," I found myself still married in my mind. My mentors tried to gently tell me that this was unrealistic. I didn't really want to date. Everyone I met paled in comparison to Martin.

For me, getting on with my life boiled down to getting on with my writing. I still thought of myself as a Hollywood screenwriter—just several thousand miles removed from the action. Still, Hollywood was "out there" and Broadway was right here. I went to see a production of *Amadeus* and caught myself thinking, "I can do that." By "that," I meant playwriting.

I bought myself a large leather-bound book. I opened it to page one and wrote the words "Public Lives." I began a love story about two artists, still in love with each other despite many years spent apart. When I finished the play, it won two large playwriting contests, one out west at the Denver Center for the Performing Arts and one at the McCarter Theater in nearby Princeton.

I didn't think of Max, my play's hero, as being a fictionalized Martin, although I can now see clearly that he was. I didn't see Catherine, the play's heroine, as a romanticized me, but she certainly was as well. On paper, and on the stage, I was letting myself have the reconciliation that I so craved in real life. In short, my playwrighting was more successful than my romance.

Domenica and I shared a two-bedroom apartment and I set up my writing station in my bedroom. It was there at a tiny desk that I labored over my magazine articles. There that I began work on a second play, this one darker than the first. Other than keeping company with other sober alcoholics, I did not get out and about in Manhattan. For one thing, I took Domenica with me everywhere, and there was always her curfew to consider. "Spinster with child" I might have been characterized during this period. My mentors kept urging me to try for a social life and I kept making excuses. Didn't Domenica need me? Didn't I need to write? Both motherhood and writing could expand to fill any number of available hours. Forget three pages a day. My brilliant career became my hobby and my companion. Manhattan was right outside my door, but I could have been living in Kansas for the amount I took advantage of it. I was a recluse. Single motherhood and time at the typewriter became my excuses for being socially anorectic. "Get out!" my mentors all but screamed, concerned that I was setting myself up for a drink out of loneliness. Finally I listened to them.

It was against my better judgment that I attended a theater party. At that party I met a lanky, red-haired actor with a cowboy's seductive drawl. If Martin was small and tightly drawn, Daniel Region was tall and loose-limbed with a wonderful offhand wit. I found myself attracted to his humor, too attracted to make my standard speech about how I was not available. Maybe I was available after all.

Daniel was a theater animal. He loved the stage and he encouraged me as a playwright. He seemed to take it in stride that I had a daughter and that she would need to be included in many of our outings. For her part, Domenica liked Daniel, which certainly made it easier on me. I liked Daniel too.

Daniel lived in a shotgun apartment in the West Thirties, a rough neighborhood by night and an empty one by day. He had furnished his apartment with a cowboy charm, mission oak furniture that he had rescued.

"You think this is nice," Daniel told me. "Where I'd really like to live is the West Village. That's what's really nice."

Beyond Bleecker Street, I had never been to the West Village, and so, on our dates, Daniel and I would explore the coveted neighborhood. We would walk the cobblestone streets and look wistfully in the windows of brownstones. It seemed their inhabitants led perfect lives. My own life seemed far from perfect. Our apartment on Seventy-first Street had flooded irretrievably due to a neighbor's renovation and Domenica and I had moved farther north to 202 Riverside Drive. I found the new neighborhood more than a little scary. Domenica did too.

I was restless on the Upper West Side and began to think that Domenica and I might do better in the Village. It seemed to have a higher per capita density of artists. I might fit right in. Perhaps, I thought, if I acted more like a writer, I would feel more like a writer. I laugh now, but then I still thought that there was a stamp somewhere that would validate my writing identity. Actors lived on the Upper West Side; writers lived in the Village. Then, too, there was the fact that I no longer needed or wanted to live close to Martin. In cozy retrospect, it is easy to see that I was at a turning point. I could admit that I had chased Martin cross-country and failed to win him back. So my choices were to go back to Los Angeles, defeated, or to try to make a life for myself in New York, closing the Martin chapter a little more gently. I decided to stay on in New York, but I would move to the Village.

Once I had my mind set on it, the move to the Village happened quickly. I found an apartment in a brownstone on Jane Street. The apartment featured a tiny office, so for the first time I was able to set up a writing station that felt professional. The window of the office looked straight into the limbs of a lovely chestnut tree. The tree was one of many that shaded the cobblestone street.

From the first, Domenica and I loved life in the Village. She attended P.S. 41 and was quick to find friends. I was pleased that her life was less circumscribed by my own, but we still had many adventures. We took long neighborhood walks, ending up on Mac-Dougal Street at the Caffe Reggio. I would sip a cappuccino and Domenica a hot chocolate. We would split a cannoli.

Bleecker Street was filled with antiques shops, and there were children's stores featuring toys and costumes tucked throughout the neighborhood as well. Nothing was better than the Village at Halloween. Jack-o'-lanterns sat in brownstone windows, witches and goblins roamed the streets. Domenica had a fine collection of stick horses and could select a fresh mount daily for our walks. We explored as far east as New York University. It was on one of these forays that it occurred to me that I could go to film school.

Martin had attended NYU film school and he spoke of it highly. During the summer they offered an intensive boot camp, and it struck me that I could learn to make my own films, independent of the studio system and being a writer for hire. I called NYU and was informed that they had one place left. It could be mine, the professor said. He admired my essays from *Rolling Stone* and *American Film*. Daniel was thrilled by the idea that I would be trying film school. He was a strong believer in art for art's sake and he thought it would be good for me to make small films on topics of my own devising. He would be willing to act in them, he said. (Daniel and I would happily collaborate for the next twenty years.)

After my mother's death, my father sold our family home and bought a large live-aboard sailboat that he anchored at Long Boat Key, Florida. His long, sunny days were spent reading and taking a vicarious thrill in his offsprings' many adventures. When I told him of my desire to go to NYU's boot camp, my father leapt at the idea. "I'll spring for it," he said. "Just keep me posted how it goes."

"Dad," I soon wrote him. "This is tough!" And film school was tough. I was fifteen years older than any of the other students and I went to class each day both excited and intimidated. We wasted no time. Our first week, we were given cameras and taught to load them and shoot them. Next we were sent into the field to make five-minute shorts. This is where Daniel and Domenica came into play, playing father and daughter. The short films had apocalyptic titles: *The Visit* or *The Divorce*. I loved making them, loved walking to school every morning at eight, wondering what secret of the film-making world would be revealed to me that day. By this point in my career I had already sold a number of feature scripts. As a screen-writer I was a moderate success, but it was much more fun to shoot films than to simply write them. Both Daniel and Domenica were very talented and they made me look good as a director. I began to toy with the idea of making a feature. What would it take?

The first thing it would take was a workable script, which I could write myself. The second thing a feature would take would be money, which was in a little shorter supply. I was making my living from magazine writing, and while it paid the rent and even five hundred dollars a month for Camouflage, it wasn't sufficient to bankroll a feature. For that I would need to sell another script to a studio.

Then, too, there was the fact that my finances from Martin were not stable. My child support varied month to month and I never knew precisely how much I could count on. I contacted a lawyer to see what could be done to make my child support steadier.

I no sooner gave my lawyer the details of my divorce than the press printed every damaging element. He was playing hardball. Both Martin and Liza, through their media representatives, denied any wrongdoing. I was painted in the press as the crazy and bitter wife. For weeks the New York papers were filled with acrimony. I felt dirtied and ashamed when I realized that my disclosures were the source of the scandal. Domenica's teacher called me in for a conference, worried about what impact the controversy would have on Domenica. Frightened and discredited, I decided to pull up stakes. How could I ever convince Martin that I had not acted with intentional malice? New York was too sophisticated and too vicious for me. I decided to go back to California. I say "decided," but the decision was more like pulling my hand back from a hot stove. New York had burned me. I wanted to run "home."

4.

oing back to California was a radical move. It meant the
uprooting of many things that I had begun to be able to
count on. For one thing, there was my exciting new
world as a New York filmmaker. For another, my magazine world.
Editors liked to see you face-to-face. For yet another thing, I had
recently begun to teach creative unblocking. I had a position at the
New York Feminist Art Institute and I was on my third round of
grateful students. I loved teaching and seemed to have a genuine
knack for it. Under my hand, students were flourishing. Blocked
directors were directing again; actors were acting; writers, writing;
and painters, painting.

About this same time I had finished a script for Jon Voight. I
had received a wildly enthusiastic phone call from his business
partner and then radio silence. I didn't know what to make of the
lapse. Maybe, I told myself, I should take a trip to California just

to explore. And so, yearning for the safety I imagined existed for me in California, I boarded a plane. It was officially just a business trip, but it was really an exploratory journey.

"Please, God, give me knowledge of your will for me and the power to carry it out," I prayed on the airplane. I thought I was talking about the Voight script. I believed I was going to be able to straighten out the politics and get on with things—things back in L.A. Somewhere over Chicago I noticed that my prayer was being answered—but not at all as I desired. I was praying for knowledge of God's will for me and the power to carry it out, and I heard, clearly and succinctly, "Go to New Mexico." I repeated my prayer and the universe repeated its answer. This was before New Mexico was chic. We flew right over it with me thinking, "Go to New Mexico? That's crazy."

What seemed even crazier happened next. I landed in California and told my best girlfriend, Julianna McCarthy, about the directive to go to New Mexico. Instead of joining me in my disbelief, Julie took the order seriously. "Here's a thousand dollars," she told me. "Go to New Mexico."

I tried getting Jon Voight on the phone, but there was no response to my repeated calls. I could sit on my duff in Los Angeles or I could follow instructions and go to New Mexico. I decided to go, but before I did, I had two lunch dates, one with cinematographer Laszlo Kovacs and the other with *Rolling Stone* writer Christopher Holdenfield. "Go to New Mexico!" they both said with glee. They gave me names and phone numbers. They advised me, whatever else I did, not to miss the high road from Santa Fe to Taos.

Trying to reach Jon Voight was making me feel crazy, just as powerless and crazy as a Hollywood screenwriter was supposed to feel, I remembered. So I booked my ticket and I flew to Albuquerque. I found it to be a nondescript town that resembled the far reaches of the San Fernando Valley. With not much ado, I moved on to Santa Fe. This was better, very beautiful, but still not "it." I was restless and discontent. This trip to New Mexico was a wild-goose chase. I prayed again for guidance and this time heard, "Take the high road to Taos." I decided to do as I was advised.

I pointed my rental car north from Santa Fe toward Espanola. I hadn't gone fifteen miles before the country abruptly became beautiful—more beautiful than I could imagine. "I am home," I caught myself thinking. And then I thought, "What do you mean, you are home? You live in New York, in Greenwich Village, on Jane Street." But did I? Piñon-covered mountains stretched in all directions. Snowy peaks loomed in the distance. Enchanted, I drove on slowly to Taos. When I got there, I called Chris Holdenfield's friend. "Do you know of any rentals?" I heard myself ask. He knew of one. A small adobe house, two-roomed, at the very end of a long dirt road. It sounded like heaven to me. My own little someplace in the middle of nowhere. Before the day was out, I had rented it. I flew back to New York to collect Domenica and sublet my Village apartment.

When Domenica recalls this first foray to Taos, her memories are not happy. She remembers missing her father and his parents, whom we also saw at least once a week. Accustomed to being the treasured grandchild, accustomed to busy city streets and store windows chock-full of treasures, she was suddenly plunked down in the middle of a sage field while her mother underwent an iden-tity crisis. "I want to go home," she would beg. "We're staying for a while," I would answer her.

Every morning as the sun rose to the east by Taos Mountain, I would go to my writing table and start to pound the keys. I wasn't writing anything in particular. I was just writing for the sake of writing, three pages a day, just to keep my hand in. Most mornings I was grumpy and lost. If the truth were known, I didn't know what I was doing in Taos either. And yet, when I prayed, I heard, "Stay and write." And so I stayed and wrote.

We were in Taos all during a glorious fall. The aspen were solid gold. The cottonwoods were saffron. To the casual eye the mountains looked aflame. One morning, as I was writing, a female character named Johnny came strolling into my pages. Without any more ado, I was suddenly writing a novel. My three pages of stream-of-consciousness morning writing had led me in a new career direction. I kept writing daily, the three nondescript pages which I dubbed my Morning Pages and then three pages of novel. By the time fall was over I had a first draft. I also had a leaky adobe house that was porous to the cold.

"Can't we please go home," Domenica begged. This time I said yes.

Back in New York, I did not feel as safe or as at home as I had hoped. The apartment building on Jane Street had acquired a new and unwelcome tenant, a drug dealer who lived just upstairs. Our landlady was drinking heavily and there was a persistent odor of rotten meat. I needed to find a new place to live. God must have been listening very closely. What I found was a spacious loft mere blocks from Jane Street. We moved into 317 West Thirteenth Street on the coldest day of the winter and I felt like something out of Dickens. It wasn't just the cold that made me feel that way. Domenica and I were broke—down to the "penny pot." I was owed money from magazines. I was still trying to stabilize child support. My trip out to Taos had been a splurge. Among other things, it had cost us Camouflage. I had been unable to afford to ship him out and my girlfriend Tracy had sadly had to oversee his being sold at auction.

"What am I going to do?" I asked my friend Gerard, who had known me since I was seventeen.

"You're going to borrow twenty-five hundred from me and you are going to get through this. What you have is a cash-flow problem. You'll get paid and everything will straighten out."

"Oh, Gerard! You really think so? Last night Domenica and I were counting change to see if we could afford going out to eat some cold sesame noodles. We just made it."

"Well, sesame noodles are delicious," Gerard said brightly. "You're going to be fine."

And so, bailed out by Gerard, I decided to give New York another try. I settled down to writing and teaching. The magazines that owed me anted up and the penny pot went back to being spare change instead of all we had. The misadventure had not been lost on Domenica, however.

"Mommy," she would sometimes ask, "are we going to eat out of the penny pot again?"

"I hope not," I would tell her. I would tell myself the same thing, doubling up on writing assignments, wondering if I could raise my teaching fees. *Ladies' Home Journal* paid more than *Mademoiselle* but had less panache. I was doing well, writing to chic young women, talking to them of their dreams and fears. I had shared those dreams until my divorce; now I was trying to be a fit mother and worrying that Domenica's home life was too splintered.

Every weekend I drove Domenica across town to see her grandparents, who had relocated from Little Italy to Second Avenue and Twentieth. Their doorman knew Domenica by name and would watch the car while I hurried into the elevator and up to their floor.

"Why, hello!" Grandma would carol, whisking Domenica inside her magic kingdom, an apartment brimming with delicious smells and tastes. Every week Grandma made special treats just for her visit. Domenica would come home stuffed, talking about ravioli and cannoli. She would be full of "Grandma says" and bits of happy chatter. Grandpa Scorsese was more stern, but he, too, doted on his grandchild. Domenica would fearlessly climb up on his lap and his stern expression would quickly be forgotten.

Like his parents, Martin had moved. He had traded his swanky midtown apartment for hipper and cozier digs in TriBeCa. Now his house was walking distance again for me and for Domenica. This was and wasn't good news. For Domenica there was no conflict. Daddy was simply Daddy. For me Martin was both my ex and the man who got away. Dropping Domenica off for a visit, it was impossible to ignore the continuing attraction tingling for me.

"Are you two dating?" a precocious Domenica demanded to know. The answer to that would have been both yes and no. Every week I looked forward to our visit and stayed just a little longer. Every week I had to remind myself that the visit had to do with Domenica, not me, and certainly not with any fancied reconciliation. One week I arrived to find one of the bathrooms festooned with frilly lingerie. No, clearly Martin was not dying on the vine—and except for Martin, the itch I could not scratch, neither was I.

With my father's backing, I had once more enrolled in film school. This time we were making a fifteen-minute short and again mine featured Domenica, Daniel Region, and a fine young actress named Mary Bell. In my film Domenica got to play out all of her troubled and conflicting emotions about divorced parents. She got to act out in all sorts of ways she didn't in real life—swearing, hiding in the bathroom to smoke cigarettes, starting up a small apartment fire. Shot on a shoestring, the film was both powerful and cathartic. Domenica was so good, I began to suspect I had a child actress on my hands. Other NYU students asked if they could borrow her for their shoots. Embedded in a world of independent films and off-Broadway theater, embedded in our creative hopes and dreams, we were starting to thrive—then I got a phone call from Martin.

"There's something I feel I should tell you," he said. "I've met someone. I've met someone and she says that you are spreading rumors about me, talking to other alcoholics about my private affairs."

As he spoke, I felt the bottom drop from my world. I thought of the lingerie in the bathroom. Clearly "the someone's." "Someone" was doing dirty laundry, but it wasn't me. Still, from Martin's tone, he was convinced he was being gossiped about, and this was nothing I could really disprove.

"I've never talked about anything I didn't need to talk about to stay sober," I finally managed to say.

We were at an impasse. Martin and his new girlfriend, soon to be a fiancée, versus me and my "alcoholics." How could I fight a rumor? I couldn't disprove what he had heard and I couldn't choose Martin over my affiliation with other sober alcoholics, not if I wanted to stay sober. My choice was Martin or sobriety. We had reached a great divide. A chasm like the Grand Canyon yawned between us. Even thinking about giving up my alcoholic affiliation, I felt too close to the abyss. Martin or sobriety? I chose sobriety. I simply had to talk with other alcoholics.

If Martin didn't feel safe with my talking to other alcoholics, a foreign culture to him, I no longer felt safe in New York, a foreign culture to me. New York was Martin's city. Or perhaps Martin's and Liza's. New York was too hard for me and too scary. I had been dragged through the newspapers there—and that caused by my own hand, hiring a lawyer for what should have been a sane and neutral transaction. Clearly I didn't understand how the game was played in New York. I wasn't a player. I was a loser. I surely felt like one.

I had gotten sober in Los Angeles, and with my sobriety shaken, it was to Los Angeles that I returned. Doing so, I left behind my fledgling career as a playwright. I left behind my work on short films. Just as I couldn't choose Martin over sobriety, I could not choose my career over sobriety either. I wanted to go "home." By "home," I thought I meant Los Angeles.

I couldn't say to Domenica, "I have lost your father again. And this time I have really, really lost him." Instead, I said to her, "You will like California. There will be a backyard for Calla Lily, your puppy, and Cloud, your cat. We'll grow lemons and avocados. There will be flowers everywhere. You'll be near Doris and Billy. We'll go riding in Griffith Park."

Because I had never been honest with them that reconciliation with Martin was my dream, I couldn't go to Martin's parents and say, "You see, he's got this really toxic girlfriend." No, to them I was the toxic one, the admitted alcoholic. Long ago I had told Grandma Scorsese, "I don't want you worrying. I will raise Domenica sober," but my attempt at reassurance had only ignited doubts. And now those doubts about my stability were coming home to roost. For the second time, I was uprooting their beloved granddaughter and moving her thousands of miles away. There was no discussion of any of this. No one suggested that I stay. Sorry as they were to lose Domenica's weekly visits, they were probably glad to have me at a safe remove from Martin.

And so I packed our things—the dog, the cat, the hobby horses—and Domenica, and I headed west. We drove first to Chicago. There we spent time with my family, still finding its way after my mother's death. To my siblings I explained my need to safeguard my sobriety and my thought that I could do that best safely back in Los Angeles. Two of my siblings were sober alcoholics as well, and they could understand my priorities. They did not say, "We're staying sober right here. Come back to Chicago and be with your own family." Instead, they wished me good luck, understanding my bond with the sober alcoholics in Los Angeles.

True to my word to Domenica, I moved her into a house with a yard. The house, a Spanish bungalow in West Hollywood, featured a towering avocado tree and some smaller lemon trees. It was walking distance to Domenica's new school, West Hollywood Elementary. It was a short drive to the Third Street Market, where we could go for cappuccinos and adventures—and I found myself yearning for adventures. After New York, Los Angeles seemed tame. The days stretched out long and empty—long and empty and the same. I did what I always did, settling in to write. My East Coast movie agent, Fred Milstein, had moved to Los Angeles as well. "How would you like to write for *Miami Vice?*" he wanted to know.

A job! A paycheck! Solvency and stability! Maybe I wasn't such a loser after all. I would love to write for *Miami Vice*, I told Fred. Although I tried to appear soignée, I was thrilled. *Miami Vice* was very hip. Everyone watched it. It was a wonderful coup to get to write for them. Producer Michael Mann had come to William Morris specifically looking for movie writers. I was one of six invited to write for him. I proposed a very dark show about incest. My idea was green-lighted.

If my days at the typewriter were filled with darkness, Los Angeles days themselves were filled with sun. It wasn't long before Domenica and I found our way to the Los Angeles Equestrian Center, where we spent long afternoons with a wicked little Welsh pony named Melody and a good-natured Anglo-Trakehner named

Gatsby. Both horse and pony were romantic dapple grays. I have a photograph of Domenica holding on to the pair of them. She looks transcendentally happy.

My hair was long, blond, and curly. Domenica's was straight and chocolate brown. We decided to get her a permanent and try for more of a mother-daughter resemblance. Her permanent came out fanned around her face like a baby Afro and reeking of chemicals. I had to slather her hair repeatedly with expensive shampoo to tame either the style or the odor. What Domenica remembers most clearly from those days is that I developed a love for quesadillas and stir-fry. Night after night we ate some variation on the theme. After the multiplicity of New York cuisine, it was quite a comedown. Our food felt bland and blond—just like California itself. We tried to focus on what we had gained and not on what we were missing.

In the backyard, under the limbs of the avocado tree, Domenica set up a jump course for her white standard poodle, Calla Lily. The dog loved the circus aspect of jumping obstacle to obstacle. Domenica jumped with her until she missed a landing and twisted her ankle. She remembers hobbling along with me as I went to script meetings with Darryl Hannah and others. I remember her comments as uncanny. "They shouldn't have killed the boyfriend off-screen," she said, correctly identifying a film's major flaw.

With the California days unspooling blue and gold, New York seemed a far world away. It seemed even farther when I met a passionate and charismatic filmmaker who wanted to live with me—and Domenica. The catastrophes of my romantic past posed no threat to him. He was the veteran of four failed marriages and was nothing if not fearless in matters of the heart. His enthusiasm swept me away. We became lovers. Then I got a call from the Denver Center that my play *Public Lives* had been chosen for a month-long workshop process. Could I come?

How could I not? My play had been chosen over six hundred others. My new boyfriend was understanding. After all, we all had to think of our careers. My sister Connie volunteered that Domenica could come and stay with her and her husband, Alan, on their idyllic "Little Red Farm" in Libertyville. I left Los Angeles with a sense of relief. I found very quickly that I did not really miss my new boyfriend. I began to have the uncomfortable suspicion that I had been looking for a Martin-alike and thought that I had found him in another filmmaker—or, to cast it in California terms, in another Scorpio.

The days at the Denver Center were long and demanding. We had three weeks to work, two to get the plays in shape, and then they were up. When I met my leading lady, I had a sinking feeling in the pit of my stomach, and that was soon validated as she quit not only my show but also her role in *Painting Churches*, which was running at the time. The Denver Center was staggered. They could not apologize enough for the damage they felt my play would sustain. Was there anyone, they wondered, who was my ideal casting for the part? Yes! An actress named Julianna McCarthy. Snowy-haired with ice-blue eyes, she had the commanding presence of a Celtic queen. I had written the part with her in my mind's eye. The Denver Center flew her out sight unseen and, once they laid eyes on her, cast her as their lead in *Painting Churches* as well. Opposite Julianna, as my male lead, I enjoyed the casting of noted theater director Laird Williamson, a bald-pated powerhouse. Their chemistry was immediate and combustible. The play fared well.

Meanwhile, I had my nightly phone call to contend with. Officially supportive, nominally a feminist man, my boyfriend actually sounded like an abandoned orphan. He knew I had to be gone, but still . . . "What about us?"

Was there an "us"? I wondered. Then I accused myself of having cold feet and being commitmentphobic. "Don't be that way, Julia!" I scolded myself, and proceeded to ignore every red flag that went up. My boyfriend wasn't "needy," as I perceived. He was just ardent, and I wasn't used to it. Yes, I was the cold fish and I was determined to warm up. He couldn't wait for me to come home.

Ignoring my misgivings, I agreed to share a house with him on my return and we soon found a beauty on tree-lined Genesee Street. I packed up my and Domenica's household. He packed up his. We marveled at how our belongings seemed to complement each other's.

All went well until the day we moved in together. We could not agree on where to place the furniture. Here? There? Neither place? Our two households, which looked so compatible on paper and in the abstract, clashed horribly in real life. Tension grew to such a peak that Domenica began tiptoeing underfoot, afraid that someone's temper was about to turn volcanic—which was an altogether reasonable fear. She began having nightmares. Fortunately, after just a few weeks, fate took a decided twist and we went with it.

During the long years of my parents' illness, I had grown very close to the brothers and sisters I was raising. Although I claimed to have no favorites, I was particularly close to my brother Christopher, and he now invited me and Domenica to come to Chicago and celebrate his marriage. Feeling a little gleeful at being able to escape our newly unhappy home, we boarded a flight and flew to the heartland. Bad news greeted our arrival. My brother's bride had walked out three days shy of the ceremony. This was a bona fide family emergency. My brother was fragile and distraught—nothing to take lightly in my family. I called Los Angeles. "I think I am needed here in Chicago," I said. "We're going to stay for a while."

"How long?" He sounded petulant.

"I can't tell. A little while. My brother's shaky."

My brother was in shock and Domenica and I were staying with him. Every day we said, "Christopher, time for breakfast . . . Time for lunch . . . Time for dinner." We led him from place to place. We listened to his recitations of what had possibly gone wrong. Gradually a portrait of his girlfriend as a charismatic neurotic began to emerge. On the telephone to Los Angeles, I had my own charismatic neurotic to deal with.

"When are you coming home?" Was he whining?

"I am not sure. I've been here only a few days."

"It seems like a long time. Are you coming home soon?"

"Not yet. My brother needs me."

And then, suddenly, "You are not coming home, are you?"

No, I was not, but I wasn't quite ready to admit it. Chicago was seducing me with its bright flags waving gaily along Michigan Avenue, its shiny river winding like a necklace amid the broad-shouldered city's architectural splendors. In between holding my brother's hand, I had written three songs with his songwriting partner, Jim Tullio. The collaboration was fun, even electric. I loved writing songs, I remembered. Furthermore, it had occurred to me that if I really wanted to make movies, I might do well to stay in Chicago. A bigger fish in a smaller pond, I could teach at Columbia College and use their filmmaking equipment just as Martin had used the equipment at New York University when he was starting out. What's more, I might be able to write about the movies for one of Chicago's newspapers, the *Chicago Tribune* or the *Chicago Sun-Times,* homes to Siskel and Ebert, respectively.

Telling myself I was just testing the waters, I showed both newspapers my clips. Both immediately offered me a job. I took the one at the *Tribune*, feeling that over at the *Sun-Times*, Roger Ebert and I would too often want the same stories. Columbia College made a place for me on their faculty as well. Suddenly I had more jobs than I knew what to do with, more steady income than I really needed, and the possibility of making a feature loomed large. In Los Angeles I faced a future of writing for the studios with scant chances of making my own films. I was one wannabe filmmaker among many. In the City of Angels it was possible to be a very successful screenwriter and never get a film made at all. Paradoxically, if I was willing to leave, if I was willing to not look like a filmmaker, I stood a better chance of actually being one. It seemed to come down to a question of character: Which did I want, to look like an artist or to be one?

"When are you coming home? You're not, are you? Have you met anybody? You have!" My boyfriend was certain he was being left for another man and not for career opportunities or because we simply were not a match. How could I do this to him? How could I leave him alone and lonely? He had an aria of recriminations. Put bluntly, I was a rat. I agreed with him on that, but I was willing to be the rat to gain my freedom.

Thoroughly the villain of the piece, I simply never went back to Los Angeles. I paid to have my belongings packed and shipped. I didn't want to face the soured music with my boyfriend and I didn't know how to face it. What was I to say, "You reminded me of Martin and then it turned out you were this horrible control freak and I couldn't even unpack my furniture?" That was true enough as far as it went. I didn't want to go any further.

Chicago seemed to promise me the brave new beginning I had

been looking for in Los Angeles. For half the amount I was accustomed to paying, I rented a large, bright, sunny apartment with tall windows in all four directions. From my bedroom I looked west toward California. From my writing room I looked north out on a romantic church spire. The kitchen looked south toward the Chicago Loop. The living room faced east toward Lake Michigan. I hung white lace curtains in all the windows.

Settled in, I one more time networked with sober alcoholics. I met a sober writer and then a sober photographer. With their help I soon met others from many walks of life, sober lawyers and stockbrokers and teachers. Throughout this time I stayed in close telephone contact with my California colleagues. I had, after all, gotten sober with their help, and I remembered again that haunting rumor about one out of two alcoholics drinking over a major move. I had again made a major move. I was determined not to drink.

Sobriety was built, I had been taught, on a foundation of helping others. One way I could help others was to teach, and so I placed a small ad offering help with creative unblocking. I quickly assembled a first class. We met in the early evening in the large living room of my apartment. I taught them what I needed to remember myself: God is the Great Artist and God is benevolent to all aspiring artists. By Morning Pages and many self-exploratory quizzes, students could help make a clearer contact with the Great Artist. Some of them were skeptical. I asked them to be willing to try. In effect their pages were prayers, saying, "This is what I like. This is what I don't like. This is what I want more of. This is what I want less of." As they wrote, Something was listening.

The class met weekly, and weekly I received reports of progress—some by leaps and bounds, some more modest than that. As a rule, my Chicago students were just as gifted as any I had taught in New

York or Los Angeles, just a little less assertive—and a little more stubborn. I was running up against the "good midwestern values"—"Don't get too big for your britches"—that made it a little hard for students to put themselves forward. Nonetheless, they did move forward. Blocked writers started writing. Blocked filmmakers began once again to make films. As for myself, I found myself writing a new play—and dreaming more and more steadily of making a feature.

For the *Chicago Tribune* I was writing steadily on the world of Hollywood and films. Every Sunday the Arts section of the paper featured a celebrity interview or a "thought" piece on the arts. I might be called upon to interview an amiable James Garner or a more highly strung Jane Fonda. I might talk to a director like the great Akira Kurosawa or Martin Ritt. For me the interviews were exercises in sleuthing. What question or questions would open up a conversation? What could I ask that hadn't been asked before or, if it had, how could I ask it differently, in a way that would give a fresh answer?

Many times a celebrity would register a double take upon meeting me. "Don't I know you?" Sissy Spacek asked me.

"Yes, but you know me as Julia Scorsese," I might reply. Often my connection to Martin and filmmaking set people at ease. I learned that for many celebrities, "the press" was something they dreaded, not trusting that they would be understood and accurately reported.

"So you do know," Akira Kurosawa said to me before opening up about the painful years in which he had been unable to get his films made.

Working for the *Tribune*, I was both an insider—I still wrote movies and had a William Morris movie agent—and an outsider, "the press." Sometimes it was difficult to straddle both worlds.

Sometimes I did not do it gracefully. I remember with particular regret an interview I did with Kevin Kline, who was playing Hamlet—to fine reviews. The paper flew me to New York to interview him in his dressing room at the Public.

Kline entered the dressing room in a rush. He had the revved-up energy of a boxer, newly out of the ring and victorious. He loved working onstage and the great part brought out his best—or nearly. I was the one who brought up the "or nearly." Seeing him, I blurted out, "You are the greatest comic film actor in America. Why must you insist on playing serious?"

Kline skidded to a halt. He took in the question and its implicit criticism of his playing Hamlet. Looking me up and down with exasperation, he finally remarked, "Clearly this is not going to be the normal interview."

And it wasn't. I had a bone in my teeth: my conviction that Kline was selling us and himself short by not doing more comic turns. Couldn't he please try to give us more comedy? His stiffened demeanor announced, "I like doing Hamlet." Like a spoiled child insisting on a treat, I begged him to reconsider.

"You're funny. No one else is as funny as you are," I told him ardently—and I meant it.

"I know who you are," he said warily. "You are the éminence grise behind Martin Scorsese."

"Nonsense. I'm not old enough," I quipped. The interview ended on an understandably testy note. A year later, when Kline undertook his brilliant comic turn in *A Fish Called Wanda*, I told myself that perhaps my tactless fervor had played a role.

When I had to fly out of town for my interview work, Domenica enjoyed the attention of my siblings, her doting aunts and uncle.

In Chicago lived not only my brother Christopher, a stellar musician, but also my sisters Lorrie and Pegi, two hot advertising copywriters. Happily married themselves, they were nonetheless sympathetic to my plight as a single mother. They were pleased to be able to help me out. As far as they were concerned, my ill-fated marriage to Martin was something from which I needed to detox. They stood ready to welcome me back from the world of fame and fortune hunters. What I needed was as much of the good old Midwest as they were able to give me. If they could help me hold down a steady job, they were all for it. Enough show business madness.

Meanwhile, show business, if not madness, was precisely what I was promoting in my Columbia College screenwriting course. "Dare to write a feature script!" I told my students. "Ignore the odds against you! It just has to be good, and a good script can as easily be written in Chicago as anywhere."

I believed what I taught. I had to believe it. I was in Chicago, too, and it was unbearable to me to think it was some luckless backwater. No, I wanted to believe it was the city of big shoulders, capable of lifting me and my work to a new plateau.

Columbia College was located at 600 South Michigan Avenue, just off the south end of the Loop. To get there, I drove past the Chicago Water Tower, sole survivor of the Great Chicago Fire, past the Tribune Tower, and past the famed Chicago Art Institute with its two great lions guarding the entryway. I drove to work on many a snowy night with the wind whipping in from the lake. I parked in a multilevel garage a block from my teaching building and scurried through the cold and the dark to get to my classroom. There, several dozen students waited for me.

"Write three pages a day," I taught them. "Write your first draft all the way through as if you were driving coast to coast, New York to Los Angeles. Just keep writing. Remember that this is a rough draft and you are not to judge it. The movie you are trying to write already exists. Your job is simply to write it down. Think of it more like dictation than like making something up. Watch your movie in your mind's eye. You will be able to see it and describe it. Take down what your characters are saying. Eavesdrop on their dialogue rather than inventing it. At three pages a day, you will have a first draft finished in six weeks. That's really very fast. Once you have a first draft, we can fix it."

Columbia students were eager to learn and willing to take personal risks. I seldom encountered a student who balked at writing. Three pages a day seemed doable to all of them. It was just long enough and not too long. My classes began to generate a steady flow of feature scripts, many of them set in Chicago and "doable." This raised an interesting question: Why do we need to beg Hollywood to make our scripts? Why don't we go right ahead and make them here?

Believing that the best way to lead was by example, I set my hand to writing a small "doable" script. I needed to make something that didn't involve many locations. I needed to make something with a small cast. It was astonishingly easy to devise such a film. Chicago was loaded with good actors. I had a fine cinematographer, Chip Nussbaum, right on the Columbia faculty. He, too, was passionate in his certainty that we could make a feature film right in Chicago.

"I'll work for free, just to have the experience," Chip told me. He worked under the tutelage of his mentor, septuagenarian Jack Whitehead, who had shot Hitchcock's second unit material. "Come on! Let's do this!" Chip would say, gathering a crew from his finest students. They would work free as well. "Do it for the experience," Chip urged students. "Do it to prove it can be done!"

From my creativity course, a filmmaker named Pam Moore stepped forward. "I'll produce," she volunteered. Through casting director Jane Alderman, I found a fistful of choice actors. For my leads, I recruited my daughter, Domenica, to play a young orphan, and my good friend Dan Region to play her newly deceased father, a highly theatrical ghost. With him, Dan brought his new wife, actress Laura Margolis.

Pam, Chip, and I planned to shoot *God's Will* as quickly as possible, during Columbia's summer break. To pay for film stock—in those days it cost seventy-eight dollars per ten minutes of 16mm color stock—we would use my check from *Miami Vice*. To pay for postproduction, we would rely on the generosity of friends and a financial helping hand from my father.

Helping hands were not all financial. Sister Julia Clare got us the use of her convent for a pivotal first sequence. She also assured us we had the use of her prayers, which we certainly needed. We were making a movie in which God was an attractive red-haired lady golfer. The nuns seemed to enjoy the idea.

I had been warned that food was the difference between a happy crew and a balky one. We did not have money for caterers, and so Pam and I set out to make casseroles among our many other jobs. Male directors often compare making a movie to a military campaign. I found it more like throwing a Thanksgiving feast, day after day after day.

Given our naïveté, all went remarkably smoothly. We shot on a golf course. We shot at a cemetery. We shot on a ledge ten stories above the lakeshore in order to approximate "exterior heaven: a viewing station." Bantering casually, our actors stood tucked like gargoyles next to an ornate cornice. Except for when the scene called for it, they did not look down. I still marvel at the aplomb of Marge Kottlisky, the older actress playing God. From her narrow and treacherous perch in "heaven," she serenely surveyed her realm.

"Weren't you terrified?" I wondered.

"That's why they call it acting."

Within twenty-one days we had the film wrapped and in the can. The performances were delightful. Chip's cinematography was beautiful, a close approximation of old Technicolor, courtesy of some tutelage from his mentor Jack Whitehead. After we wrapped we took a two-week breather before heading into edit. It was during this breather that the unthinkable happened—our sound reels were stolen.

Stolen? Yes. Our sound technician was a young but talented student. He had left the reels unguarded in his car and somehow someone had made off with them. That was the story. Chip, Pam, and I found it hard to believe. We thought it more likely that somehow he had botched the sound and didn't want to admit it, but he stuck to his story. What was worse, the theft had happened right after we wrapped and he had waited two weeks to tell us. The trail would be cold.

Who would want sound reels? I called the police. They listened but made it clear they had bigger fish to fry. I searched the Dumpsters near the student's house. In an empty Dumpster I actually found some sound reels—but they were not ours.

Now what? I had used all of my savings and a considerable amount of everyone else's time and talent. Friends suggested we reshoot, but we didn't have the resources to do so. The very thought seemed overwhelming. There had to be some other solution.

I screened the silent footage. The performances were delicious. Watching, I supplied the dialogue in my head. After all, I had written it, shot it, and knew it well—so well, it occurred to me, that I might be able to cut the film silent and dub it later. European films were frequently dubbed. If I managed to cut and dub our film, it could be released in Europe and on the festival circuit. It was better than nothing.

Initially I gave the footage over to a gifted documentarian who had said he would help to cut it. He was another faculty member at Columbia and he also yearned for feature work. Sandwiching us in amid his documentary assignments, he worked slowly and carefully. I waited on pins and needles to see what we had, but when I saw his meticulous work, it was clear that to edit documentaries and to edit comedy required separate skills or perhaps a differing sensibility. I took over the editing myself. In a small room at the east end of my apartment I installed a flatbed and set to work. I found that I loved cutting. It was just like writing: choice, choice, choice.

After a several-month hiatus to shoot my movie, I went back to work at the *Tribune.* In my absence, the editorial personnel had changed. The new editors were deeply suspicious of me and my skills. Inadvertently I had crossed that midwestern line of acting too big for my britches. Who did I think I was, shooting a feature film? And besides, wasn't there a conflict of interest? Writing about movies *and* actually making them?

Who did I think I was? This was an excellent question. The *Tribune* job became too uncomfortable for me to keep, and suddenly I was in Chicago without any regular Hollywood contact. I was teaching my creativity workshops and I was teaching at Columbia. I took up running daily in Lincoln Park, and as I ran, I would pray. "Dear God, please guide me . . . dear God, please show me the way. . . ."

Meanwhile, my father had decided to come north for the summer to avoid hurricane season in Florida, where he was still living aboard his sailboat, anchored in a picturesque lagoon. He moved in with me and Domenica. He had arrived just early enough to play a priest in the final sequence of *God's Will.* He had been there to absorb the blow of the sound being stolen and the frustration of what to do next.

"Just don't drink over any of it," I told myself. "Just stay sober and keep on cutting. Maybe something good will come to pass after all." I couldn't imagine what.

Good did come to pass. It was the unexpected deepening of the bond I had with my father. My father had been a photographer in his college days and he was very interested in my ill-fated film. Like me, he was reluctant to just scrap the whole project. If I cut the film myself and could work out some reasonable budget around the dubbing, he would help me out with the postproduction costs.

Our days took on a pattern. I would be up early to write my Morning Pages and head to the editing room. A little while later my father would drink a steep cup of black coffee and then be ready for breakfast. Breakfast involved a quick walk across the street to Jerry's, a nearly all-black diner which featured good scrambled eggs, sausage, and grits. After breakfast we would take Domenica over to a small stable tucked underneath the elevated tracks. There she would happily spend her days.

We had managed to bring Melody, the naughty little Welsh

pony, with us from California. Domenica and I both hoped that with enough love and attention, Melody would reform, returning our love and kindness with some of her own.

"Nonsense," my father snorted as he came to know the pony. She was just a bad apple, and the sooner we traded her in for a good one, the better. Melody came from a famous pony farm near Racine, Wisconsin. My father had the idea that we should call the farm up, explain that Melody wasn't working out, and see what they wanted to do about it. "They need to make good," he said stubbornly. "They advertise lovely children's pets and that pony is a demon. Sooner or later Domenica is going to get hurt. We can't have that."

No. We couldn't. I called the farm and explained our troubles with Melody. My list of woes were met with astonishment. "Why, we always found her sweet as a lamb," the farm's owner protested. "But bring her back and I will see what else I can find you. Although I tell you, I don't think I have a thing." We arranged to have Melody shipped to Racine while we ourselves drove.

En route to the pony farm, Dad, Domenica, and I stopped by to see another pony, also advertised as tractable and sweet. Not too tractable and not too sweet, it turned out. When I mounted the pony, he felt my weight hit the saddle and took a few nasty, twisting bucks before I could get settled. Off I came, slamming into the ground, and the fall was a bruiser. Melody seemed like an angel by comparison.

"I don't think he's right for my granddaughter," Dad said mildly. And then to me, "Are you okay?"

I was okay. A little battered, a little bruised, and very, very chagrined that a mere pony had managed to throw me. Oh, well, I consoled myself. He was a pony of the Americas, half Appaloosa, and Appaloosas, like my former horse Camouflage, were known to be ornery. We declined the offer to try again.

"I've been thinking and thinking," Melody's pony farm owner exclaimed as we limped up the hill to her barn. "I got a bad debt paid for by a little Arab named Kelly, a dapple gray, four years old. He should turn out to look like a pony hunter. Of course, he's not a Welsh like Melody, but he might be the best we can do."

Throughout this conversation, Domenica was hovering near my hip. She had tried to be brave about Melody's ill temper, but now that there was a chance of another pony, she was very excited.

"I like dapple grays," she announced, sounding very grown-up and like the horsewoman she longed to be.

"Well, he's right over here," said the owner as she led us across the indoor arena to where a slender gray was tethered. "He doesn't know very much and I think he might even be a little bit slow," she warned. "But he's nice."

"Nice" was the magic word. Domenica crossed to the gray, and he regarded her with interest, extending a velvety muzzle to be stroked.

"Hello," Domenica whispered, enchanted by his friendliness. "Hello, you."

My father watched carefully. He wanted this pony to be right. Finally satisfied that the pony was genuinely good-hearted, he signaled to the farm owner. "I'll give you Melody and a dollar," he offered. The sale was closed.

And so, with a safe pony to love and work with—she renamed him Walter Mitty—Domenica spent long days at the stable currying and fussing. I myself spent long days in the editing room, currying and fussing with my film. My father would sit quietly in the living room, absorbed in the newest Dick Francis. Numbering

Domenica's white standard poodle and white Angora cat and my father's soot-black Scottie, Blue, ours was an unusual but happy household.

With my nose happily to the grindstone of editing, I couldn't afford to indulge in doubt. Yet doubt was something that eddied at the edge of my consciousness. What was I doing in Chicago? Now that I was no longer working for the *Tribune*, no longer writing about the world of movies, I found myself immersed in a city that was immersed in sports. The Oscars were the one race I watched closely, not the doings of the Cubs or the Bears, but even my siblings were sports fans. They went to ball games while Domenica and I went to the movies.

"Just keep working, Julia," I told myself. My creativity workshops were growing larger. My film was growing longer. "It's all all right," I told myself. "One day at a time."

And so, one day at a time, I learned to read lips. Squinting at my film, I savored stories of the great old comic directors who had reportedly cut their films silent so that they could focus on performance and not on sound. To this day I do not know if these stories were true, but they were certainly comforting. Most of my cast were stage actors, and they tended to stay very close to the script I had written. Ad-libs were few and far between, and I found that as I worked I became able to decipher those as well.

Waiting for me to cut the film, Pam Moore did something extremely valuable: she kept the faith. While she may privately have despaired, to me she was a steady lamp of optimism. "Of course" we would finish the film. To this end she enlisted the support of Ric and Keri Cokin, who owned a postproduction facility. We would need to dub our film once it was cut. We would need to bring back our entire cast and have them act their scenes all over again in the sound studio. There, at microphones, they would watch the film projected in front of them on a large screen as they sought to duplicate or improve the performance they gave while we were shooting.

One more time I was lucky with the Cokins. They knew I was shooting on a shoestring and they agreed to defer payment against a share in the film's eventual profits, if any. I began to feel that the film was well named. It clearly seemed to be God's will that the little movie actually reach completion. In this I had to have faith, and faith was something that took a little working at.

Chicago was a bustling, extroverted, sports-oriented city, but I began to feel a strong need for solitude within it. I started going on long, slow runs, winding my way along the lake front or through Lincoln Park. Running, I would seek guidance. I would take a stride and pray, "Please guide me." As I became lean and fit, my prayers seemed to be more clearly answered—as if by improving my body's fitness I was also improving my spiritual radio kit. In my daily Morning Pages, I would "send," and on my daily runs I would "receive."

Some of what I began to receive was uncanny psychic guidance. I began to "know" things that I had no way of knowing. I'd always had vivid dreams and strong intuitions about people, but this was different. While I prayed daily to have God make of me whatever was useful, "psychic" was not a label that I took to easily. It made me feel a little crazy. It was about this time that Domenica won her first writing contest. Her winning entry? A short story about a little girl who had a witch for a mother. I was not amused.

How would Domenica like it if she really had a witch for a mother? I wondered. What if I were struck ever more deeply psychic? Might I not end up back in Venice Beach, California, wearing purple robes and beads and wandering the boardwalk? The more I prayed about it, the more my psychic "hits" seemed to increase in frequency and accuracy. As my ESP escalated, so did my anxiety. I already felt isolated living in Chicago. My psychic adventures made me feel more isolated still. What was God up to with me? I was afraid to find out. I wanted to be a writer—and maybe a director. I certainly didn't want to be a witch.

Enter Barry Cecconi, a wise, shrewd, and humorous therapist. I went to see him hoping to have my psychic gift removed. Instead, he told me in no uncertain terms that my psychic gift was just that, a gift, and that it might very well be permanent. He suggested I try living with it instead of living without it. He asked me, "Don't you have any role models for someone who is both psychic and sane?"

I thought immediately of Sonia Choquette, a psychic I had met once when she was teaching a workshop on manifesting creative dreams. Married and the mother of two, Sonia seemed eminently sane. A pretty brunette with lively brown eyes and a ready smile, she dressed trimly, favoring sweaters and slacks. There were no billowing robes and beads that announced "I am special; I am different." No, to judge by appearances, Sonia was reassuringly normal. I called for an appointment.

"You see," I told Sonia when we met, "I am afraid that I have been struck psychic."

"Everybody's psychic," Sonia said gently. "Being psychic is normal. We are all intuitive beings. It's just that most of us are not open to our sixth sensory input." She gave me a reassuring smile. We sat in her lovely book-lined study. The afternoon light was bright and steady.

"Lately I have known all sorts of things I have no way of knowing," I told her.

"But you do have ways of knowing. You're just not used to using them. Why don't you let me be your teacher? I can teach you how to live with your gifts as a normal part of life."

"But I am scared."

"You don't need to be scared. Being psychic doesn't need to be something strange and threatening. I'm not strange or threatening, am I?" Sonia arched a delicate brow. A small smile played around her lips.

"No. You seem quite normal."

"And so will you."

I went home from my consultation relieved and a little excited. Perhaps if Domenica's mother had to be a witch, I could be a good witch, like Glinda from *The Wizard of Oz*.

But it wasn't quite so simple. I no sooner walked in the door and sat down at my writing desk than I heard a firm instruction, or "marching order," as I had come to call them.

"Phone Sonia," the directive went. "Ask her about the book."

"Book? What book?" I thought with my everyday rational mind. Sonia had mentioned no book. I had no way of knowing that a book even existed. Still, the marching order was firm: "Phone Sonia and ask her about the book."

Reluctantly I obeyed the directive. I didn't want Sonia to think she had become involved with a needy flake, a wannabe psychic who would phone her relentlessly with all manner of received messages. My marching orders seemed not to care about my reservations. "Phone her. Phone her. Ask her about the book," they kept on. And so I phoned her.

"The book?" Sonia gasped. "How do you know about my book?"

"I don't know," I told her. "I'm psychic. Remember?"

"It's just that the book is my darkest secret," Sonia laughed. "Nobody knows about the book."

"Well, I am supposed to ask you about it."

"No!"

"I'd like to see it."

"No!"

"Come on. If I can be a fledgling psychic, you can be a fledgling writer."

"Well," Sonia answered reluctantly, "I suppose that's fair."

Sonia had written a book, but two "friends" had been discouraging about it to her. One had gone so far as to ask her if English was her second language. Now she was embarrassed, so embarrassed that she sent her husband, Patrick, to hand over the maligned manuscript—and so began a friendship of mutual mentoring. I thought Sonia's book was good, rough around the edges perhaps, but wasn't any first draft?

"I'm ready to work on your book whenever you are," I told Sonia.

"You really think it's a book?" She was afraid to trust.

"Yes." I hoped my voice carried the conviction I felt. I "saw" her book published and doing well.

"It doesn't read like English is my second language?" Sonia tried to sound offhand, but I could hear that she had been really hurt.

"No. It does not. Your friend was just being mean."

"You're sure?" Her voice sounded a little lighter.

"I'm sure."

"You think I should try again?"

"Yes, I think you've got a book here. It just needs some work."

Sonia had work for me to do as well. She encouraged me to do written readings for some of my friends, those who were curious about my newly unfolding psychic gifts. I found this prospect as frightening as Sonia found the book. And yet, it was fascinating. One of my first "clients" was a lady editor. When I first inquired,

"What do I need to know about her?" I was "told"—and then "shown"—pomegranates. I thought incredulously, "Pomegranates? She will really think I am crazy." But Sonia had taught me not to censor the psychic flow, and so I wrote out, "The first image that seems to be important is pomegranates." I mailed off the reading to the editor, fully expecting her disbelief and discouragement. Instead, I received a breathy phone call.

"I cannot believe that you got it about the pomegranates," she gasped. "When I was a little girl, I just loved them. I used to carry them in my pockets!"

"Really?" I was as impressed as she was.

"The rest of the reading seemed dead-on too. You may really have a knack for this."

"I think I'll stay mainly a writer."

"Well, of course you've got a knack for that too."

I was glad to hear her say that. I had recently written a play, *Four Roses*, set in an alcoholic treatment center, dealing with the fates of four woman patients. The play had been given a reading at Victory Gardens Theater. Chicago was a town used to Sam Shepard plays, and the feedback I got was discouraging: "Where are all the men?"

"Don't let it throw you," estimable director Robert Falls took me aside to whisper. "It's just a feminine play and they're not used to that."

But the criticism did throw me. I liked the play as it was and couldn't see adding in any men. Was I being stubborn or true to the play? I couldn't tell. (This question was successfully answered years later when the play was produced as written in Los Angeles, where it garnered fine reviews.) Chicago was beginning to be really hard for me. I was used to being accepted as a writer. In Chicago I had two strikes against me. The first was my sex and the second was my sobriety. The Chicago theater crowd was a macho, hard-drinking bunch. Even the women were macho and hard-drinking. Put simply, I didn't fit in.

"Don't worry," Sonia predicted. "You're going to write a book and that book is going to bring you great renown."

If great renown was in my future, it wasn't in my present. Without the steadiness of the *Tribune* check, times were tight. My alimony was long since done with, and I needed and depended on Martin's child-support check, which came faithfully but never a moment too soon. If I wanted to buy Domenica an extra treat, I had to ask him for extra funds. In this he was generous. I would mail in receipts and sometimes written reports on the special occasions. I told myself that it was good that Domenica was being brought up out of the limelight. Time enough later, I said to myself, for her to have to deal with second-generation fame. Little did I realize, Domenica was having just as much trouble fitting in in Chicago as I was. Her peers at Lincoln School sniffed out her vulnerability as the child of divorced parents. "Your father lives in New York?" they asked her. The word I did not want to use for myself or for Domenica was "lonely."

We lost ourselves in books. She read horse stories. I read books on spirituality and on addiction. I was restless, irritable, and discontent, and all that seemed to help me was prayer. "Please guide me," I prayed.

Domenica and I were invited to a neighborhood party. It was crowded and loud. Sitting on a back couch, sipping a soda, I still felt alienated as the talk around me swirled from sport to sport. Suddenly Domenica appeared at my elbow.

"Mommy, c'mon. There's somebody you should meet."

Reluctant but curious, I followed Domenica into the partying throng. She stopped at a pool table where two men were faced off. One of the men bore a striking resemblance to F. Scott Fitzgerald. The other man, black-haired, Irish, and handsome, grinned and then winked at Domenica.

"Him," she said. "His name is Mark."

"I'm Julia," I told him. "Domenica's mother."

"Hello, Domenica's mother. I'm Mark Bryan. Pool?"

"I don't play."

"Tell your mother that's too bad," Mark said to Domenica. I could see that she was enchanted with him and I could see why. He was tall and burly with a quick laugh. He had dark, mischievous eyes. He included Domenica in his conversations. Around Mark, no one was a wallflower.

"We're moving to a new house," Domenica volunteered.

"Maybe your mother would like some help with that," Mark offered.

He knew how to close a deal. If I wouldn't play pool, he would still get me to play ball. I agreed to let him help me move—from our apartment into a snug town house. What I didn't realize at the time was that on moving day, he would take over the entire operation.

"You're doing it wrong. You need to rent a bigger truck. Just let me handle things, all right?"

There was no arguing with Mark. He was much too charming to argue with and, too, he happened to be right. I had rented too small a truck. Doing things my way would be costly in the long run.

"Go ahead," I told him. "You run the show. Better late than never."

And so Mark orchestrated our move. I didn't realize it at the time, but it was actually the start of a trend. With Mark around, things would get better. Somehow, from someone on that crowded moving day, Mark learned that I was a writer—in his words, "a real writer."

"I didn't just help you move to hit you up for a favor," he said. "But I have some pages I wonder if you could look at. I've sometimes been told that I could write."

"How many pages?" I didn't want to get saddled with too much.

"About a hundred." He sounded suddenly shy.

"Typed?" I didn't want to try to decipher someone's handwriting.

"Typed."

"Okay, I'll look at them."

"Great. I have to go to the Orient on business, but I will be back in a couple of weeks. We can talk about them then."

With that, Mark left, although he was back the next day to drop off his packet of pages. The new town house was three stories high and I settled in uncomfortably. I missed the sunshine and views of the old apartment. The new place was modern and more cost efficient, but it was much darker and I wasn't sure I liked it. Domenica's bedroom was on the second floor and mine was on the third. We seemed too far away from each other. My family was pleased that we had moved to the town house. It seemed more solid to them than our apartment had. Perhaps we were going to become real Chicagoans, they thought.

Instead, I felt more and more alienated. In our old apartment, with its expansive views, I could pretend that we were nearly in Los Angeles, or nearly in New York. This new town house was clearly smack in the middle of Chicago, where I increasingly felt I had no business. "Oh, my God. What have I done?" I thought. To distract myself, I opened Mark's package of pages.

I expected to be bored. I expected to be critical. Instead, I was quickly swept up by Mark's world. I learned he had tried a number of professions from contractor to working on the trading floor. None of them quite fit. Ambitious and clearly energetic, he described his entrepreneurial adventures with humor, rue, and frustration. To my eye he was a born writer. He had a naturally powerful, even riveting, style. He wrote about his wild bachelor life, his adventures with "the ladies," and I found myself both attracted and repelled, even frightened. As an artist I was attracted. As a woman, and a sober woman at that, I was put off. Mark was clearly a ladies' man, and I felt in danger of becoming one more notch on his belt. Still, he could really write. . . .

I called a writer friend of mine from California. "Listen to this," I said. I read him an excerpt from Mark's pages.

"Whoever that is can really write," my friend opined. "Who is he?"

"That's just it. He's this perennial bachelor, a real lady-killer, and I am afraid if I go near him, I'll fall for him."

"Sounds like you've already fallen for him."

"Oh, no!"

"Oh, yes. At least he can write."

5.

ark's writing ability was a hook for me, and I knew it. As with Martin and even as far back as my high school boyfriend John, I fell for talent, not just for looks, and Mark had both. "He could use a little encouragement," I caught myself thinking, and then I thought, "Julia! Be careful!" My relationship with Martin had begun with my thinking he needed a little help with his bumpy script. In my experience, a little help could very quickly become a whole lot more, and I was wary of another overwhelming involvement. Besides, weren't Domenica and I doing well enough on our own? We had the stability of family and sobriety to anchor us. What was a little loneliness? Small price to pay for safety.

Mark felt anything but safe. By his own pen he had described his checkered past with women. Married once as a teenager with an unplanned pregnancy to contend with, Mark was sadly estranged from a teenage son, Scott, to whom he wrote long, unanswered letters. In his pages he wrote brilliantly and bitterly of his dashed hopes, the Ivy League education gone glimmering when faced with the grim realities of teen fatherhood. No, Mark did not want to be "captured" again. He wanted to be footloose and free and he had a whole bevy of women willing to be Miss Thursday or Friday or Saturday. "Count me out," I told myself firmly. Besides, there was the movie to think of, and it was time to start looping.

Daniel and Laura traveled back to Chicago from New York. I reassembled the cast of Chicagoans. Early every day we would travel to the Cokins' studio, where they would project the film I had cut onto a large screen. The actors would stand at microphones and, line by line, recreate their performances. Most of the time, the lines they had to say were the lines as scripted. Occasionally an ad-lib would intrude. "Oh, dear God, what did I say?" the actors would groan. We would piece together what they had said. From my hours in the cutting room, I was adept at reading lips. To everyone's amazement, little Domenica was crackerjack at reconstructing her lines.

"She makes it look so easy," the grown-up actors would complain.

When the studio got too tense, Domenica would unreel a couple of cartwheels across the carpeted floor. We consumed a steady supply of diet orange sodas and diet colas, but there were times when something stronger seemed called for.

"Just hang in," I would urge "my" actors then. "We're getting there."

Where we were getting was a finished movie, with every single sound in it, from the rustle of a silk dressing gown to the "thwack" of a golf club, artificially created. Ric Cokin was obsessive in his drive to get the sounds right. His wife, Keri, worked by his side. Producer Pam Moore was a quiet and thoughtful presence, calm at all times despite her concerns that we might not be able to find distribution for a looped picture.

Meanwhile Mark came back from the Orient. His business there had been frustrating to him. A man of ambition and potential, he had repeatedly endured dashed hopes. He was at loose ends, and that worked to my advantage. To begin with, I told him that he could "really" write.

"You're sure?" He sounded dubious yet hopeful.

"I'm sure." I probably sounded cranky. It was enough work to have read the pages, now was I expected to convince him?

"You're not just saying that?"

"Why would I do that?"

"Oh. I had that done to me once."

With a bit of prying, I got Mark to tell me the details. They were sordid. He had once been encouraged by a writing teacher as a teenager, only to have that teacher reveal a covert agenda of getting him into bed. No wonder he was so suspicious. He wanted to believe my assessment, but he wasn't sure he could trust my character. I felt confident that I would never misjudge bad writing for good—but as to my character? Mark was attractive and I was tempted despite my good judgment.

"You've made a movie?" Mark was intrigued and perhaps a little impressed.

"Yes. I've made a little movie, but we need to find distribution for it."

"I could help with that. I'm a good salesman and I've always been interested by the movies."

The hook was set both for me and for Mark. He wanted to be taken seriously and I took him seriously. He was both smart and hard-driving. What he needed, I thought, was a focus for his considerable energies. Then, too, I craved a little more fun and Mark was nothing if not fun. We each had what the other wanted. He came on board to help with *God's Will*. Pam's tireless work got us accepted into the Chicago International Film Festival and Mark's networking got us the largest crowd in the history of the event. Domenica and I went to Neiman Marcus and bought mother-daughter outfits to wear to opening night. Our big event was screened at the Music Box, an art deco gem of a theater, well suited to the thirties comedy style of the film. We wanted to look our part.

My brother Christopher, known in music circles as "Chicago Hambone," had worked long and hard to craft an excellent original score for the film. The theater was jammed with his well-wishers, with Mark's wide-flung network of friends, with Pam's and the Cokins' business associates, and, most important for me, with my father, who had bankrolled the film's postproduction but declined to view the film "until it is actually in a theater." Now it was.

From start to finish *God's Will* had taken two years and cost about $100,000 with many costs deferred against future profits, if there were any. With the film being looped, we had scant hopes for American festivals or distribution. A period-style comedy, and looped, we weren't Sundance's cup of tea. We were pleased when the film was accepted into both the Munich and London film festivals. "*God's Will* Hit in Munich," ran the *Variety* headline. In London we garnered fine reviews along the lines of "Julia Cameron is not Noël Coward, but she is funny."

Our American reception was much harder to take. In Chicago, our hometown, we received no major reviews. In Washington we opened at the Kennedy Center to a dire review by a youthful reviewer from my old alma mater, *The Washington Post*. Despite the review, the film played well to a standing-room-only audience. As one viewer remarked to me, "I thought this wasn't supposed to be funny! Is this the same film they reviewed?" Yes was the answer. I had been hoping for a hometown-girl-makes-good reception, but that I didn't get—at least not in print. My unfavorable press made me crave a drink. I felt humiliated and despairing.

"Dear God, please keep me sober," I prayed as I walked for an hour in Rock Creek Park, hoping that the flora and fauna would soothe my ego and calm my spirit. Something did. Despite cravings for alcohol, I didn't pick up a drink. "There has to be more to life than me and my brilliant career," I prayed. "Please give me some equanimity, some strength, and some resilience." My prayers were answered.

Pam and Mark were very disappointed by the Washington reception of our film. Pam was graceful and quiet. Mark was angry. He hated to lose a bet, and he was betting on me. The Cokins remained steadfast and determined. One morning they phoned me to say they had found distribution, a tiny but upwardly mobile company named Double Helix. Although it wasn't the level of deal we had hoped for, we were thrilled to have a deal at all. So many fine independent films never acquire distribution. Even looped, ours had. This was a real, though small, victory.

"You're not George Cukor," Martin told me, viewing the film. "But this film should get you your second directing job. What you really need for the style of comedy that you're after is a cast of those great thirties' character actors, and they're gone. Domenica is the best thing in the film."

I agreed with Martin about Domenica, but we disagreed what to do about it. She seemed to me, her doting mother, to be an artist to her fingertips. She loved to draw, write, and act, and I thought she should be free to try all three. Martin was horrified by the idea of her becoming a child actor. He would cast her in small parts in his own movies, but he didn't want her to have a real career. "There's no future for too many child actors," he explained his position. "And there's too much rejection."

Domenica, meanwhile, had attracted the attention of the estimable Geddes Agency. They signed her up with my parental proviso that her parts would be very carefully chosen. Little did I realize that Martin was quite right and that there could never be enough "protection" for the bruises of a child's acting career. Then, too, there was the fact that I was not ideal casting as a stage mother. It was my clash with Francis Ford Coppola that cost Domenica her part in *New York Stories.*

As the veteran of Martin's artful sets, I was horrified by Coppola's treatment of his actors. He blared at them over a loudspeaker. He kept them waiting for hours. This was intolerable to me. This judgment showed on my face, I am certain. With my "the emperor has no clothes" attitude, I was simply much too obtrusive a mother to have on the set. Domenica suffered as a result, and soon she was let go.

Now we really were adrift. Martin was extremely upset by Domenica's loss of face. Domenica herself was rattled and did not know if she wanted to keep on acting. Wanting her to be able to put her miserable experience behind her, I enrolled her in Evanston's famed Piven Theater Workshop, home to the talented Cusacks, Joan and John. I hoped that work itself would heal her creative wounds.

Meanwhile my own life was turbulent. Just as I had feared, I did fall for Mark. He fell for me, too, but that didn't mean he wanted to be monogamous. I might be his girlfriend, but there would be other casual flings. Mark was a player, and I didn't want to play.

"I'm too old for this," I protested to my friends. I was forty and Mark and I had celebrated my birthday with a romantic getaway to the Hotel Raphael on the curve of Lake Michigan.

"I don't want you to feel over the hill," Mark told me. "You are not over the hill."

If we were both agreed that we were young and vibrant—an attractive idea—then Mark didn't need to settle down because we were too young for all that. What we weren't too young for was some good, productive work. I believed in Mark as a writer, and I innocently suggested he might want to try taking my creative un- blocking class and see if that didn't get him back to the page.

Against his better judgment Mark agreed to take the course. He was already taking graduate courses at Northwestern, and my course seemed at first to be mere frippery on the side. I had assem- bled a diverse class that included others as volatile and high-powered as Mark himself. We were to meet once a week at my town house and proceed as I had proceeded for nearly ten years, unblocking through the use of Morning Pages and a series of carefully cali- brated exercises.

"Where are the course notes?" Mark wanted to know. I ex- plained to him that there weren't any, that I "was" the course. It was an oral, not written, class.

"But what if I have to miss a class? How will I make it up? I have to travel a lot, you know," Mark protested. At the time he was manufacturing a small radio in Korea as well as pursuing an advertising master's at Northwestern.

"If you miss a class, you miss a class. You might want to try not missing any," I retorted.

"Oh, come on. If my professors at Northwestern can write up class notes, so can you." Mark was insistent and persuasive. He wasn't above guilt-tripping me about my lack of professionalism. Class notes were the least I could do. . . .

And so I did class notes. Every week before we would gather, I would think about what material I wanted to cover that week and then I would think about Mark. What did that bastard need to know in order to unblock? I would ask myself. Essay by essay I assembled my thoughts. Mark became quite the taskmaster, given to coming over several hours early on class day just to make sure I had written something up that he could put on the computer and then print out for his classmates. For the first time in my years of teaching, handouts became a regular part of class. I no longer simply taught off the top of my head. I had formal notes, and even if no one but Mark appreciated them, I enjoyed the process of writing them up. It was actually pleasurable putting my theories on the page.

The class that Mark was a part of was particularly high voltage. I was excited by their potential and very pleased when they all buckled down to work. I found using the weekly essays to be grounding. True to his word, Mark missed a class or two due to out-of-town travel, and I had class notes to give him to help him make up the work. Little by little, week by week, the class began to loosen up, energies were freed from long-standing blocks, and everyone began to take on modest new projects. For his part, Mark began to write again, and it became a question of what he would settle on to write next. He began with a series of monologues, which he read at Chicago's ubiquitous open mics. His work met with great reception, and both he and I were encouraged.

"I think you are on to something with this unblocking," Mark told me. "I think you could help a lot of people. I think you should keep writing on your theories. I think you should make them a book."

And so, as much to please and seduce Mark as for any loftier reasons, I wrote on. Based on my long teaching experience, I divided the course into twelve weeks. Experience had taught me that was the amount of time necessary to "cook" a class. At Mark's urging, I sent a copy of my manuscript to my agent.

"Julia, what on earth are you doing?" my agent shot back. "Who would be interested in this? You're a movie writer. Go back to writing movies."

But I didn't want to go back to writing movies. A born entrepreneur, Mark had convinced me that I was on to something with my little book, which I tentatively titled *Healing the Artist Within*. I began mailing packets of my class materials off to blocked artists who needed them. I mailed packets to Los Angeles. I mailed packets to Switzerland. Everywhere I sent the work, requests for more packets came back to us. Mark and I began to photocopy "the book" in batches, sometimes fifty or a hundred copies at a time. It wasn't cost effective. We had to charge twenty dollars for a manuscript, but students were not complaining about the price. There was a real hunger for the information I had to share.

"I see you becoming very successful with this work," Sonia encouraged me in a reading. "I see you becoming renowned as a teacher. I see you teaching large groups of people. You'll move to the Southwest. Your own creative work will continue to flourish."

"Enough about work!" I wanted to tell Sonia. "What about my romantic life? What about me and Mark?"

"He loves you," Sonia told me. "He's just fighting the snare."

The snare? I was the one who felt snared. Mark continued his bachelor ways and I began to feel trapped. How could I love a man who didn't love me back or, if he did love me, fought loving me? We would have great stretches of romantic and harmonious time and then, just as we were particularly close, Mark would stage a fling.

"His flings don't mean a thing," Sonia assured me. Her assurances fell on deaf ears. Feeling conventional and pathetic, I was hooked, hurt, and furious. I wanted out.

"He does love you," Sonia would repeat.

"He has a hell of a way of showing it," I would fume.

I talked to my girlfriends about my dilemma with Mark. I talked with them until they were sick of it. "I think you're addicted to him," one of them finally burst out.

Addicted? I did feel hooked. "Addicted" did not seem like too strong a word. I knew what to do about addiction, I thought. Quit it cold turkey. And so I packed my suitcase and booked a flight to New Mexico. I would go to Taos and shake it out. Leaving Domenica in the custody of one of my sisters, I got on the plane. Maybe sagebrush and mountains would hold enough romance for me.

"I think she's had it," friends told Mark about my departure. "I think you've pushed her too far and she is gone."

Where I had gone was an old adobe motel called El Pueblo. It lay on the north outskirts of Taos and was walking distance to shops, galleries, and the town square. On one of my first days in town, I found a small metaphysical shop called Merlin's Garden.

The bulletin board outside the door held cards for astrologers, massage therapists, Reiki practitioners, channelers, and a psychic named Lois West. I took her number and called for an appointment. She would see me that night at nine. Meanwhile a tremendous storm moved in from off the mesa. Lightning walked on pronged legs. Great sheets of rain swept in. Undaunted, I drove five miles north of town to the bed and breakfast where Lois rented herself a room.

"There's this man," I told Lois.

"There's this man and this book," she corrected me. "You are writing about the connection between spirituality and creativity. This is an important book. Do you know what I am talking about?"

"I have been writing something," I told her. I reached into my briefcase and brought out the manuscript. I read a few passages.

"Yes. That's it," she corroborated.

Like Sonia, she saw the book as "important" and widely read. Like Sonia, she saw my writing this book as being a significant part of my destiny. The book would shape my future identity. I needed to keep on writing.

"And the man?" I could not resist asking.

"The man loves you, but I can't tell you what form the relationship will take. That is best determined by the two of you."

I thanked Lois West and with lightning still crackling on the horizon, I drove back into town. Maybe, I thought, I would grow into the spinster I feared, or perhaps a wise old crone. My future as a writer seemed assured and my future as a woman seemed not to matter very much to anyone but me. Still, I was determined not to be addicted, and so despite every craving to the contrary, I did not contact Mark. Instead, I spent long days walking the dirt roads out toward the pueblo.

"Please give me knowledge of your will for me and the power to carry it out," I prayed as I had been taught to pray.

At the north end of Taos, tall fir trees grace the road. A little farther on, there are cottonwoods. Out by the pueblo, there are rolling fields of sage, fragrant and sturdy. I walked and prayed. I prayed and walked.

"Relieve me of the bondage of self," I prayed. "Take away my difficulties."

I wrote and I prayed and I walked some more. I asked God to restore me to sanity, by which I largely meant "about Mark." I did not want to be the further victim of what felt to me—despite all psychic reassurances to the contrary—to be unrequited love. What I was asking for was the gift of detachment, a renewed faith that life would unfurl as it should unfurl, that the universe was a user-friendly endeavor. I prayed more casually too: "C'mon, God. I don't rebound easily. Martin took me more than ten years to get over. Don't let this be a repeat."

And then the phone at the El Pueblo rang. It was Mark. I found myself talking to him with the detachment I had prayed for. "I'm in a withdrawal," I explained to him. "I don't want to be addicted to you. For right now I have to say all bets are off."

"You're in a withdrawal?"

"Yes. I am treating our relationship as an addiction."

"But there's so much that's good. It's not just an addiction!"

"It's an addiction for me." I explained to Mark my theory that he was addicted to multiplicity and I was addicted to him. He could do whatever he chose to do, but I knew that I had to withdraw. I couldn't really give him any assurances about the future. I would need to play my cards as they lay.

"What's happened to you?" Mark demanded. "You're different."

"I'm just unhooked. I have to go now."

And I went. As gratifying as it was to get the call from Mark, I knew that our relationship had no future if he continued to play the field. I had discovered through self-inventory that sexual triangles got me instantly hooked. If a relationship with Mark meant anything, it meant constant triangles as the games played out between me, Mark, and Miss Flavor of the Week. No, I could not afford it. Mark might be right that there was much that was good about our relationship, but I was also right that there was much wrong. No, as things stood, I could not afford Mark.

Meanwhile, although I didn't know it, Mark was deciding his bachelor days were over. "Julia's different. She's changed," he told our friends. "There's something about her now. It seems she can take me or leave me. I've got to have her." I continued my time in Taos, walking and praying. Mark called again.

"I'm in withdrawal," I repeated to him.

"Explain it to me."

"Maybe you should read about it."

"There's a book?"

"Yes. I'll send it to you."

And so I sent Mark a book that detailed sex and love addiction. I had diagnosed myself as hooked on him. He could choose to see himself or not in the book's pages. With me as a declared addict and him as the object of my addiction, all bets were off anyway. For both of us to form a healthy, nonaddictive relationship, we would both need to come to the conclusion that there was true love hidden in our addictive bond. Such a conclusion seemed like much too much to hope for and so, speaking for myself, I wasn't hoping. I considered Mark a part of my addictive past. He was free to do as he chose.

"She really is different," Mark continued to tell our friends. Meanwhile he embarked on reading the book I had sent him. He could see clearly the passages describing my prior addictive behavior. He could see my need to undergo withdrawal.

"I respect your choice," he told me long distance. What he did not tell me was that he was making some choices of his own. He, too, would reconsider his sexual conduct. He sensed my newfound freedom and he respected it. He wanted that freedom for himself.

I came back to Chicago willing to be celibate and solo. What I wanted was a sense of wholeness, and my withdrawal period was giving me that. Mark, meanwhile, wanted to see me.

"I don't think you should throw the baby out with the bathwater," he told me. "I think you should consider that there were many healthy and nonaddictive elements to our relationship. I think you should consider that we just might be good for each other. Think about it. I am in withdrawal too."

Mark had caught me completely by surprise. Instead of what I had expected—anger at the suggestion that his freedom was being curtailed—I found myself dealing with an emotionally sober man who sounded quite reasonable and, yes, quite persuasive.

Could he be right? I asked myself. Was it true that our bond held as much health as addiction? I thought of Mark's talent as a writer and the way that his gifts had drawn me in. Perhaps there was a sober artist hidden beneath his freewheeling ways. Perhaps I should give him—and us—another chance.

Mark got sick. He had a bad case of the flu. My heart went out to him and I decided to be an angel of mercy. I would take him chicken soup and ginger ale. Surely I could do that much? I got to Mark's house to discover I wasn't the only female who had hoped to play Florence Nightingale. He was well stocked with supplies.

There was practically a line out the door of young lovelies hoping to help him. Far from experiencing a saintly spirit of service, I was sick with jealousy. My hard-won emotional sobriety teetered and then collapsed. I was hooked again and I knew it.

"God grant me the serenity to accept the things I cannot change," I prayed. "God grant me the courage to change the things I can. God grant me the wisdom to know the difference."

Mark called. "Where did you go? You just disappeared," he accused.

"I am in withdrawal," I reminded him. "I didn't want to get rehooked."

"Well, thanks for thinking about me."

"Oh, I think about you."

"You do?"

"I wish I didn't."

"Maybe we should talk a little. I mean, if you are thinking about me, I can't be all bad, can I?"

He had a point. I thought not only about his writing and the talent I dearly hoped he would develop; I thought also about all the help he had been to me on the movie *God's Will*. There was also the not-so-little factor that Domenica seemed to adore him. Her cat liked him. Even her picky dog, Calla Lily, seemed to be besotted. Could they all be wrong?

Mark wanted to see me. He had reached a few decisions and some of them might be of interest to me. I told myself that if I were very careful, I could see him. I wanted to hear what he had decided and what, if anything, it had to do with me. We arranged to meet.

"I don't think it's emotionally sober for me to continue to play the field," Mark started off. "I have decided to give up 'les girls.'

What I have in mind for myself is a committed, monogamous relationship. Are you interested?"

I was interested. I didn't like the way Mark made it sound, as if he were looking for a relationship with just anybody, but despite that lapse in tact, I was interested.

"I'm interested," I told him.

"Great. That's great." Mark closed the deal as though he had just acquired a choice piece of real estate.

"I see you teaching in large venues," Sonia now told me. "Unity Church will afford you a wonderful opportunity."

Encouraged by Sonia, egged on by Mark, I placed a call to Unity Church. The Reverend Sara Matoin was in charge of programming, I was told. I made an appointment to speak with her. At the scheduled hour, I took Mark with me. Nothing if not a persuasive salesman, his rapport with Reverend Matoin was immediate.

"Julia teaches a great course," Mark told her. "She uses a spiritual tool kit. I am sure many of your congregation would be very interested. I'm a graduate of Julia's course myself." He went on to enumerate the writing he was doing, the way he felt more clearly guided in his choices, more empowered in his life. Reverend Matoin was interested.

"Could you teach a regular weekly course?"

"I could. The course lasts twelve weeks. And I would ask Mark to teach with me." This last was a brainstorm. I suddenly saw that it would be much healthier to teach large classes with a male-female team. Those with mother issues could relate to Mark. Those with father issues could relate to me. Together we would split the "magic teacher" projection in half and the class might emerge far healthier.

"Two for the price of one?" Reverend Matoin joked.

"Exactly. Two for the price of one."

And so it was set that Mark and I would begin teaching at Unity Church. I was an old hand at teaching, although not in such large groups. A newcomer, Mark was firm in his opinions about how classes should be taught. Our students now received the hand-bound "book" of class notes as well as weekly handouts that tracked their progress and told us how well certain favored tools of the course were working. In front of the class, Mark and I soon found our feet as a teaching team. Like Desi and Lucy, we swapped humor and some gentle barbs. Although I sometimes felt a little stifled, I generally enjoyed teaching with Mark. From the front of the class it was easy to see who related best to a male teacher and who to a female teacher. "Good job," we often told each other when the class went particularly well. Although I had been teaching for years, "teacher" was a new identity for me. I had more often thought of myself as an artist among artists.

"Let's go to Ann Sather," Mark would say as we drove home after class, and so we would make our way to the famous old Chicago restaurant that specialized in Swedish cooking: large bowls of home-made soup, cinnamon rolls dripping frosting, friendly waiters.

"I think they're getting it," Mark would say as he spooned down his soup. He loved teaching. He might have a sheaf of papers with him; he enjoyed giving the class questionnaires.

"Of course it's working," I would say, a little miffed that Mark acted like the course was a new invention instead of what it was— something tried and true for nearly a decade.

Both Mark and I could be keyed up on teaching nights. Until we caught on—"teaching nerves"—we had terrible arguments in the car riding to the church. Burned-out from our fight, I would arrive to teach frazzled and fuming. Mark would be serene and chatty, having simply blown off steam with our tiff.

"God guide me. Show me what to teach," I would pray. Far more than Mark, who loved a lesson plan, I tended to teach from the seat of my pants, listening for guidance and improvising as I went. Between the two of us and our divergent styles, the classes seemed to thrive.

Domenica, too, seemed to be thriving. In Mark she found a ready ear for all of her troubles at school. At his suggestion, she entered therapy, a happy decision as it turned out. She liked having "her" therapist. Once a week I would drive her up to Evanston, where Sheila Flagherty-Jones maintained her practice. With someplace to vent, Domenica became less volatile. Her native high spirits returned to her and her creativity flourished. Again at Mark's instigation, her father flew in from New York to do some Daddy-daughter sessions. It seemed to me that Mark was a born parent. With Mark and Martin so actively on the scene, I felt a little left out. I was "just" the mother. I told myself, correctly, that all of the masculine attention was good for Domenica. I could also see that Domenica was good for her father and Mark.

Although we still lived separately, increasingly, Domenica, Mark, and I functioned as a unit. Sometimes they would gang up on me, as when they decided my beloved old Chevy Blazer was too shabby and that what they wanted was a Jeep Cherokee. I began to settle into the idea that we were a sort of family—until Mark got a call from his own family that sent him hurrying back to the East Coast.

"They need me," he explained his decision to pack up and move to Maryland and help his two brothers put together a real-estate deal.

"I need you," I felt like saying but didn't. It seemed clear to me that Mark was fleeing the life we were building together. He saw it differently and thought it perfectly possible to pursue a long-distance relationship. His was an army family, and long separations came with the marital territory. He would be back, Mark told me, every month or so for a long weekend.

I hated Mark's decision to go east. I thought he was abandoning both me and Domenica. I thought he was doing a creative U-turn on his gifts as a writer. If I had had things my way, he would have remained in Chicago, faithful to his unfolding as a writer. What did real estate have to do with anything? I fumed. By "anything," I meant "Art." Mark felt it was a once-in-a-lifetime opportunity. He wanted to see his brothers make good and he felt that he could help them. And so he left.

Without Mark I felt more than ever adrift in Chicago. Although I kept in touch with my West Coast friends, I didn't really feel I belonged back there. I didn't know where I belonged. I felt rootless. Restless, irritable, and discontent, I tried to console myself by stepping up my spiritual practice. I read widely and I prayed. I was seeking the courage to change the things I could.

"What you need to change is your own profile," announced my friend, lawyer Michele Lowrance. She suggested I teach a creativity course at her swank downtown loft. She would fill the class with the crème de la crème, Chicago's movers and shakers: let me try teaching at the top.

And so convened one of my favorite creativity classes, filled with judges, lawyers, and stockbrokers. Highly ambitious and equally frustrated by their elusive dreams, this class tried the spiritual tools with skepticism. As one broker explained, "I don't believe in any of this kind of thing, but since I have paid good money for this course, I am going to give it my best shot." That turned out to be more than enough.

By the time the class was half completed, my stockbrokers were trying their hand at writing. My favorite judge had taken up sculpting, and my most verbal lawyer had decided to try some stand-up comedy. On the phone to Mark, I would talk about the class. I wanted him to feel my life was glamorous without him.

"We need page numbers for this book of yours," one stockbroker complained, and so I turned my hand to shaping the class notes into something more overtly bookish. I added quizzes and fill-in-the-blanks. I began to see that the class itself held valuable stories to be used for others.

On nights that I wasn't teaching, I felt lonely in Chicago. Then I hit on the idea of taking a night course and signed up to study the works of Carl Jung with a renowned Jungian scholar, John Giannini. I saw immediately how Jung's concept of synchronicity fit in with my own experience as a teacher. When students used the tools of Morning Pages and a weekly Artist Date, they had the support of synchronicity working on their behalf. More and more often they were in the right place at the right time. I told them they could count on it. Giannini was a mesmerizing teacher. I found myself strongly attracted to his ideas, concepts I tried to share with Mark long distance.

"This is a bit hard" was all Mark would allow about the progress he and his brothers were making. Domenica and I undertook the long drive east to go visit him. "I've been writing something," Mark told me when I arrived. I saw with excitement that it was a screenplay, *The Light Rangers*. Thrilled with what I read, I knuckled down to help Mark in shaping his script. As we spread papers across the floor and juggled scenes, Mark's brothers hovered nearby. They were both threatened and interested by Mark's "other" life. If real estate sounded like pie in the sky to me, show business sounded that way to them. Mark was caught squarely in the middle, believing in both.

Visiting with Mark, I began to doubt that he and I belonged together. His family was large, loud, and boisterous. His nieces and nephews were plentiful and lovable. They welcomed me and Domenica with open arms, but we still felt like aliens among them. One night at twilight we went for a crowded car ride through an evening lit by fireflies.

"Isn't it magic?" Mark's niece wanted to know. It was magic and I began to feel that I had lost Mark to the pull of family ties and the "magic" of the countryside he was living in.

Back in Chicago, still living on a shoestring—my teaching money and child support—Domenica and I moved from our town house to a small but inexpensive shotgun-style apartment. With many small rooms opening one onto the other, it was almost like a doll's house, miniature but well suited to me and Domenica and my diminutive father, who would stay with us when he came north from Florida for visits.

My classes at Columbia College were going well. My creativity courses were flourishing. I missed involvement in theater and satisfied this itch by writing plays, but I saw scant hope of getting them put up in Chicago. "God, please guide me," I would pray, feeling that both Domenica and I were increasingly out of place. Her father was a source of renewed notoriety for her. He had crafted a film, *The Last Temptation of Christ,* that was met with controversy. At school Domenica faced the prying and prodding of her classmates, who knew her father was controversial or, worse, ungodly. Some even threw rocks at her, jeering at her from bus windows. Chicago was no longer such a safe backwater for her to be raised in. Her father's fame—or, as some said, his infamy—touched Chicago as well.

Mark came home for a weekend visit. He set foot in the new apartment, and it was immediately apparent that it was the wrong scale for him. A graceful man, he nonetheless tripped over our velvet Victorian furnishings. The household was too feminine to suit him. "What are you doing here?" he asked.

"Trying to save money," I answered. "Trying to stay out of debt."

"You're making yourself smaller," Mark warned. "What I think you need to do is concentrate on making more money. Why not teach at Northwestern instead of at Columbia? I am sure the money is better."

"Don't talk to me about money," I fumed. "You and your brothers are chasing a big deal, expecting a magic wand to touch your lives and make everything okay."

"Leave my family out of this."

"You are chasing a big deal."

"That's the American dream you're putting down."

But I had the bit in my teeth and wanted to run with it.

"C'mon," I said to Mark, "can't you see that chasing a big deal is drunk? Money drunk?"

The moment I coined the phrase "money drunk," I felt a small electrical tingle. What would happen, I asked myself, if you viewed money through the lens of addiction theory?

"Money drunk?" Mark picked the phrase up and turned it over. He, too, was intrigued.

"People become as intoxicated with money as they do with any other addictive substance," I went on. "It's like the different kind of drunks. Some people are Big Deal Chasers. Some people are

Maintenance Money Drunks. Some people are Poverty Addicts. Mark," I said excitedly, "I think we should explore this. I think this should be a book!"

I didn't see it at the time, but I was throwing Mark a lifeline. His deal back in Maryland was increasingly going sour, spoiled by the intricate local politics they had stumbled into. Despite their intelligence and their drive, Mark and his brothers were being foiled at every turn. Local developers were used to having a monopoly, and they were determined not to share a piece of the pie.

As Mark's real estate deal unraveled, he would travel back to Chicago once a month, increasingly discouraged. I refused to hear his discouragement. The world of writing lay ahead of him, I believed. In writing it was a meritocracy. Surely with his talent he would succeed. In the meantime, we had the new book to work on, and I was excited by the ideas we were exploring.

"Let's go for coffee and do some writing," I would say. And so, sipping at cappuccinos in a series of sidewalk cafés, we would lay down page after page of our money theories. Mark had long been fascinated by the world of high finance. As I had in Hollywood, he had watched many high rollers crash and burn. He was eager to help people be "money sober." Elbow to elbow, we wrote page after page, chapter after chapter. I had no doubt the book we wrote would be published.

At Mark's urging, I sent a new literary agent a copy of the creativity manuscript. To my delight, she phoned back, interested. "But it's too impersonal," she said. "I'd like to see more stories and more about you."

At first I balked. I wanted the creativity book to be like an owner's and driver's manual. I wanted it to be straightforward and factual, as simple as "Try doing it this way. It works." Mark convinced me that a more personal book might help more people, and so I went carefully through the manuscript, adding stories to illustrate my points. This was a lengthy and painstaking process. When I finished, I mailed the manuscript back to the agent. After a month or more, I heard back from the agent again, but the news was not what I had hoped.

"I cannot represent your book after all," she said. "Our agency represents Natalie Goldberg, and we think there might be a conflict of interest."

I was stunned and saddened. I knew Natalie Goldberg's work and didn't think it really bore much resemblance to my own. I said to the agent, "Natalie herself would be generous in a case like this. I think she would say there was room enough for all of us on the shelf."

The agent sighed. "I suppose you are right about what she would say, but this is just business. I am sorry."

I got off the phone daunted and discouraged. Mark handed me a business card with another agent's name and number, Susan Schulman. He explained, "I was in Transitions Bookplace about a month ago. Howard, the owner, asked me if you had a good agent. I got the card from him. Call her."

I didn't want to call, so Mark did. He got Susan Schulman on the line and then handed the phone to me. I gave Susan a quick précis of my checkered past as a journalist and a screenwriter. I told her a little about the book.

"Send it to me," she suggested. "I seem to always get one good manuscript each Christmas."

"What did she say?" Mark wanted to know, the salesman in him frustrated by my lackluster pitch on my own behalf.

"She said send it."

"Great! So we'll send it!"

It was Mark who actually sent the manuscript off. He had no patience with my hesitation and reticence. He wanted the book in the world. "It can help so many people," he insisted.

Bent on helping other people, Mark did not see what I did— that he himself needed help. Back in Maryland, the shenanigans of local politicians put him and his brothers out of business. What began as a great opportunity turned into a high-risk situation where they were lucky to escape with their reputations and personal finances intact. Dismayed and disillusioned, Mark moved back to Chicago—"back to us," I thought—and focused his ferocious entrepreneurial energies on the two books we had in hand. "Let's just be writers," I told him, little recognizing that for Mark writing would never really be enough.

One cold January day the phone rang in my Chicago apartment. It was Susan Schulman, the literary agent. "It happens every year," she said gleefully. "I get one great book every Christmas and this year it is yours. I'd like to represent you and I'd like to send your book to Jeremy Tarcher." Schulman went on to explain that Tarcher was a creativity press, perhaps America's most noted one. She thought the book would be a match.

"We're working on another book you might like to look at," I told Schulman. "It's money viewed through the lens of addiction theory."

"That sounds interesting too. Send it on."

And so we sent off a first draft of our second book, *Money Drunk/Money Sober*. I was eager to get back to fiction from nonfiction and immediately began work on a screenplay. Mark, meanwhile, goaded me to call Northwestern's film department to see if perhaps I could join their faculty rather than teaching at Columbia.

Northwestern replied that they were seeking a writer in residence. With my résumé, I was just what they were after.

"I told you so!" Mark crowed. He was thrilled that I had tripled my Columbia salary. A believer in name brands, he was also glad to have me associated with Northwestern, arguably Chicago's most prestigious teaching venue.

For my part, I loved the Northwestern campus with its towering trees and graceful buildings. My own classroom featured tall windows and a very long trestle table for students to gather around. I convened my first class and found my students to be bright, ambitious, and discouraged. They found the faculty highly critical and nonsupportive. They were learning a great deal about how to take films apart but very little about how to make them. I had my work cut out for me.

The first thing I needed to do was get my class emotionally sober, restored to a sense of optimism. I would teach them both the tools of creative unblocking and of screenwriting, I decided. We would start with our daily quota of three pages and proceed from there. What I was after was actual feature-length scripts. I believed my students had talent enough to write them. They just needed to find a way to write that was nonpunitive and nonself-conscious.

To my delight, my students flourished with this "into the water" agenda. Three pages a day, no more, no less, they began writing out their tales. Although it sounds like a modest amount, three pages a day is actually a very fast writing clip. It means ninety pages in a month. It means a finished first draft in six weeks.

"You're artists!" I told my students. "Enjoy yourselves. Have fun with dialogue. Learn to eavesdrop. You'll hear wonderful stuff."

Egged on to write freely, my students began writing very well. Freed to write rough drafts, they found a new ease in all of their academic writing. Ripples began to spread through the film department. What was I up to with this creative unblocking? My students became a spirited lot, hardworking and hard-writing. They began to win contests with their work. Something was going right.

In addition to my Northwestern teaching, I began teaching weekly writing circles as well as creativity courses. I rented an office on Belmont Avenue and I began to feel a bit like a one-woman school. The classes I taught on Belmont were small but intense. My students were middle-aged but highly motivated. Their work was often quirky and surprisingly powerful, as for example the essay that mother-of-two Cokie Evans wrote about her love of speed.

If my students were speeding along, I, too, was speeding. In addition to Northwestern and my classes on Belmont, Mark and I cotaught a course at Chicago Filmmakers. As I had at Northwestern, I grounded the class with creativity tools. One more time I found myself able to awaken in my students a passion for their work. Feature-film scripts poured forth. "What is it that you do? We've been trying for years to get people to write like this."

"I believe that they can do it."

Believing that my students had it in them to be great writers, I was naturally excited to read what they were writing. Mark and I often found ourselves exclaiming excitedly, "This is great! Listen to this!" as we read through students' work.

Still, I was teaching too much and too often. There was no time for the well to fill, little time for me to do my own writing. I began to get cranky and irritable. "I need to make things," I complained to Mark. "I need to write something that's just my own."

The phone rang constantly. Teachers, it seemed, were meant to be on tap. Students wanted more than I felt I could give. Mark was baffled by my balkiness. He loved teaching, thrived on teaching, and loved any and all human contact that came from it. There was no such thing as "after hours" for Mark. He would take a call at any hour of the day or night. He loved helping people. By comparison, I began to feel like a real misanthrope. Mark's heart seemed to me to be larger than life. He wrote long letters to his son, Scott, letters that were never answered. "That's not the point," Mark would say. "This isn't about what kind of son Scott is, it's about what kind of father I am." This stance seemed to me to be both idealistic and brave.

Spring, in Chicago, comes after a long, hard winter and is a glorious time. Fruit trees blossom in the parks. Tulip beds catch fire and blaze with beauty. It is a time for long bike rides along the lake, meandering walks through Lincoln Park Zoo. It is almost impossible to be depressed during a Chicago spring, and yet I was managing it.

"I've got to get out," I told Mark. "I need to go to Taos. I need to hear myself think."

If Mark felt comfortable and happy in crowded and busy Chicago, I yearned for the empty sage fields and lonely dirt roads of New Mexico.

"All right. Go then," Mark said. "I'll take care of Domenica."

As soon as my teaching year at Northwestern ended, I booked a flight to Albuquerque. I was out at O'Hare Airport, sitting in a boarding lounge, when a man's voice began to speak to me. I grabbed a pen and paper. I began to scribble along, chasing the voice. It belonged to a homicide cop named Elliot Mayo. It spoke with confidence and great individuality. They called my flight and

I hurriedly boarded. All during the several-hour flight, the voice talked on. By the time we landed in Albuquerque, I had filled a notebook. In the airport's gift shop I bought another, wondering if the voice would pause long enough for me to get to Taos, a two-and-a-half-hour drive north. The voice did pause and I drove north feeling exhilarated. At last I was writing again, really writing.

Arriving in Taos, I checked into the El Pueblo. My lodgings held a small sitting room, a small kitchen, and a neat bedroom. Through my windows I could see Taos Mountain. I was right next door to Dori's Café, a favored haunt of Taos writer John Nichols. I could go there and both eat and write. The voice started talking again, and I took a notebook with me to Dori's, where I ordered red beans and rice and kept on scribbling.

I wrote until Dori's closed. Exhausted but happy, I went back to the El Pueblo. I was hoping the voice would let me sleep. Before I went to bed I called Domenica and Mark. "I am writing!" I reported happily. They sounded a bit grumpy and abandoned, but I was determined to ignore any negativity. I was writing!

Booked for a week's stay, it became clear to me that I was writing something larger than the time allotted. I woke daily, went to Dori's, settled in at a table, and wrote all morning. At lunch I was joined by my girlfriend Ellen Longo, an astrologer and accountant whom I had lived next door to on my very first stay in Taos. Ellen loved Elliot Mayo. She couldn't wait to hear his daily adventures. "What happens next?" she always wanted to know. I told her I would have to write to find out.

After lunch with Ellen, I would write all afternoon, pausing about four for a longish walk out toward the pueblo. The air was fragrant with piñon and sage. The walks gave me time to pray and to mull. My life back in Chicago was lopsided, I realized. I was doing too much for other people and not enough for myself as an artist. My writer was starved for exactly the kind of time it was enjoying in Taos, long hours with nothing to do in them except write, write, write.

"Mommy, when are you coming home?" Domenica wanted to know. I had stretched my one week into two and then three. The novelty of having Mark care for her had been displaced by missing Mommy.

"I'll be home soon," I promised.

"When?" Mark wanted to know. He, too, sounded bereft.

"This weekend, but when I come home we have to make some changes. I can't just teach all the time. You can; I can't. We're different."

"Just come home."

By then I knew that I was halfway through a crime novel. I was determined that when I got back to Chicago, I would not abandon it. Taking one last, long walk out toward the pueblo, I prayed, "Dear God, please give me the strength to be true to myself." And then I went home.

Home had a surprise waiting for me—a big surprise.

"I think we should get married," Mark unexpectedly told me. "I think we're good together." Evidently my absence had given him some thinking time. I had plotted a novel while he had plotted the course of our lives.

I knew what Domenica's vote would be—and the cat's and the dog's. My own vote seemed to be almost after the fact. We were living like a family, and getting married just acknowledged that fact.

"Yes," I told Mark.

Once we agreed to get married, we set about consolidating our households. We had two separate apartments to fold into one house. We would need writing room as well as living room, and Domenica, on the brink of adolescence, would need space of her own as well. I thought it would take a long time to find agreeable housing, but on my very first day of looking, I found a snug yellow coach house with room for all three of us. Mark and I decided to marry at midsummer. That gave me a scant two months to prepare.

I called Laura Leddy, a student of ours who had evolved into a true friend. "I need a dress! I need a dress for Domenica! I need flowers! What kind of wedding should we have? Oh, Laura!"

With Laura's help, I planned a country wedding. Guests would picnic on fried chicken, cole slaw, baked beans, potato salad, and pies, lots and lots of pies. Of course, my bridesmaids were anything but countrified. They were a clutch of urban beauties swathed in hyacinth blue. Mark and I decided to get married at Unity Church, where we were teaching our creativity course, and we decided to invite our students to the wedding. It was to be a big, casual, heartfelt affair, a community celebration. The details of planning it threatened to inundate me. I panicked.

"I need to write," I told Mark. "I have to finish my novel."

"You'll finish your novel," Mark tried to placate me.

"I mean I have to finish it now!" I yowled.

"Do what you need to do, but I'd say a wedding is a pretty important priority."

"You don't understand me!"

"Oh, yes, I do. Go write."

And so, with Mark's grudging blessing, I began to write every day at our local coffee shop, the Half and Half. Sometimes alone, sometimes with Laura writing across the table from me, I would race page after page, following my detective hero, Elliot Mayo, through his increasingly dark and labyrinthian sorties into Chicago's underworld. I do not recommend this, but I was writing flat-out. With the wedding looming, I had a deadline. I did not think that Mark would appreciate having a novel unfolding in the middle of our honeymoon, most especially as dark and violent a novel as mine was shaping up to be.

My family was excited by my impending nuptials. They were relieved that I had found someone who would take me on with all of my "intensity" and all of my "ideas." Although they loved me, my family thought of me as just this side of crazy. To be honest, I thought of myself that way and was constantly monitoring myself to be more "normal." With Mark in the picture and my life taking on increasingly solid associations like my job at Northwestern and my teaching duties at the church, my family heaved a collective sigh of relief. Maybe now Domenica would be "okay."

Mark's family was more shocked than mine at our union. To their eyes I was more suspicious, a divorced woman with a child, and the product of time in Hollywood. They found it exciting that Martin was famous. They found it exciting that Domenica was semifamous. They knew that Mark had big, glittering dreams and they wanted him to have them. If I was part of what it meant to Mark to be successful, okay, then, let him marry me. But make no mistake, Mark's was a military family, in which the men wore the pants and gave the orders. I was just a little too uppity to be good casting as wife material. They hoped Mark knew what he was doing.

June gave way to the heat of July and I was now in the home-stretch on my novel. Amid fittings for dresses and decisions about flowers, I continued to rendezvous daily with Laura and my book.

A few final plot twists and the book would be finished. A few more weeks and I would one more time be a married woman. My father and Mark seemed to get along well, and this mattered to me. Mark and my brother Christopher shared an ironic sense of humor. I was glad for any and all the ways that Mark and I seemed to be a good fit. A lingering symptom from my time with Martin was that I did not trust my own judgment when it came to men.

Our wedding day dawned bright and blisteringly hot. I thought I would melt clinging to my father's arm as we walked down the aisle. Mark and I said our vows in front of a large congregation. Many of our students were grinning with jubilation. They had felt us to be a match, watching our chemistry as we taught together. "I told you so," their victorious winks and high signs seemed to say. In our wedding pictures Mark and I both look exhausted but happy. Domenica, in a grown-up apricot silk gown, looks happiest of all.

For our honeymoon Mark and I traveled to Taos. As we drove in down the Rio Grande canyon, three beautiful rainbows arched overhead. I was ecstatic with this little bit of art direction from the Higher Power. I wanted Mark to love Taos as much as I did.

"Three rainbows," I kept exclaiming. "They must be just for you."

"They must be." Mark smiled back. "I can see why they call this the Land of Enchantment."

We had a scant week for our honeymoon, hardly time to walk and drive the beautiful landscape. I would have stayed on, but Mark was due back in Chicago and then off to Russia. He had been invited to be one in a group of entrepreneurs asked to help bridge the knowledge gap in the new Russia. It was an exciting business opportunity for him. He planned to teach our creativity work on a boat trip on the River Volga. For my part, I planned to miss him and finish my novel.

As it turned out, finishing the novel was much easier than miss-ing Mark. My hero, Elliot Mayo, was faced with the known dan-gers of the netherworld. I found myself faced with the unknown dangers of my own paranoia. For the weeks that Mark was gone, I spent my insomniac nights twisted with insecurity. Was Mark run-ning away from our new marriage? I wondered. Would he, like James Bond, meet with curvaceous temptation? His business asso-ciate knew Mark as a bachelor playboy. Would it matter to him that Mark was now a married man? For that matter, would it mat-ter to Mark? Where had my trust gone? I asked myself.

After my time in Taos, I felt claustrophobic back in Chicago. The little coach house felt tiny. Domenica and I were both let down after the wedding to have Mark gone one more time and this time so very far away. I knew that for my daughter, having a real, on-the-premises, live-in father felt very important. I felt the same way about having a live-in husband.

Mark came home to banked anger. I resented having missed him. I was relieved to learn that his sexual temptations had been success-fully navigated. "I told them my wife was a poet," Mark explained. "They love poets and I shared some of your poems with them."

But if Russia was behind Mark, it was not out of his system. He wanted to put together entrepreneurial opportunities. He rented an office on Belmont, where I taught, and set to work making phone calls to the men he knew from the board of trade. Mark was filled with enthusiasm. He worked long days and longer nights.

"He's back but he's not back," Domenica summed it up. She was angry.

"You're back but you're not back," I told him. I was angry too. "And what about our projects?"

Susan Schulman was trying to place the creativity book, and she had hopes Tarcher would publish it. Additionally I had written a small cop film called *Closer Than You Think.* We planned to produce it in Chicago, but writing books and making movies now seemed like small potatoes to Mark. He was involved in world politics. Movies paled by comparison.

Summer simmered into fall. I finished my novel and sent it off to Susan Schulman to put it up for sale. I returned to my still-too-heavy teaching load at Northwestern, Chicago Filmmakers, and Unity Church and on a private basis. It was now like pulling teeth to get Mark to do a writing session with me. I insisted that we finish polishing our money book. I couldn't bear to see our promising projects abandoned, but his passions lay elsewhere.

"Oh. All right," Mark said, settling into the harness of joint writing again. Despite his reluctance, he was writing better than ever. Struggles with solvency spoke to his compassion. It wasn't too long before we had a finished draft of *Money Drunk/Money Sober.* We sent it off to Susan.

It was a brilliant autumn that year. The trees in Lincoln Park were a deep crimson flared with gold. On chilly fall nights I would drive to the Green Mill, Al Capone's old bar, and there I would participate in something called the Poetry Slam, in which poets went up against other poets like boxers. It was a real Chicago-style beer-and-brawl environment. To hold the boozy crowd's attention, you had to be good. Week after week, I tried out new material. My colleagues were poets Tony Fitzpatrick and Mark Smith, well-known fixtures on the slam circuit. Their work was macho yet sensitive. I hoped my own was tough-minded as well.

I was working on a book of poetry that Mark Bryan would collate and publish for me called *The Quiet Animal.* Among his many roles for me, Mark was a superb muse. Something about him set the writer in me off and running. It was very efficient of me, I sometimes kidded, to have married my muse.

With Mark hard at work on his Russian endeavors and me hard at work teaching and writing, one might think that the little coach house would settle into happy productivity—but that was not to be. One night, as we were settling in for a quiet evening, Mark got a phone call from his sister. She was distraught—and who wouldn't be? Her husband of many years stood suddenly accused of child abuse. She loved him and she didn't know what to do. Were her children at risk?

Mark got off the phone tremendously upset. He could not in good conscience leave his sister alone to fend for herself with such a terrifying problem. There were four children involved, Mark's nephew and nieces, whom he loved. "What are we going to do?" Mark asked me. "They can't stay with him. The kids need counseling."

Whether Mark said it first or I did, the answer seemed obvious. Mark's sister and the children would need to come north and get help. Within days we had found them an apartment two houses down from the little coach house. It was, I hoped, just enough distance for them to have a separate household and yet feel safe.

When Lorna and the children arrived, they were shell-shocked. Used to living in the beautiful West Virginia countryside, they were suddenly thrust into the urban heart of Chicago. They missed their dog. They missed their friends. Mark swung into action. He got the children qualified counselors and he got a good therapist to work with his sister.

"She loves her husband," he would say, in obvious pain.

"That doesn't mean she can stay with him," I would counter.

Domenica, too, felt a sense of loss, not gain, with the cousins' arrival. Before they came, Mark had been "hers"; now she had to share him with other children.

"Try to be generous," I would tell Domenica. "They're not here forever, just until things get straightened out."

"Well, when will that be?" Domenica had a point.

There was no magic wand that we could wave to ease the pain of Mark's family. Reeling from the shock of the accusations, they tried hard to reach a grounded sense of truth. Could the accusations be true? The vote on this ran one way one day and the other way the next. The accusations had come from more than one source. It seemed they had to have some validity.

Mark worried that there would be a vendetta. Lorna's husband was foreign, and foreigners weren't easily accepted under any terms in the hill country where they lived. His work as a night watchman was both solitary and dangerous. Mark feared the worst and then beat himself up for fearing it.

"Why do I have this crazy feeling?" he would wonder aloud.

But Mark's feelings weren't crazy. They were premonitions. Late one night the phone call came that Lorna's husband had been murdered—castrated and then burned to death as the hill people took justice into their own hands, declaring him guilty as accused.

Lorna and her children went back home. They refused to stay up north in the city, blaming themselves and their absence for what had happened.

"Mark, we tried," I told him. But he was inconsolable. Like his sister, he had a lingering sense of self-blame for his brother-in-law's death.

"Maybe we shouldn't have brought them north," he said. "Maybe we shouldn't have broken up the family."

"What if the accusations were true and you left the children with him," I would counter. "I think you did the right thing. I know you tried."

For Mark, mere trying was not enough. It was with great reluctance that he watched his sister take her children back to the scene of the crime. "They'll be stigmatized." He worried about the children.

It was probably inevitable that with Mark's focus on Lorna and her children, Domenica would choose to act out. For several years she had safely gone to spend schoolday afternoons at the stable. Now, suddenly, there was trouble in the form of an older boy who had a crush on her. The boy drove one of the carriages that were a tourist attraction on Michigan Avenue. He invited Domenica to ride with him. This meant leaving the safety of the stable. It was an adventure Domenica could not resist—and she was flattered to have caught the eye of a handsome older boy.

Mark drove to the stable to pick up Domenica for dinner and quickly sniffed out the situation. He did not want his stepdaughter hanging out with any carriage driver. For one thing, the boy was too old. For another, Mark had his suspicions that the carriage drivers smoked dope.

"You are off-limits, young lady," Mark told Domenica.

"I don't know what you're talking about," Domenica countered— but she did know. In fact, she had been as much frightened as flattered by the older boy's attentions. She was relieved when Mark drew a line.

"He's too strict," she complained but without much conviction. Mark meanwhile was squarely focused on her again and now he had bigger fish to fry. Domenica belonged in private school, Mark felt. He took his case to Martin, explaining the advantages of the private school, scholastically and socially.

"All right. Count me in, I'll pay for it," Martin said, and so Domenica transferred to Francis W. Parker, a fine, arts-oriented school, where she was slightly more at home among her classmates. Socially they were more advanced than she was, and this initially made her feel shy, but before long she found a few kindred spirits, whom I called "baby artists," and so school and the social whirl became easier for her.

If Domenica's life was growing a little easier, Mark's and mine was growing more difficult. One more time I was over-teaching and under-writing. One more time the cost was depression. For his part, Mark was having a hard time finding investors for his Russian enterprises. To those he approached, the Russian economy still looked too risky. As the rejections piled up, Mark, too, became disheartened.

Instead of being a snug haven from worldly woes, the little coach house began to feel like a pressure cooker. I missed Mark's help on creative projects and I began to have the sinking feeling he was on a wild-goose chase with his Russian venture. Mark wanted the family to have financial stability, and to him teaching looked like one way to accomplish it. When I would talk about needing more writing time, he would point out that he himself was putting in long days. We lacked sympathy for each other's perspective. As the little coach house was blanketed with heavy winter snows, Mark and I suffered from dispirited moods.

"You need a horse, Mom" was Domenica's diagnosis. "You need something that is just plain fun."

As it happened, Domenica had a particular horse in mind, a small, showy chestnut Arabian with four white stockings and a blaze. The horse was named Captivate, and he belonged to an NBC newscaster who had won him on a bet. Captivate was spirited and much too much horse for the novice rider to handle. He was up for sale at what can best be described as a steal. I bought him.

Now Domenica and I both went to the stable in the afternoons. We both took turns in the ring working the kinks out of our "ponies." Around and around we went. Such riding was better than nothing, but it made me yearn for the luxury of trails and the great outdoors. The addition of a horse made Chicago feel even more claustrophobic to me.

"There's a tenured slot coming up in the film department at Northwestern," Mark told me his version of good news.

"But I don't want to be tenured."

"Sure you do. Salary, benefits, for that matter prestige—"

"I am not really comfortable at Northwestern. I don't think that a lot of the faculty likes me. Even if I tried for tenure, I'd never get it."

"You could try."

"Well, maybe."

It was true that I was increasingly uncomfortable at Northwestern. Unlike Columbia College, where the faculty had largely been composed of working filmmakers, Northwestern leaned heavily toward film theory. Many of the faculty knew a great deal about how to take a film apart but precious little about how to put a film together. There I was in the midst of them, a working screenwriter who had just shot a feature film and looked likely to shoot another. My students appeared to be fountains of creativity. Feature scripts were pouring out of them and they were beginning to win national attention. No, I did not fit in. I couldn't face it squarely, but I was envied and resented. My lack of academic credentials were held against me. "All" I had was my résumé as a working film-maker.

The winter in Chicago is always long and dark, but the winter that year seemed to be colder and darker than usual. Bundled in scarves against the wind, I would walk to my classes on Belmont. In a small, cozy room my students would pile the wooden table with the writing of the week. They were becoming ever stronger and more daring. The pieces they wrote were suitable for publication and for literary contests. Every week we would stir the pot deeper still. Some of my most timorous students grew bold on the page. It was very rewarding.

At the same time, my movers-and-shakers creativity class moved on to ever more adventurous endeavors. The judge who wanted to sculpt began to study with a master sculptor. The lawyer who loved comedy began hosting her own radio show. The socialite who wrote "on the side" now tried her able hand at how-to beauty books.

On cold winter afternoons, when evening fell by four thirty, I would meet Domenica at the riding stable and together we would take our turns going round and round. Domenica had shaped Walter Mitty, her gray Arabian, into a fine model hunter. With the help of my sister Libby, an equine portrait artist, she had also acquired Ing, a bay Thoroughbred jumper. I would work with little Captivate, whom I had renamed Jack Merlin, after my friend Ed Towle's detective hero. Domenica would work with her jumpers. We did well spending our mommy-daughter time with the horses.

By six we would head home, usually to find Mark still hard at work. I enjoyed cooking and we would often invite friends to dinner. After dinner it was homework for Domenica and private time for Mark and myself. As much as we hated to admit it to each other, our days were productive but unrewarding. Mark was disappointed by his Russian work. For him it was one more worthy dream gone glimmering. I missed having a creative peer group. Being the teacher meant I was supposed to be the one with answers, and I found I had many questions, chief among them "Why am I not more happy?"

Spring came and with it my predictable rejection for a tenured faculty position at Northwestern. The very attempt was a nightmare for me. I explained my creativity theories to a room full of skeptics. The department chair noisily ate all the way through my presentation. Instead, they chose a young woman with a dearth of professional credentials, though she did hold a master's in film studies. Cynically, I felt the game had been rigged. Mark, on the other hand, was shocked by my rejection. He had not seen it coming as I had. I had learned my lesson in rejection from the *Chicago Tribune.* The Chicago message seemed to me to be: be good but not too good. Do not rock the boat and do not make your colleagues uncomfortable. When I directed a feature film, I was too uppity for life as a reporter. When I developed my own creativity theories and practiced them on my students, I was too uppity for an academic.

"You're not happy," Mark diagnosed me, accurately.

"No. I can't see what I am supposed to do with myself in Chicago."

"But you're doing a lot. You're writing poetry and screenplays. You're teaching. What else do you want?"

I wasn't sure what else I wanted. I had grateful students. An ample enough income. My very own Arabian horse. My husband was tall, dark, and handsome. Not to mention smart, kind, and generous. What was my problem? Where was my gratitude? As spring turned toward summer, I began taking long bike rides along the lakefront. As I pedaled, I prayed, "Dear God, please give me a sense of direction. Please show me what it is you would have me do."

On cue, Susan Schulman called. "I have good news," she said with her typical understatement. "Jeremy Tarcher wants to publish your creativity book."

I took the news calmly. I always take good news with an absolutely flat affect—something that can hurt and puzzle people until they come to expect it. I found myself pleased but not precisely surprised. Mark, by contrast, was over the moon. "I knew it!" he crowed. "I knew it should be a book! How great!"

Susan explained that there would be an editorial call from Jeremy "just to make sure you are on the same page," and then there would be editorial notes and rewrites. "It will go fine," Mark promised Susan. He was determined that I should make a success of the book.

When Jeremy Tarcher called, I found him tart, astringent, amusing, and inspiring—an invigorating mix of a man. He explained that he would be sending me a memo that gave his overview of the book and that he had certain questions and areas where he wanted me to elaborate.

"He sounds great," Mark pronounced when I filled him in on the call. "He sounds really brilliant. I like him."

With this brief conversation Mark stepped comfortably into what would be a managerial role regarding what would become *The Artist's Way*. I might have written the book, but he had "seen" it. In a very real sense, it was his brainchild and he had ambitions for it.

Susan Schulman rang us again. She had more good news. She had placed *Money Drunk/Money Sober* with a good small press. There was just one problem: both of our books were due simultaneously. Would we be able to handle doing two books at once? We both thought yes.

When my memo from Jeremy Tarcher arrived, it was very long

and detailed. He had thoughts on every chapter. I was going to have to really buckle down to work to give him what he wanted and needed. In order to work in such a concentrated fashion, I felt I needed an office, somewhere out of the house if Mark was going to be working at home.

And Mark was going to be working at home.

We quickly decided that the best way to work on two books simultaneously was for each of us to take one and see it through. In this way, editors would not be confused by whom they had to deal with. And so I left the house every day and walked two houses down to a small apartment I had rented as office space. Mark settled in at his desk and we both tackled the chapter at hand. At lunch we would ask, "How's it going?" We would each hope that the other might answer, "Fine." At night we would talk over the day's work. We both wanted to be current on each of the books, although we really had to keep our focus on just one.

Working with Jeremy's memo, I would occasionally take offense at the way something was phrased—and Jeremy could be quite picky. Mark was wonderful at defusing my defensiveness. "Maybe this is what he meant," he would say. Somehow, coming from Mark, I was able to hear what was intended. Sometimes I had to laugh at my own volatility. For a professional writer, I could certainly be thin-skinned.

Day by day and page by page, I responded to Jeremy's notes. I explained and clarified. I lengthened and elaborated. After a month or more of this, my little manuscript had nearly doubled. Mark was making similar progress. Unlike Jeremy and myself, who tended to work on the page, Mark and his editor forged an active phone relationship. They hammered out the final draft of the money book with many lengthy conversations. I would come home from my office and hear Mark on the phone hard at work with his editor. She was as tenacious as a small terrier, and the book was a healthy tug-of-war between their two sensibilities.

In addition to my writing, I had my teaching to contend with. It was difficult to show up for work at Northwestern feeling like a persona non grata. It took all of my professionalism to continue to carefully mentor the talented students I had there. Meanwhile there were scripts to read for Chicago Filmmakers and the ongoing writing and creativity courses I was teaching. Mark seemed to have endless stamina, but I felt myself flagging.

"Our life is full," Mark would say with satisfaction.

"It's too full," I would counter. My gratitude was at a low ebb and my nerves were on edge.

Our phone rang constantly with calls from our many students. Mark seemed to thrive on the hubbub. He loved being dead center of a swirling melee. Not for me, all the commotion. I craved quiet and space. Our little coach house seemed overstuffed with life. I felt there was no space for my dreams.

"I need a vacation," I told Mark. "I am going to finish up work on the creativity book and then take myself out to Taos."

"What is it with you and Taos?"

"I am happy there. I can hear myself think."

"I think fine right here."

"That's you. Maybe we're country mouse and city mouse and you are city mouse."

"Maybe."

"Is it okay with you if I go? Can you take care of Domenica?"

"Of course I can take care of Domenica. We'll have a good time."

Taos became the carrot I held in front of my exhausted nose. Finishing up at Northwestern, I comforted myself with images of sage fields rolling to the horizon. Reading through my students' scripts, I told myself that soon I would catch the scent of piñon on the wind, soon I would see mountains and hike out near the sacred land of the pueblo. But "soon" did not seem soon enough.

"What's wrong with you?" Mark would ask, worried.

"I'm tired."

"Go ride your horse."

I would go to the stable to ride, only to find that the stable felt claustrophobic as well. Piloting Jack around the ring, I would catch myself thinking, "This isn't working. I am riding in circles. I am thinking in circles. I am living in circles." I would come back from the stable frustrated and sad. This in turn frustrated and saddened Mark. Desolate—and for what seemed to be no good reason—I went to see Sonia Choquette.

"You're right on track," Sonia told me. "The book you are working on is going to change your life. It's going to help more people than you can imagine. Just keep plugging away at it. The work you're doing on it is good."

"But why am I so sad? Why am I so restless?"

"I see you moving to the Southwest. You will love it there. I see a job for Mark and continued success for the two of you."

"But Mark's happy in Chicago."

"I see the two of you in the Southwest. I see a great deal of Mark's future good coming to him from the Southwest. Try to have some faith. Everything is unfolding exactly as it should."

As he did every summer, my father came north from his winter home aboard the sailboat on Long Boat Key, Florida. I was very glad to see him. He always helped me to parse things out. This summer he felt, as I did, that I needed some time in Taos. "Just go," he told me, and so I did.

Oh, the relief of being back in Taos! I had finally finished the creativity book and my long and tiring year of teaching. With Mark watching Domenica, I was free again to walk and to write. I settled into the El Pueblo and began my daily regime of walking and prayer. "Please guide me," I prayed. "Please show me the way. Please guide me. . . ."

My prayers seemed to be unanswered. Or they seemed to be answered in an impossible way. Every day I fell more deeply in love with Taos, the sight of the silver-green sage, the scent of the piñon. A sudden rain would wash the valley. A rainbow would arch overhead. It all seemed impossibly beautiful: the changing face of Taos Mountain, the walking rain stalking in across the mesa. I particularly loved the black-and-white magpies that would balance lightly on a fence post. "I want to live here," I realized on one long walk. "It is just so beautiful."

Mark, Domenica, and my father were back in Chicago, waiting for me to return, but I didn't want to return. The more I walked, the more I prayed, the more clearly and certainly I knew that I was "home." On the phone with Mark I heard his puzzlement. What was wrong with Chicago? We were surrounded by friends and opportunities. He loved Chicago. True, he had been unable to interest Chicagoans in his Russian venture, but there were other fish to fry. Chicago was the city of big shoulders, the land of opportunity. Mark loved it there.

"Come home," he said now. "It's beautiful here, full summer. We can bike-ride along the lake."

"I just want to stay a few more days," I pleaded.

"Well, we all miss you."

"I miss you too."

My final days in Taos were spent dreaming. What would it be

like to live here? God felt so close when I was out walking. Praying for guidance seemed natural, no mere exercise. The more I prayed for guidance, the more I knew that I needed to move to Taos. But what about Mark? What about Domenica? Would it be right for them as well?

When I got back to Chicago, I again immediately felt trapped. I told Mark I had to talk with him, really talk with him, and when we sat down, I laid out the case for Taos as best I could. "We have two books coming out," I told him. "We are writers and teachers and we can write and teach in Taos. We don't have to stay in Chicago. Maybe we have outgrown it."

"I don't feel I've outgrown it," Mark said. "Maybe you have."

"I want you to go to Taos by yourself and see how the place feels to you."

"But you just got back."

"I want you to go. Take some walks. Feel the land. See if you don't think you could be happy there. I think it would be good for Domenica. She could have a real high school experience, homecoming and football."

Mark saw that I was serious and he agreed to take an exploratory trip. He would stay at the El Pueblo, where I always stayed, where he and I had both stayed on our honeymoon.

The days with Mark gone were days of pins and needles for me. Every day I would wait for his check-in and I would say, "Well? What do you think?" I did not know if Taos would be able to work its magic on Mark. Viewed objectively, it was just a small town. Whatever romance it had might speak just to me. And then, one summer evening, Mark called and said, "It was a good day today. I see what you see here. Is your dad there?"

Mark had spent the day looking at Taos real estate and he had come to the conclusion that with my father's help we might be able to buy. This was one rung above my dreams come true. I had assumed that if we moved to Taos, we would be looking for yet another rental. To my surprise, my father agreed with Mark that we should buy, not rent, and he further agreed to put up the down payment. Now it was up to Mark to find a property where we could have horses and yet be close enough to town for Domenica's school friends to be able to stop by.

"You'd better come out," Mark's next call ran. "I think I've found it." And so I went back to Taos to look over the properties that Mark thought were suitable and one in particular which he felt should be ours. I was hoping for a romantic old adobe, but Mark had found a stucco house with a barn and paddocks, a scant mile from Domenica's high school just on the edge of town. The property had five acres, room enough for a whole herd of horses, and a large covered porch that looked west and north toward Taos Mountain and the sunset.

"You have to picture it fixed up a little," the real estate agent said apologetically as she showed me through the house. Indeed, the furnishings were terrible, the draperies worse, and the paint job a terrible mess. "Don't buy me" the house all but announced, and still, if I stood in the heart of the house long enough, I could sense what Mark had sensed there, a happy future life for the three of us.

"Well, what do you think?" Mark wanted to know.

"I think you've found it. I think I can fix it up. I think we might be really happy here," I told him.

Whisk! Mark and my father swung into action. "We'll take it," they told the broker, eager to take the house off the market. Papers were faxed. Money was wired. It was settled. We were buying the Taos house and moving there. We could take possession right after

Labor Day. Mark and I came back to Chicago with a clutch of photographs to show Domenica and my father. In the photos, the little ranch looks ramshackle but charming. We knew just how we would fix it.

Our Chicago friends were desolate. They planned a huge and elaborate going-away party. The guest list was enormous, reflecting the size of our Chicago life as teachers and community members. The night of the party, Mark and I found ourselves swept up by two emotions: anticipation and regret. Our Chicago life had been rich and our friends were beloved. The excitement of the party didn't entirely mask the sorrow underneath. We were really going.

All of the belongings from the little coach house fit into one large U-Haul truck. Mark would drive this truck and I would follow in the Jeep. We bought walkie-talkies to stay connected, but they would prove to be useless on the open highway. We drove convoy fashion, slower than Mark would have liked, as fast as the unwieldy truck would allow. The trip took three days. Mark and I each drove alone with our own thoughts.

Domenica had gone out a week early to be the guest of my friend Ellen Longo, whose son Erin would be her guide at her new school. Each night on the road, as we pulled into our lodgings, Mark and I would check each other's emotional temperature after the day's drive, then we would call Domenica.

"How are you? How is it?" we would ask, hoping that she was approaching her new school with enthusiasm.

"It's weird, but I am okay," Domenica bravely responded. She was actually in shock and soldiering through. Her new school was one-third Hispanic, one-third "Anglo," and one-third Native American. It was a far cry from posh Francis W. Parker back in Chicago.

Mark and I pulled into Taos from the north side of town. This meant we drove past a long string of souvenir shops hung with Indian blankets and guarded by cow skulls.

"What is he thinking?" I wondered as Mark piloted the big truck into the town's small streets and finally onto the narrow dirt road leading to our new house.

"Welcome home. We're not in Kansas anymore," Mark exclaimed, swinging down from the truck.

After the city of Chicago, the quiet of Taos was very noisy. Coyotes howled in the darkness. At dawn songbirds burst into song. A searching wind jangled the wind chimes that we hung on our large covered porch. It seemed there was music everywhere. Church bells tolled frequently across the countryside. Taos Valley was predominately Catholic and the bells called worshippers to mass. Added to all of this was the singular sound of water. Taos Valley was irrigated by an acequia system, ditches and gates hundreds of years old that carried water from icy mountain streams to the fields where it was needed. The rush of flowing waters pried through windows and accompanied conversations.

The first thing for me was trying to find some sober alcoholics to talk with. Fortunately this proved easy. When I had first lived in Taos, sober alcoholics were few and far between. Now I quickly found several people with whom I enjoyed an easy rapport. Mark made friends even more easily than I did. Seemingly from out of nowhere he found a group of men who helped us with the moving in and the setting up of our household. Their laughter boomed through the house. It made Taos feel less like a terrible risk and more like an adventure.

September sped past. Domenica joined the volleyball team and reported that her teammates were cutthroat competitors. The horses arrived, their shipping paid for by Martin's generosity. We bought a load of hay and several bags of feed. Mornings began now with feeding the horses and getting Domenica off to school. A writing day then loomed ahead of me. Mark took a job working with troubled adolescents at a mental health clinic. He had to commute to work, but his drive took him along the flank of the Rio Grande River, and he enjoyed the views.

One of Domenica's first school science assignments was to make a bug collection. Taos Valley was filled with creepies and crawlies of all sorts, ranging from seldom seen tarantulas to the more common and more deadly brown recluse and black widow spiders. Finding these creatures was a quick baptism by fire into the realities of where we were now living. I am happy to say that Domenica's bug collection was large and impressive. We may have felt squeamish, but it didn't show in her exhibit.

Autumn in Taos Valley is glorious. The cottonwoods flare yellow. The aspens shine bright gold. Evenings turn chill and the smell of piñon fires begins to scent the air. In the mornings, plumes of smoke can be seen curling up above the adobes. Our house featured two fireplaces and a woodstove. We laid in a supply of firewood and began to enjoy the business of laying a morning fire. Mark was good at building fires. It was wonderful to lie in bed weekend mornings with a fire crackling in the fireplace a few steps away.

After going through many possibilities with Jeremy Tarcher, it was decided to call the creativity book *The Artist's Way*. The first books off the presses were beautiful, and for the first time I had real books from which to teach. As I had in Chicago, I placed a notice in the local paper advertising a creativity workshop. I offered a set fee or reasonable barter. My phone rang off the hook and our first class was assembled. We had painters, musicians, clothing designers, writers, and photographers. We offered them a weekly class held right in our living room with a crackling fire for commentary. Our living room windows looked north to Taos Mountain, whose summit was often wreathed in clouds. It looked lofty and mysterious, a suitable home for the Great Creator. Our class thrived.

The previous owners of our property had allowed the fields to fall into disrepair. Mark spent much of that first autumn supervising the digging of new ditches and the laying of pipe where needed. We would be rewarded in spring by green and verdant fields, but just then the work of restoration was costly and difficult. Mark found an old Hispanic man who remembered the best placement of ditches for the flow of our land. Half in Spanish, half in English, the work progressed. There was a sense of urgency because soon snow would be on the way.

"Take time to ride with us," Domenica and I would plead. Rides, to us, were a source of wonder and adventure. On our very first trail ride, Domenica and I had been walking placidly down a narrow dirt road on Walter and Jack, when suddenly Domenica piped up, "Look, Mommy! Tarantula!" Sure enough, a large bow-legged tarantula was strolling across the road just ahead of us. Yes, we loved riding.

We would saddle and bridle our three horses and take off as a family, first riding the dirt roads through the sage fields and then, higher up, the twisting trails leading through the mountains. Mounted on surefooted Arabs, Domenica and I had no difficulty with the terrain. Mark was riding Ing, a long-legged Thoroughbred for whom the going was tougher. Add to that the fact that when Ing spotted a straightaway, Mark had his hands full. Still, the rides were glorious. We would surprise flocks of wild bluebirds. Magpies would keep pace with us, teasing the horses along. Sometimes we would spot large hawks riding the thermals—even eagles. There was always the danger of flash floods, and we had to take care, as we sometimes rode the bottoms of twisting arroyos, always alert for snakes.

Winter comes early to northern New Mexico. The first snows blanket the peaks in October, while the leaves are still ablaze. By November the fiery colors are gone and the beginnings of a winter wonderland are taking form. Mark was determined that we should enjoy the long winter. Early one Saturday he snuck out of the house and attended a ski swap. There he acquired ski paraphernalia for himself, myself, and Domenica.

Taos is famous among skiers for its formidable mountain. Intermediate runs at Taos are said to be as hard as expert runs elsewhere. Mark determined that if we were to learn to ski, we should not be frightened or injured. And so, one snowy Saturday, he announced that we were all going over to Angel Fire, a more gentle ski resort some twenty-five miles away through beautiful twisting canyons of fir trees. Mark was in his element as we drove the canyons. He loved being the leader and having a new adventure to share with his "girls." Domenica and I were both more than a little intimidated. Mark was a natural athlete, and by day's end he was plunging down the slopes. We were more timorous, sticking to the beginners' runs. The beauty of the Angel Fire Valley was breathtaking. As we rode the lifts, Domenica was enchanted, "Mark! Mommy! Look!"

As winter deepened, the canyons became more impassable. Skiing remained a special occasion, and we went as often as we could. Meanwhile, on a daily basis, Mark was driving the treacherous canyon that cradled the Rio Grande. On his daily commute, which took an hour each way, he navigated rock slides and mud slides and sudden dense snowfalls. It was during one such snowfall that I heard a knock at my front door. I opened it to find a stranger holding a tiny, wriggling black puppy. "Is this your dog, ma'am? I found it in the road." I reached my arms out to take the puppy. Although I faithfully trekked through snow to ask all the neighbors if they had lost him, that little dog was instantly mine. Maxwell Perkins, I named him, after the legendary editor.

"I know we don't need another dog, but we do need an editor," I told Mark when he arrived home wreathed in snow and gloom from his hard day's work. He wanted the clinic to be far more than a glorified baby-sitting service for difficult youth. He wanted it to offer genuine therapeutic help, a tall order.

Looking back, it seems we should have seen that Mark's job was a danger to all of us. He had spent his own years as a troubled teen and now he was counseling youngsters more troubled than he himself had been. He took his work with them very seriously and their cases would weigh on him well after the long drive home. With our horses and our skiing, Domenica and I were living in wonderland. Mark was living in an increasingly dark terrain, where it seemed no amount of strength or wisdom was sufficient.

"What's wrong?" I would ask him, missing his normally sunny and adventurous nature.

Mark didn't really have an answer. While I thought of his counselor's job as something that would lend credibility to his future dust jackets, Mark was feeling less and less like a writer. More and more, he felt defined by his ill-paying work. He began to internalize the turbulence of his wards. His optimism was leached away.

I was accustomed to Mark's strength and resilience. He was so clearly an artist to me that I could not understand his identity becoming confused. He had a wonderful idea for a new book, *The Prodigal Father*. In it he would argue for a return of fathers who had abandoned their children. He felt he had abandoned his own son.

"I didn't think there was a place for me. I didn't think Scott needed me, not once his mother remarried and he had a stepdad," he said, "but I think I was wrong. All children need their fathers— and all fathers need their children."

Believing this, he himself was working hard to bridge the long gap of years without his son. He continued to write to him regularly, little knowing that his former wife, out of bitterness and misguided love, was sheltering their son from the letters.

Increasingly Mark became absorbed in the subject matter of his book. He found Taos to be a town filled with abandoned children. Single mothers were everywhere. Fathers were few and far between. It wasn't long before Mark, with his characteristic charisma, had attracted a small band of bright, fatherless boys who looked to him for guidance.

"It's so simple," he would bemoan. "They need a father to teach them things like how to wax a car."

So Mark would teach the boys how to wax a car. He took an interest in their stories. If they craved a father, Mark himself craved fathering. He was Pied Piper to a band of adolescent boys. The writer in him would hear their stories of abandonment. The counselor in him would try to help.

"What would you think," Mark asked me, "if I went back to school?"

The question startled me. I thought of us as writers for which we were plentifully outfitted with talent and needed no further credentials.

"I'd like to go to Harvard—if I could get in, that is. I'd like to study and I'd like to have some real credentials."

I wanted to say, "But we just got here! We're home! We can make a life here through writing and teaching." Instead, I listened to Mark's dreams with a growing sense of unease. He wasn't happy and I didn't know how to make him happy. Listening to his dream of further education, I wondered if it wasn't too late for that. He had been president of his class, a brilliant young man bound for the Ivy League, when he got his girlfriend Patty pregnant. They married in disgrace. His dreams of Harvard had been buried under the reality of teen fatherdom. He had lost that early marriage and with it contact with his son. Patty had soon remarried and Mark was displaced by the new father.

Couldn't he accept these terrible losses and move on? I wondered. Couldn't he try to make a new life with me and Domenica? I was blind to the depth of Mark's yearning, his deep-seated desire to make something of himself and in terms that meant something to him. Where I had my artist's identity, Mark had a deep respect for academia. Where I had Domenica, Mark had the haunting absence of his own son, Scott.

And then Scott reentered Mark's life. He turned eighteen and his mother gave him the long-accumulated letters. In them he read of Mark's desire to know him, to be a real father and not just some shadow from Scott's childhood. After grappling with his deep distrust, Scott, like Mark, reached out. A link was forged. Scott came west for a weeklong visit. In the photographs of that visit, Scott and Mark look almost like brothers. Mark was that young when he fathered him.

The bond that was forged by that visit was quickly tested. Scott was a troubled young man who needed every pinch of guidance

Mark could give him. Mark, for his part, longed to be able to give more than mere guidance. He wanted money, lots of money, enough to pay for Scott's education, enough to somehow make up for the years apart.

Domenica took to her stepbrother with an open heart. In some ways she seemed older and wiser than Scott, certainly more settled in a stable identity. Mark worried that the two young people would fall in love. He feared a repeat of his own teen years for Scott. Domenica, happy with the boy she was dating, was baffled and offended by Mark's concerns. She was glad to have a brother. She didn't need another boyfriend.

Winter closed in. We were in a snowy world that seemed a million miles from Chicago. I missed my friends Laura and Sonia, while Mark missed his friend Gary, who had been our best man. Domenica missed Dan Evans, a neighborhood boy who had been such a good friend to her back in Chicago, but she did something about it—she invited Dan to join us in Taos for Christmas break.

It was on a snowy morning just after Christmas that Dan came inside to find Domenica and say, "Your horse Walter is lying down in the snow. Is that normal?" It was not normal. Walter was in the throes of a bad, potentially deadly colic. Mark rushed to his side and heaved Walter to his feet. "C'mon, boy. Walk with me," he pleaded. "Walk with me." Walter took a few unsteady steps. Domenica and I frantically phoned the vet.

"We have an emergency," we told Tim Johnson, the vet, who sprang into his truck and drove the ten miles from his clinic to our little ranch. Mark managed to keep Walter on his feet but staggering. The vet arrived and gave Walter a powerful shot of bute. We waited but Walter was still in agony—nothing Dr. Johnson did seemed to help.

"We need to take him to Albuquerque," Dr. Johnson said. "If we keep him here, he's gone. If we take him there, it's ten thousand dollars."

Mark and I did not have ten thousand dollars to save Domenica's pony, but her father, Martin, did. I called him.

"Take Walter to Albuquerque," Martin said. "I'll pay for it."

And so we loaded Walter into the vet's trailer and followed caravan style in our cars. At the Albuquerque clinic, the operation was long and tricky. Several feet of Walter's intestine were removed. It was touch and go, but Walter was tough, and with Domenica at his side begging him to pull through, he valiantly turned the corner back to life and made it.

Winter shifted into spring. Turbulent winds swept the valley. Turbulent winds swept our household as well. Mark was increasingly distraught over his job working with adolescents. He had many ideas about how to improve the facility but lacked the clout to see his changes implemented. Increasingly he saw Domenica in terms of the pathologies he dealt with all day.

"I'm your daughter, not your guinea pig!" Domenica yelled at him. She wasn't a troubled teen. She was a teen, period. She resented being seen in pathological terms.

As the atmosphere around our house persistently darkened, so did my own writing terrain. One more time taking up the tale of Elliot Mayo, I found myself writing a story of sexual obsession. Elliot was involved with strippers and small-time thugs. This world was tawdry and dark. Northern New Mexico was coming into bloom, but I was living on the mean streets of Chicago.

One Sunday morning Mark spotted an article in the Santa Fe paper that talked about Joseph Di Pienza, a visionary educator who was building a film school with the help of Greer Garson.

"Call him," Mark urged me. "You could teach for him." The idea of being involved with a film school was very attractive to me. I called Di Pienza, who promptly hired me. It was a 150-mile round-trip commute through the treacherous canyon to teach in Santa Fe one night a week, but oddly, the long trip seemed worth it. It kept me with one foot in the outer world. Santa Fe was less isolated and more sophisticated than Taos. It fit better with Mark's picture of what success looked like, and working again within a filmmaking community gave me a sense of continuity that was important to me. With family life feeling precarious, I one more time turned to work for a sense of stability and self-esteem.

That spring it felt like all three of us were searching for something. We were restless. We were frustrated. We were discontent. Mark, Domenica, Julia—we all yearned for a bond that seemed to elude us. One Saturday Mark surprised me and Domenica by taking us on an excursion to a nearby Morgan farm. He knew how we loved horses and Morgan horses in particular. He thought the adventure would do us all good.

Unlike most of New Mexico's ranches, which featured barbed wire and unpainted boards, Roy-El Morgan Farm sported snowy white fences and carefully cultivated gardens. The main house was a graceful adobe, and beyond it lay the paddocks and show barns, home to fifty-plus very fancy horses. The matriarch of this domain was a gracious and elegant woman named Elberta Honstein. Her daughter, Debbie Seebold, functioned as a trainer of champions. Mark, Domenica, and I entered the biggest barn as if we were entering wonderland. Row by row the alert and polished Morgans extended their velvet muzzles to our touch.

It was in the third and final barn that we found what we didn't know we were looking for. There, in a spacious back stall, we encountered a glistening dark bay yearling named Mistery.

"Oh," I breathed. "He is so beautiful." Mistery seemed to preen under our attention.

"Would you like a closer look?" Debbie asked. She unlatched the stall door.

"Yes," Mark answered for all of us. "We would."

With that, Mistery was led from his stall. We drew in our collective breath. At sixteen-two hands, he was tall for a Morgan and he was growing still, Debbie assured us. He had a finely chiseled head and an extra inch or two of neck—ideal for jumping.

"How much is he?" Mark abruptly asked.

"Mark!" Domenica and I exclaimed, both of us enchanted by the yearling's powerful charisma, both of us certain we could never afford him.

"He hasn't had a lot of work. I could let you have him for—" Debbie named a price.

"What about in installments?" Mark persisted as Domenica and I stood there mute and overwhelmed.

"We could take installments," answered Debbie after a pregnant pause.

"We'll take him," Mark said.

Taking Mistery turned out to involve certain prerequisites. Elberta Honstein wanted to be assured that we could safely handle such a green horse, and so she required Domenica and me to come for a series of lessons. Under Debbie's watchful eye, we would each put Mistery through his paces. Lessons finished, we would repair to Elberta's kitchen for homemade pie. In addition to Elberta and Debbie, there were Debbie's two daughters, Elberta and Erleen.

Domenica loved them immediately, and the feeling was reciprocated. Soon Domenica received invitations to come to the Roy-El Farm and travel with the group to horse shows. This was a great adventure into a specialized world. The Roy-El horses were champions, primped and pampered to perfection. Domenica became an expert groom.

I have photographs of Mistery's arrival at our little ranch in Taos. He looks like a young prince stepping from the trailer, head held high, surveying his domain. And then there are the pictures of me riding him for the first time. A smile lights my face. Mark has given me my dream horse.

In return I tried to give Mark help and encouragement. While I still thought it was good that he had the structure and the income from the job working with kids, I was always glad when he was writing. He didn't write as regularly as I did, and when he did, he became happy and excited. His ideas were good, he believed, and worth money. Time proved him right.

His book idea *The Prodigal Father* sold for a sizable advance, more than double what we had received for both *The Artist's Way* and *Money Drunk/Money Sober*. This was cause for celebration, proof that we could make it as writers, but Mark kept the money to himself. I was hurt and baffled by this decision, another clue that we were no longer a unit moving together in an agreed-upon direction. Although I still couldn't see it clearly, Mark's job made him feel small. He needed to feel—and was—someone far larger.

Spring in the Sangre de Cristo Mountains is an erratic time, cold one day and warm the next. Spring flowers bloom, only to be buried under snow. The snow melts quickly and the flowers blaze again. In our marriage, Mark and I were experiencing the same tricky weather. Our trust in each other's goodwill was being slowly eroded.

As is so often the case with me, I could face on the page what I could not face in life. I set my hand to writing a marital tragedy, *The Animal in the Trees.* The play that emerged was dark and bleak. The female lead was a selfish woman—a charge that I was leveling at myself.

Seeking any avenue that might lead us to some spiritual comfort, Mark and I attended an evening prayer circle run by Larry Lonergan, a spiritualist medium. The circle met in a small room with large windows looking out to the Sacred Mountain. When the time of the service came for messages, Larry, a tall, good-natured man, faced me gravely. "I'm sorry," he said softly. "Your marriage will not endure." Wind rattled the windows, but my shiver was more than physical. Both Mark and I were irate at these bad tidings. We had gone to the circle seeking comfort. We left more estranged than ever.

Mark continued to work at the clinic, and the work environment there steadily worsened. By temperament an idealist and a visionary, he felt increasingly at risk. Many nights he would come home from work angry. Domenica and I were unable to cheer him up. He projected his work difficulties onto us. We became the enemy. He suspected us of the worst behavior. We got tired of protesting our innocence.

"I am not the kids you work with," Domenica would say. "I am not drinking. I am not doing drugs. I am not screwing around. I am me, Domenica. Remember?"

I, too, wanted Mark to remember. I was his loyal wife, wasn't I? I was in his corner, couldn't he see that? But no, he could not. He began to mistrust me in my friendships with men. Stubbornly I fought his suspicions just as I had with Martin's. I thought I had a track record of loyalty and that I didn't deserve to be questioned, but Mark was questioning everything. His writing was hard and came in fits and starts. His long days at the clinic left him with little creative energy. He was often snappish and discontent. There was no luring him out now for a family horseback ride. "Fun" had left his vocabulary.

Spring moved toward summer. My father planned to come for a long visit. I flew to Florida to drive back with him. When I got off the plane, he met me looking tiny and frail. A handsome man, he was aging suddenly and dramatically. His chestnut hair had turned to silver. His beard was grizzled. I wanted very much for my father to think everything was all right. He had, after all, bought us our house. I wanted him to think it was a happy one.

Mark and I had continued to teach creative unblocking. In our last class before I left for Florida, we had done an exercise called U-turns. In it, we remembered art forms that we had abandoned. Doing it with the class, it suddenly dawned on me that it had been nearly twenty years since I had written a short story. In 1974, I had written a short story called "Zita." My then best friend Judy Bachrach had read the story and told me, "If you publish this, you will ruin your career." No matter that I had scant career to worry about at the time. I took Judy's words to heart and buried the story in a desk drawer, never to write another. Nearly two decades had ticked past. I had written in many other forms but never another story.

Now, driving my father's white Probe across Texas, I heard a voice in my head. The voice said, "Karen's new life began ten miles west of the Pecos River. That's where she said to Jerry, 'Pull over. NOW.'"

"Daddy!" I exclaimed. "I think it's a short story. You drive!"

And so, as my father drove the long miles across the panhandle, I scribbled in my notebook. It was a short story, the first of twenty-odd short stories that came through one right after another, like planes landing on a newly cleared runway. I was ecstatic. I loved writing short stories again. My father was amused and patient. The stories would become my book *Popcorn: Hollywood Stories*.

My father and I arrived back in Taos late in the afternoon. I was eager for him to see the house, even more eager for him to see the land. My father loved flora and fauna. He was delighted to step from the car and onto the property I was so proud of.

"We're home, Dad," I announced—but my father seemed painfully short of breath. A heavy smoker, he felt weak and dizzy at altitude. I helped him into the house.

"Jim, glad to have you here," Mark greeted Dad. He ushered him into the house, hefting his bag. Like me, Mark was eager to show off to my father exactly what his money had bought and how well we were doing at husbanding it.

"Oh, Julie B. This is very nice," my father said as he made his way through the house to the large covered porch that looked north to Taos Mountain. We had positioned some comfortable chairs, a picnic table, and an ashtray for him. Wobbly, he took a seat. His demeanor immediately set off Mark's alarms. Mark's father had run military hospitals, and Mark knew sick when he saw it.

Domenica was late to arrive home. She had lately, very happily, discovered the attentions of Ken and Nancy Jenkins, a husband-and-wife teaching pair who directed many of the high school's drama productions. With the Jenkinses, Domenica was suddenly swimming in her own water, cast in a production of *Winnie the Pooh*.

"Grandpa!" Domenica caroled as she came in the door. "And your little dog, Blue!" She bent to kiss first my father and then his ink-black Scottie. "You're here! You're here! Did you see the horses yet? Do you want to go for a walk?"

"Not just yet," my father demurred. This drew a sharp glance from Mark, who noted his shortness of breath.

"It's the altitude, Jim," Mark explained. "We're at seventy-five hundred feet here. You need aspirin and water and you may need some oxygen—"

"I like your view." My father cut him off.

But Mark was right to take Dad's difficulties seriously. Over the next few days my father visibly weakened. I did not want to believe that the altitude was too much for my father. It had simply never occurred to me. Buying the Taos place, I planned that my father would, as he always did, spend summers with me. Casting ahead, I thought that when he was "old," he would come to live with me— but not if he couldn't breathe.

Over the next week we tried everything to make Dad comfortable. Nothing helped. His shortness of breath was chronic. Finally, at Mark's insistence, we took him to a doctor. "Has anyone else mentioned emphysema?" the doctor wondered. He fitted Dad with an oxygen inhaler.

My father was a tough and feisty little man. Rather than submit to the diagnosis, he made one of his own. He would leave. And so, after what felt like the briefest of visits, he got into his little Probe and headed north to Colorado, where he would turn east toward Chicago. We got a call from him from Fort Collins, Colorado. He was lost. Could I come north, find him, and drive to Chicago with him? I said I could. Mark drove me to Fort Collins, where I found my father at a little motel, still short of breath.

It took several days to drive my father to Chicago. Mark held down the fort with Domenica but, as always happened when I was absent awhile, they wanted me to hurry back. Once in Chicago with my father and my siblings, I found it was not so simple as just hurrying back. My father went to see another doctor. This time the diagnosis was worse. Yes, he had emphysema, but he also had a tumor on one lung. The tumor was inoperable and presumed cancerous. It would take a while, but my father would die. He declined treatment of any kind. He did not want radiation or chemotherapy. He wanted simply—and stubbornly—for his allotted days to run their course. There was no budging him from his decision. He would die a "natural" death, and when he did die, his remains would be willed to science. He had made up his mind.

I flew back to Taos, leaving half my heart in Chicago with my father. I found Mark deeply troubled by his work—or his lack of it. The clinic continued to be in the throes of upheaval. "I see what we ought to do, but I am low man on the totem pole," he complained—correctly. In the meantime Domenica was invited to spend much of the summer traveling with the Honsteins and their horses. She was thrilled by this opportunity. The horse-show world was an exciting one, and the Honsteins usually came home champions. For my part, I was glad to see Domenica with something to focus on other than boys. If her horsey world meant she would be a late bloomer, so be it.

Summer in Taos is marked by sudden storms, and I began to feel that our household was also seized by sudden squalls. Mark and I began fighting. He lashed out at me out of frustration at his world. I was frustrated by his frustration. Why couldn't he be happier? It seemed to me he was writing well, and writing well always made me happy. But not Mark. Our world was too narrow and claustrophobic and provincial for him. He began to feel our life—and life in Taos in general—smacked of escapism.

"How can we make Mark happier?" Domenica and I asked ourselves. Predictably, we came up with a plan that in retrospect seems spectacularly wrongheaded. Instead of saying "Quit your job at the clinic. Write full-time. Go to Harvard if you need to," we decided he needed more fun in the few leisure hours he had. What was more fun? A horse. We found Mark a beautiful bay mare, a true cowboy's dream, far more surefooted and trailworthy than Ing, the horse he had been riding. Mark named his new mare Scarlett and seemed to genuinely love her. We took a few long rides as a family with Scarlett leading the way, nimble as a cat. It was quickly clear, however, that Mark was seized by a darkness that no new possession, however wonderful, could touch.

The clinic was becoming an increasingly volatile place. Torn apart by his feelings of conflicted loyalty—he wanted to stay there and help; he wanted to quit and be done with it—Mark soldiered on. Domenica immersed herself in the drama department at school. She was very happy acting instead of acting out, as so many of her peers were. I wasn't acting out either. I had no desire to have an affair and survive my marriage that way. I did, however, find Mark increasingly difficult company—just as he found me.

My solution to Mark's and my distance was to try drawing closer to my new Taos friends. They were a wildly varied lot—artists, for the most part and New Age practitioners of many stripes. I was good friends with Larry Lonergan, the spiritualist medium, with my friend Ellen, an astrologer, and with a tarot reader/metaphysician/astrologer named Rhonda Flemming. If the going was rough at my house, I would ask one of them for a reading, hoping to discover some new strategy or, at the very least, some new explanation. I didn't eat out. I didn't buy expensive souvenir trinkets. Readings were my one indulgence, one that Mark greeted with a curious mix of open-mindedness and skepticism. Increasingly he made late evening phone calls to his old friends back in Chicago, many of them traders. As I tried to work on the small picture, Mark tried to work on the big picture. As I tried to burrow more deeply into our new home, he threw himself lines back to our old life, where his version of himself had made more sense to him. I knew Mark was tormented, but I didn't know how to ease his torment. I would try to lure him into our new life, only to have him reject it. Many of my new friends struck him as flakes. He hated to see me being "gullible."

As I always had, I turned again to nature for solace. I began taking the dogs on long walks through the sagebrush. Mark had found us a 1965 Chevy pickup truck that I named Louise. I would herd the dogs into the back of the truck and drive to a deserted dirt road, where I would pull over and let the dogs run free. No matter where I walked, Taos Mountain dominated my view. "Please, God," I would pray in its direction. "Please guide me. Please show me what to do."

I struck up a friendship with a café owner named Dori Vinella. A tall, warm, golden-haired woman, she was a pillar of the Taos community. I began going to Dori's café, home to many writers, to work. I would sit at one out-of-the-way table and John Nichols at another, both of us toiling away with words. We didn't speak to each other, just nodded acknowledgment, "You again." Both of us wanted our "office" to be private.

Although she catered to writers, Dori herself did not write. "I am just a muse," she would laughingly say. But what a muse! Nichols's work poured forth, a steady writerly stream. For my part, I asked Dori how she would feel if I hosted a poetry night once a week in her café. She was game, and so "Wordplay" was inaugurated, gathering a half dozen to a dozen poets weekly, sharing our works in progress at an open mic.

The Artist's Way had been out nearly a year and was slowly and surely gathering momentum as a word-of-mouth best seller. Even before the book was published internationally, Artist Way groups began popping up on the Internet. We learned there were clusters forming in the jungles of Panama, in Australia, all over the British Isles. In America, demand for the book consistently outstripped the size of the modest printings. Potential readers had to order the book and then wait weeks for delivery. The first of what would be a steady stream of thank-you letters began to arrive, forwarded from Tarcher.

"Your book changed my life," Mark and I read with wonder and satisfaction.

Odd little packets began to arrive. People would send children's books, slides of their sculpture, greeting cards, and even decks of tarot cards they had designed. I would get small boxes containing thank-you earrings or necklaces, all handmade by artists newly at work or back at work. Sometimes we would get a video: "This is the film that I shot" or "This is the pilot for my TV show." Sales climbed past one hundred thousand and began picking up velocity. "Do you teach workshops?" inquiries came in. Yes, we did teach workshops. I began to travel and teach.

Meanwhile, Mark continued to work at the ever-more-volatile mental health clinic. In his evening and weekend hours he was writing *The Prodigal Father*, but his editor was proving to be a difficult and capricious man, wanting first one thing and then another. There was little satisfaction to be found anywhere. No amount of beautiful scenery could console Mark for his lack of meaningful work. Increasingly, he felt Taos was a dead end for him. He was underemployed, working more, he felt, as a glorified jailer than a counselor. This bruised his idealism as well as his ego. Furthermore, the facility felt more and more like a powder keg to him, with sharp divisions among the staff.

What we needed in all of this was a little comic relief. It came to us in the form of a Brittany spaniel whom we named Jake. To begin with, Jake specialized in breaking and entering. We would come home and find Jake mysteriously in the house. He had leapt in through an open window or slipped in through an unlocked door. (Security in Taos was loose.) Or we would sit down to dinner and find Jake staring soulfully at us through the window. Jake was a beautiful dog, clearly purebred, and we could not believe he was truly homeless. Sure enough, a little footwork revealed that he belonged to a gay couple who lived across the field from us, although he clearly felt he belonged with us. We became used to Jake's visits. We would round him up and return him to his owners, only to have him reappear the next day. One day no Jake appeared. We missed him. Another day went by and then another with still no Jake, and we began to get worried. Finally Mark burst out, "You don't think they've taken him to the pound, do you?" We were alarmed. Yes, Jake was annoying and intrusive, but he was also lovable—so lovable, we went to the pound. Yes, there was Jake, whom we promptly adopted.

Safe back at home, officially our dog, Jake took his duties very seriously. First things first, there was the matter of the cat, Mangela, a plump black cat Domenica had adopted. Jake couldn't accept the presence of the cat. His manner said, "How could our other dogs have neglected the important priority of ridding the house of cats?" Jake took after Mangela with a vengeance. Mangela began hiding on Domenica's closet shelf.

"You have a choice," I told Domenica. "Either Mangela or Jake but not both." After tearful deliberation, Domenica chose Jake and we found Mangela a home with a woman who doted on her—and bragged ever after about how much happier she was with her than with us.

Jake was an excitable, emotional dog and he quickly became Mark's alter ego and companion. When we went horseback riding, Jake would come along, ranging in great speedy loops ahead and behind us. Mark would hoot with pride at his dog's antics. At moments I would hope that all was well with us again, but these moments were fleeting.

An uneasy spring and difficult summer turned to fall. Mark and I began coteaching at the College of Santa Fe. Thanks to Joseph Di Pienza's vision, *The Artist's Way* became a required course for all incoming freshmen. It was exciting to teach together again. Watching our students blossom was like having a vast and varied garden. We enjoyed the flowering.

We were not alone in noticing our success. Mark was approached by a Santa Fe mover and shaker, the man who had franchised est. What would we think, the man wondered, about franchising *The Artist's Way*? How would I like to be a huge success like Tony Robbins? He made millions, and, so we were told, there were millions to be made. Mark was very interested. To him money was an integral part of success. He was an entrepreneur at heart. I was not.

"I think the Artist's Way should be free," I ventured. "I think it should be like Alcoholics Anonymous, that anybody with a book and a desire to be unblocked should be able to start an Artist's Way group."

Mark thought I was wrong. He cited the fact that therapists were beginning to facilitate circles and to charge money for the groups they convened. "We should have some part of that," he felt. "And people need guidance."

"Mark, I will never make art if I have to administer a financial kingdom," I told him. "If I have to worry about who is paying us our fee and whether or not they are doing things properly, I won't have the time or energy to be an artist anymore."

Mark disagreed. He thought of the Artist's Way as an entrepreneurial venture, a product he wanted to develop to its fullest commercial potential. I thought of the Artist's Way much more in terms of a movement like AA. I thought it could grow by itself with very little centralized guidance. I didn't want to be a clearinghouse for problems and questions. I felt the book itself was guidance enough.

Looking back, it is easy to see that our issues around the Artist's Way indicated great differences in our personal identities. As an artist, I thought of the Artist's Way as being like a work of art— it could stand on its own. As an entrepreneur, Mark thought of it as a brainchild that needed nurturing and guidance to be properly exploited.

I had dedicated *The Artist's Way* to Mark and truly felt that without his stubborn instigation it might not have been written. It was Mark who first envisioned the importance of the book and, as sales continued climbing toward the million mark and beyond— two million plus as I write this—Mark hungered for credit for the work he had done. We had, after all, stood shoulder to shoulder printing and binding the early copies of the book. We had taught together using the text that I had written but that Mark had insisted be written.

When the Artist's Way concept began exploding into more and more clusters all over the Internet, Mark's frustration reached the boiling point. "We should at least have a Web site of our own," he insisted. I wanted none of it. I felt that if we had a Web site we would have e-mail and that if we had e-mail to answer no art would get made. I needed to protect my writing time and my identity as an artist, not as a teacher. Mark, on the other hand, hungered to teach and advise. My position was thwarting his true nature.

Domenica was cast in *The Skin of Our Teeth*, and her father flew into Taos to catch her performance. He stayed uptown at the posh Taos Inn. His presence set the town abuzz. Domenica was thrilled that he had come to see her, but now she was identifiably the child of someone famous. She had enrolled in Taos High School under the name Domenica Cameron, so her father's arrival on the scene shattered her anonymity. Fortunately, Taos was more able to take Martin's identity in stride than Chicago had been. Taos, after all, was a town filled with artists, some of them famous in their own right, all of them too hip to be visibly starstruck.

Martin's visit went well, to my relief. He returned not too long afterward to share Christmas break with Domenica. We decided to give him a Christmas experience that he could not get in New York. With Mark at the wheel and the rest of us bundled up to our necks, we drove into the mountains to harvest a Christmas tree in the deep snow. We were determined to show Martin the magic of Taos. I wanted him to approve of the life Domenica was having far from the glare of the urban spotlight where his celebrity was a constant and very difficult variable.

The winter deepened. Intense snowfalls made Mark's commute difficult and dangerous. I would hover near the door when he was overdue home, as if I could will him into safety. I could no more will him into safety than I could will him into happiness. We had sudden sharp, escalating fights that seemed to come from out of nowhere and take us no place good. We tried, in our good moments, to work on our fighting style. We would be much happier if we just called each other "you dumb jerk" rather than taking out our intellectual rapiers.

Domenica had found a new group of friends featuring four hyperbright boys: Ezra, Ian, Justin, and Louie. More and more often, the boys came to our house for their after-school relaxation. Mark was as much a part of the draw as Domenica. He drew the boys out in long conversations. Domenica, understandably wanting to be the focus of their attention, began to feel meddled with. Her concerns were largely brushed aside. Sober, articulate, and interested, Mark seemed to fill a void in the boys' lives. Could that be bad?

In the meantime, Domenica and I both felt a void in our life with Mark. If there had been some slogan like "The family that plays together, stays together," we might have been able to put language to our feelings. The darkness from Mark's job was a cloud overshadowing our lives. He would come home from work tired and discouraged. In his new clinical language, a language he would use when we fought, I thought Mark was suffering from "depression." Call it that or call it the mean reds, he was not himself and we could not seem to lure him back from the abyss.

While Mark was trying to just survive a life he no longer liked or understood, I was trying to make a new life for myself in Taos. From the classes that we taught, I gathered a small group of friends: Dori, Sambhu Vaughan, and Peter Ziminsky. From my spiritual explorations, I found others: Larry and Rhonda and Pam Hogan. From my poetry nights, I garnered still others. From my days writing at Dori's, I eventually made the acquaintance of John

Nichols. A splendid writer, he captured my admiration. He had enjoyed great success as a young novelist, publishing both *The Sterile Cuckoo* and *The Wizard of Loneliness*, then endured a long dry spell. Throughout his publishing drought, he continued to write, and eventually his fortunes turned again with the success of *The Milagro Beanfield War*, adapted to film by Robert Redford. A seriously political man, Nichols additionally collaborated with Costa-Gavras on *Missing*. Like me, John wrote daily, year in and year out. Sitting across the room at Dori's Café, I felt a sense of camaraderie and shared values.

Mark had a difficult time with my affection for John. He worried—and I think correctly—that I romanticized him. When John fell ill, I did whatever I could think of to help him, making pots of homemade soup and the occasional pie. The truth was, there was no need for me to play Florence Nightingale. John had a beautiful young lover who hovered near his side. A flamenco dancer, Miel was sensual enough to rally any man's will to live.

If my friendship with Nichols was hard for Mark, my friendship with Crawford Tall proved to be a breaking point. Like me, Crawford had a hard-drinking past, and like me, he was determined to stay sober. Both of us had shared drinking time with Hunter Thompson, and we shared a sense of humor as well. Just at that moment, we needed it. My household was tense. Crawford's life was worse. He was in love with a woman named Susan who was embroiled in a nasty divorce.

"Just don't drink," I told him—the same thing I told myself.

To me, Crawford was a colleague and comrade in arms. A bush pilot and builder, to Mark he was a charismatic figure who had captured my imagination. I felt that I was a needed sounding board for Crawford. To my eye, we were helping each other to stay sober. Mark turned a deaf ear to my explanations.

"He's in love with someone else, not me," I protested to Mark.

"You're the one spending time with him," Mark countered.

"He needs a friend right now," I answered. "If you'd give him a chance, you'd like him."

"I don't like him."

"But Mark—"

But Mark would have none of it. He felt I was out of line pursuing a friendship with Crawford, to his eyes an available single man. He felt I was engaging in "emotional infidelity," an emotional if not physical affair. With Mark on the warpath, I became both defensive and rebellious. I deserved to be trusted, didn't I? I had a right to friends. If he felt better about himself, he wouldn't feel so bad about John or Crawford. He should look to himself, not me. I felt he was policing my behavior and indulging himself in sophomoric jealousy at my expense. He was paranoid, I thought, and I was determined not to give in to his demands, which I saw as controlling.

Then Mark announced that he wanted to take a trip to Chicago. With a strange feeling of foreboding, I watched him drive away from our house. Officially, I thought it was good that he take the time to go to see old friends. But as the days of his trip ticked by, I couldn't shake my sense of apprehension. There was nothing I could articulate, but something felt very, very wrong. Then Martin called to talk to Domenica and I found myself suddenly spilling out my heart to him.

"Martin, I think he's going to come back from Chicago and leave me!" I sobbed. Martin listened carefully. "My marriage is over. I know it." This was the first time I had articulated such a fear, even to myself, but as I wept, it felt less like a fear than an inevitable reality. Mark was going to leave me. He had gone back to Chicago to gather his resolve.

Mark phoned from Chicago. He sounded like his old self, warm and humorous. His visit had been great, but he was coming home. He missed me. The call was warm and comforting. There was no mention of a divorce. I chalked up my fears to a writer's overactive imagination and was glad to open the door to him when he returned, genial as a big bear, happy to see me, filled with greetings from the friends he had seen, friends we had shared.

It was as strange and terrifying as being drenched by a cloudless sky. Once inside the house, Mark's mood shifted, and he struck out like lightning.

"I'm leaving," he said. "I want a divorce."

6.

It wasn't a fight. It was something worse than a fight: a declaration. All of the frustration, all of the mistrust, all of the bitter acrimony were gone from his voice. He was simply done. He was simply leaving.

I don't remember the rest of this day with anything like clarity. Mark took a few things and left. I don't know exactly where he went. To a motel? To his friend Carl's? I was too numb to fight with him—or, for that matter, for him. He said he was leaving and I let him go. I didn't hurl myself at him, begging for a change of heart. I knew better. His tone was very clear. There would be no negotiating a new decision. Clean as the cut from an ax, we were over, our marriage was done.

"Mark left," I told Domenica when she got home from school.

"Oh, Mommy," she said, and put her arms around me.

Beware the Ides of March, they say, and I believe it now. Mark left on March 15, and I spent the next month going to my bed at seven o'clock at night, sleeping like I had been clubbed. "Just don't drink," I told myself. "Don't use any drugs." Telling myself "This, too, shall pass," I tried to put one foot in front of the other, writing daily and going for my walks. Spring alternated with leftover winter and many days my walks were bitter cold. I fought for stability both for my and for Domenica's sake.

"Guide me," I prayed. "Guide me," and I suppose now that I was guided, I didn't pick up a drink. I didn't take any recreational drugs or fall into an ill-considered affair. In truth, I was too shattered to even be tempted by any of it.

I learned that I was said to be having an affair, two of them in fact, one with John and one with Crawford. This was wild fantasy, but it made me infuriated and heartsick. "So much for enlightened Taos. So much for friendship," I fumed. There was nothing much I could do to combat the rumors, and so I was branded a scarlet woman. In the wake of Mark's leaving, in the face of all the ugly talk, people left me pretty much alone. Sympathy was not with me. As the grapevine had it, Mark was the wronged party.

Ironically, both of the men I was said to be involved with had little cause to see me in those days. I had been a friend in need and a friend indeed, but both John's health and Crawford's involvement found solid ground. I wasn't really needed any longer as they settled in happily with the women of their choice. I was glad for them and too undone myself to feel lonely. "Lonely" didn't begin to cover my emotions. "Lost," "shocked," "bereft," "traumatized" came closer.

In spite of the turmoil of my personal life, my professional life seemed to be jetting merrily along. As the author of the increasingly well-known *Artist's Way*, I was suddenly sought after as a font of wisdom. Spiritual centers across the country began inviting me to come to teach. I agreed to go when Mark and I were still married and I had a solid home base. Now in the throes of a painful divorce, I wondered what wisdom, if any, I had to share with people. Certainly my wisdom had eluded me with Mark.

Cast as a "spiritual teacher," and desperate for answers myself in the wake of the loss of Mark, I embarked on a series of ill-considered fasts. I wanted enlightenment and I wanted it now. Fasting promised huge spiritual breakthroughs, so fast I would. I simply stopped eating and lived on water and "green" juice. I went as long as a week or ten days without solid food. I went for very long walks, praying with every footfall. Although I didn't see it at the time, mine was a punishing regime. My life made no sense to me. I wanted God to speak in a loud, clear voice, in plain English. I read spiritual books voraciously. Reading was the one thing for which I had an appetite.

Winter finally gave way to a late and glorious spring. Domenica attracted the notice of John Newland, an esteemed Hollywood director, newly retired to Taos. Taos is a magnet for artists of all stripes and Newland had found himself living in Taos to suit his painter-wife, Areta. He had directed many greats, among them Anthony Hopkins and Patricia Neal. I first encountered Newland's work when I went to the Taos community auditorium for an evening of monologues. Expecting some Shakespeare and perhaps some Sam Shepard, I was astonished by the evening that unfolded. The monologues were edgy and brave. The material was fresh and unfamiliar. The actors were astonishing. "Who did all this?" I caught myself wondering. Someone pointed out a tall, white-haired man. I made my way across the crowded auditorium to introduce myself.

"I know who you are," Newland said when I offered my hand. "You're Domenica's mother and very talented in your own right, I understand. Let's have lunch."

We agreed to meet the very next day at the Taos Inn. I arrived in the high-raftered bar moments after Newland. He had seated himself in a window to enjoy the afternoon light. When I reached the table, he stood up, towering over me.

"So," he said brusquely. "First let's talk about your daughter. Does your ex-husband have any idea what a talent she is?"

"I am not sure," I answered.

"I didn't think so. She needs to be working. She's the real animal."

Newland could not have chosen a swifter or surer path to my heart. I, too, believed that Domenica was "the real animal." I, too, longed for her father to recognize her gifts and encourage them. What was wrong, I wondered, with a little nepotism? But Martin wanted Domenica to make it in the business under her own steam, seeming not to understand the burden that carrying his name brought to any encounter.

"I don't think Martin wants Domenica in the business."

"Too much rejection?"

"Exactly."

"Well, she's in the business whether he likes it or not. She's a born actor—and I do know what I am talking about." Lunch ended on a decidedly conspiratorial note.

Newland took Domenica under his wing. Excited to be cast in a community theater production, under his hand she played a lead in *The Petrified Forest*. The production included an older man, who made a pass at her, frightening her badly. It also included Ezra Hubbard, initially her friend and then, as their feelings deepened, her first serious boyfriend.

As the calendar moved toward summer, my teaching commitments came due. My fasting had left me weak and vulnerable and still unenlightened. Reluctant to leave Domenica, who promised she would be "fine," I drove the one hundred and fifty miles to Albuquerque and boarded a plane for Los Angeles. Trying to fit my new casting, I had packed several simple silk smocks that came to my ankles. Designed by Jo Dean Tipton, they were what I called "creativity dresses," inscribed with fanciful spiritual symbols and words. Wearing Jo Dean's dresses, I at least looked like a spiritual teacher. It was a start.

How could I do this to myself? I wondered, looking over my teaching schedule and realizing I was slated to teach four events in three days. One of those events was scheduled for six A.M. I was already shaky with fatigue. How did I think I would manage? The flight into Los Angeles was bumpy, and so was my mood.

When I arrived at my friend Ed Towle's house, he took one look at me and ushered me toward the guest bedroom. "Get some rest," he ordered, dismayed to hear I would be getting up at four.

At five the next morning I slipped out of the house and piloted my rented car toward Beverly Hills. "The Inside Edge" met at a posh hotel. I didn't feel very posh myself, but I was trying to be game. Once in the hotel, I was intimidated by the large crowd of participants, all of whom seemed to be preternaturally attractive, uniformly bronze and fit. They flashed each other dazzling, snowy white smiles. Hoping to collect myself, I retreated to a tall Queen Anne's chair in the lobby. I was hiding there when I saw Tim Wheater enter. A tall, thin, bald-headed man, he loped across the lobby and into the ballroom where the event was to be held. I watched him go as if I had just sighted a rare and exotic animal. Who was that? I wondered.

"He's on the bill with you," I was told. "He's a sound healer—whatever that is. You go first, then he's the entertainment."

"No, no," I thought. "He should go first. After some sound healing, I should feel ready to speak."

And so I leapt up and ran into the large hall where Wheater was just checking his sound.

"Would you mind going first?" I asked him. "Oh, I'm Julia Cameron, and I don't really think you should be the dessert."

"I'll be glad to go first," Wheater said, a flicker of interest crossing his face.

We looked around for our host, a tall, genial man who agreed to our shift of agenda. The clock ticked toward six. We took our places. The host introduced Wheater, who stepped to the mike.

"Good morning, ladies and gentlemen," he started off. Introducing himself and his Indian instrument, a harmonium, he launched into a hypnotic series of sounds. All around the large room, conversations dropped to a whisper, then to a halt. Clearly, this strange man was someone to pay attention to. Gliding vowel to vowel, Wheater finally crescendoed into three resonant "oms." The room was totally still as I stepped forward to teach.

"I'd like to talk with you a bit about creativity," I began. "It's really very simple. Creativity is a spiritual matter"—and the rest went smoothly. I spoke for perhaps half an hour, ending to resounding applause. As participants rushed forward to thank me, I found myself thinking, "Where is Wheater? I need to get a contact number for him." To my relief, I saw that he was busily signing CDs. When I finished with my own well-wishers, I crossed to his side.

"Let's trade numbers," I told him. "I'd like to work together. In fact, I would like to work together this weekend if you are available."

With a slightly quizzical look on his face, Wheater handed me both a CD and his phone number. When I looked at his CD, *The Yearning*, a shock ran through me. From the CD's cover, my own eyes stared back at me.

That night I drove from Los Angeles to San Diego, where I was scheduled to speak again. Rebecca, the woman who drove me, was trained as a Hawaiian healer, and I was lucky that she was. We no sooner arrived at our hotel room than a sudden chill swept over me. I began to shake, both hungry and fatigued.

"When is the last time you ate?" Rebecca wanted to know. I couldn't really remember. Before I was scheduled to teach, I tended to fast, hoping for greater clarity. Fasting made me lose interest in food. I lived on water, lots and lots of water.

"I think you need a hot bath," Rebecca announced, "and some dinner. Here, what does that CD sound like? Maybe it will relax you."

But *The Yearning*, composed by keyboardist Michael Hoppe and featuring Tim Wheater on alto flute, did much more than just relax me. It made me weep. All the pent-up tears about Mark came out in a wrenching torrent. It seemed I was crying for my whole life and then not just for my life but for everyone's. Going where words had been unable to, the music reached directly into my heart. I felt all that I had been too numb to feel before. My tears seemed unending. Rebecca, who had seen such kriyas before, took them in her stride. I was having a "breakthrough" not a "breakdown," she assured me. Wrought by nerves and unable to sleep, I spent a long, frightening night, alternating between a tepid bath and bed, listening to the CD over and over again.

"I think it's safety music," I explained to Rebecca between sobs. Somehow, the music seemed to reconcile all the grief of living and of dying. (I would later learn from Hoppe that the music was used in birthing rooms and in hospices.) As its soothing sounds washed over me, I felt myself knitting back together. Serenity replaced sorrow. Calm and centered, I was ready to go out and teach.

"Your music is remarkable," I told Tim Wheater later that day when I reached him by phone. We agreed to meet for an evening and to work together at a large weekend workshop I was teaching at Agape Church.

The evening I spent with Tim was one of intense energy. I told him that I was a sober alcoholic and newly separated. I learned that Tim was British, that his father had left when he was still a young child, leaving him to be raised by a fragile mother. Music had saved his sanity as his mother's health spiraled out of control. Scholarships got him through school, where his precocious talent led him to another precocious talent, Annie Lennox. With her he formed a soon-to-be-famous group, the Eurythmics. He toured with that band to world acclaim, trying not to listen to the still, small voice inside him that kept insisting he was a composer as well as a player. According to the voice, he had his own music to make.

While we picked at our plates of Thai food, Tim continued his story. No matter how he tried to ignore it, his still, small voice had grown larger and louder. "You're crazy, Tim," his friends told him when he tried to tell them about the voice. Crazy or not, he decided to quit the band at the very apex of its fame to go off on his own to see what his real music was. The music in his head and heart became a series of albums, which he made on a shoestring. One of his albums, *A Calmer Panorama*, became a sudden, massive hit. Immediately Tim found himself once more catapulted to the top of the charts. This time he was sought after and lionized as both a composer and a player. All was going well—until the day he drank poisoned water.

At the time, Tim was living in a remote and pristine part of Cornwall. His was a rustic cottage with water that came from a communal village well. While Tim had been away touring at the Montreux Jazz Festival, the village water supply had been accidentally poisoned. When he arrived home, Tim drank a large glass of water and instantly his lips began to burn, blister, and swell. He was struck numb, his mouth unable to form simple sentences. Panicked, he reached for his flute. When he touched the instrument to his lips, it was as if he had never played a flute before. His famed facility was gone, simply vanished. He could not play the simplest of melodies. He could not find a note.

"Without music, I didn't know who I was," Tim explained. The next three years were a nightmare of doctors who could find no cure and bureaucracies that could offer him no help. Finally, desperate and despairing, he struck out on a pilgrimage to India.

"I didn't care if I lived or died," Tim explained. "Without music, I didn't know who I was." Put simply, Tim had a death wish, and he threw himself into dangerous circumstances and locales. He slept in snake-infested hovels. He rode rafts down raging rivers, inches above the boiling waters. And then, one night at dusk, as he was walking through an ancient city, he heard the sound of a woman's singing—soulful and hypnotic. It drew him to a dark alleyway and down that alleyway to where he found the source, a pregnant woman singing in prayer.

"Her song sounded like nothing I had ever heard," Tim recalled. "It was so beautiful, so spiritual. I found myself thinking, 'I may not be able to play the flute, but I can still sing.' I decided then and there that I would begin to use the gift of the voice God had given me—little did I realize then that the voice was healing. What the woman was doing was called toning. Over the next year I taught myself how to tone—and I accidentally toned myself well. The feeling in my lips returned. The paralysis subsided. Slowly and methodically, I taught myself to play the flute again. But I play the alto flute now, lower and slower. . . ."

I listened to Tim's saga, thinking about how similar our stories were. Like him, I had been struck with a fatal illness, in my case alcoholism, and in seeking spiritual help for that disease, I had been led, step by step, into my life as a teacher. I sketched this out for Tim, debriefing him as if I were an astronaut. We finished dinner and stepped onto the street. I spotted a package store and suggested we go inside for water—my precious water, far more appetizing to me than the Thai food, which I had left largely untouched.

Entering the store, we ran directly into a young alcoholic-addict who was staggering out. His eyes were blurred. His manner was desperate.

"Spare any change, man?" he asked Tim. He lurched into Tim's chest, and Tim caught him gently by the arms.

"I have something better, man," Tim said calmly, and leaning his head close to the young man's heart, he began to tone. At first the young man seemed about to bolt, then he suddenly relaxed, swaying slightly, then standing stock-still. As I watched, his eyes cleared. His wildness disappeared and clarity eddied back into his gaze. Tim stopped toning and stepped back, mission accomplished.

"Thanks, man," the young derelict said. "Whatever it is you did, thanks." With that, he walked slowly off.

"What is it that you did?" I asked Tim.

"I just prayed for him," Tim said. "I just told him that God loves him."

It was getting late. Tim and I drove home through the Holly-wood Hills.

We stopped at a scenic overlook and admired the sparkling city laid out below us.

"You're very special," Tim told me. I felt the same for him.

Two days later, in Santa Monica, Tim joined me to teach several hundred people. Unrehearsed and instinctive, our partnership was instant and effortless. We did not plan what we would each teach. We simply alternated. Our bodies of work fit together like hand in glove. "I would love to work with this man," I thought to myself, but he was due back in England, and so I faced a long season of teaching alone. Suitcases, airports, and classrooms became my re-ality. Often overwhelmed, I tried to remember to pray and walk to keep myself in balance.

Back in Taos, after my teaching tour, I faced the dregs of winter. The days were cold and gray. My mood felt the same way. Mark was rumored to be dating—a glamorous, younger blonde. I re-turned to my routine of writing and walking. Now I wore a Walk-man on my walks and listened to the music of Michael Hoppe and Tim Wheater. One day, as I was walking, I hit upon the idea of inviting them to Taos—surely, I thought, there was a wonderful audience here for their music. "Part Merlin, pure magic," I adver-tised the concert in *The Taos News.* I was eager to show off Taos to Tim. He was eager to play in a new venue, and so was Hoppe.

Concert day dawned gray and cloudy. A late snow was due. By midafternoon the flakes were swarming. This was something worse than a snow shower; it was a belated blizzard.

"Don't worry. They'll still come," I assured Tim and Michael, who worried that their flight in might have been in vain.

Come they did. With snow drifting in the streets, curious Taosenos still mobbed the little auditorium, filling it near to overflowing. I introduced Tim and Michael, then retired to one side to let them weave their magic—and magic it was. For two hours, as the storm raged outside, they cast a spell of calm and safety. Hoppe played keyboards and projected his grandfather's stunning Pre-Raphaelite-style photographs. Tim played the flute and then the harmonium. The audience was enchanted and so was I. I have a photograph of Tim and myself taken backstage at that concert. We are dressed idiosyncratically in oddly similar clothing. We have our heads tilted together and we look like two happy schoolchildren, amused partners in crime—playmates.

When Tim and Michael left the next day for Los Angeles, I did feel I had lost my playmates. I loved their music so much, it was difficult not to feel the same affection for its creators. I wanted to spread the good word about both of them. Tim left behind with me a small toning tape, and I asked him about making a toning tape for wide distribution. To my delight, he agreed, and I happily set about assembling the project, crafting a powerful cover using the art of Paul Pascarella, a marvelous painter.

My involvement with Tim and Michael became the talk of our small town. Mark was divorcing me, but he remained temporarily in Taos, in an apartment that I drove past daily. Taos is a small town, and I was regularly informed of his doings—and he of mine. He was not yet ready to divorce our body of work. He cared about what I was up to, and he really didn't approve of any of it. Who were these strangers I was dragging home to Taos? He worried that they might be too New Age and airy-fairy. It seemed to me that he was concerned lest I lose credibility. If I became known as a New Age flake, it might cast a long shadow over his dreams of Harvard and intellectual legitimacy.

After the late snows, spring came in grudgingly, not quite trusting that it was safe or welcome. I was beginning to find my feet, quite literally. My daily walks stretched longer and I continued to listen to Tim's music as I trudged. One late afternoon, as I made my way through the fragrant sage, I had this thought: "Tim's music is just like my music except inside out." The thought brought me up short. "My music"? What was I thinking? I had no "music." I was forty-five years old and, surely, if I were musical, I would have known it by then.

Back at the house, the thought persisted. I stormed angrily around the kitchen making dinner. Music was a painful subject for me. Growing up, I had been carefully taught that I was nonmusical. "Let your sister have the piano," I had been told. My sister Connie, my brother Jaimie, my brother Christopher, and my sister Lorrie all played the piano with ease. Furthermore, at Christmas, when we gathered around the tree to sing carols, they achieved harmonies with grace. "Is that you, Julie?" I was used to being shushed.

During the worst days of my marriage to Martin, I had taken to writing songs. In those days I heard lyrics but no melodies. I poured my heart into the words. I partnered with my brother Christopher and a composer friend, Jerry Frankel, who wrote the music. Now, in my Taos kitchen, I had the unlikely thought that I myself had "music." Angrily, I swatted the thought aside.

Early the next morning, writing my Morning Pages, I received a one-line directive: "You will be writing radiant songs." Once again I brushed the thought aside. Once again I was angry. "I am not musical," I almost said aloud. The pages persisted. "Wouldn't it be fun to write a musical about Merlin?" I answered back in my head, "Of course it would be fun, it would be great—if I were the least bit musical. Thank you for sharing!"

Like most people, I had taken the gauge of my probable talents and I had taken the word of my family that music was not among them. True, I loved music. True, whenever I wrote about imaginary lives, I wrote down "torch singer." But loving music did not mean I could write music, I told myself. That, surely, was far too much to hope for.

As the wildflowers and lilacs began to bloom, I found myself with many other thoughts on my mind. Domenica had fallen deeply in love. Her sweetheart, Ezra, was a magical young man—sweet, fierce, humorous, and engaging. Like Domenica, he had captured the eye of John Newland. At Newland's invitation, he began studying acting with him through the University of New Mexico. I often sat in on Newland's classes. It was a joy to watch him jump-start actors, pulling performances out of them like rabbits out of a hat. Both Ezra and Newland fired Domenica's and my imaginations. We began to feel almost like a theater troupe—a small, happy band of coadventurers.

As April became May, I was one more time called away to teach, another lightning tour, this time ending in Boulder, Colorado. Reluctantly I left Domenica behind again. I packed a small bag and set out. One more time I turned to fasting, hoping for more ease and clarity in teaching. The crowds I taught were large, and I felt their dreams and disappointments deeply. I took my teaching very seriously and strove in the course of a workshop to give those attending optimism and hope. I felt an obligation to be "inspiring" and "wise." The demands I set for myself, coupled with the fasting, left me fragile and exhausted. So I was in shaky condition when I arrived in Boulder to stay with my friends Terrell Smith and Kekuni Minton, who lived in an Alpine house set high on a mountainside.

"You need a rest," Terrell announced, looking me over with a loving eye. She put me right to bed. I slept a deep and exhausted sleep straight through the night, and when I woke late the next morning she had more advice for me. "Why don't you take yourself for a nice walk, maybe down to the stream?"

Obedient, I set out in the direction Terrell indicated. Sure enough, I shortly came upon a clear, fast-moving stream, twisting and twirling its way down the mountainside. There was a large rock near the edge of the stream. I sat on that rock and listened to the music of the waters. Suddenly another music came over me. I heard a song unfurling, lyrics and music, as if some spirit were piping it to me. The song was beautiful:

My green heart is filled with apples.
Your dark face is filled with stars.
I am the one that you've forgotten.
You are the one my heart desires.

So, dance to remember me.
Sing to remember me.
Dance till your heart can see who we are.
Dance to remember me.
Sing to remember me.
Dance till your heart can see who we are.

I am the lake that has no bottom.
You're the sword that leaves no scars.

I am the water sunlight dapples.
You are the light from distant shores.

So, dance to remember me . . .

I leapt to my feet and went racing back up the mountainside. I flew inside the house and found my friend. "Terrell," I announced, "I heard a song!" Quick as a wink, Terrell thrust a tape recorder into my hands. Breathless, I sang the little song into the machine. Excitedly, we played it back. The song had a lilting, Celtic flavor. It was radiant, just as the pages had described.

Driving home from Terrell's to Taos, I was hit by a mountain snowstorm. Just as I crested La Veta Pass, I heard another song. One more time, the song had a Celtic leaning:

In the greenwood, shadows lengthen.
In the greenwood, rivers flow.
In the emerald heart of darkness,
Lovers know the things they know.

In the greenwood, stars are distant.
In the greenwood, stars are near.
In the greenwood, lovers listen.
And they hear the things they hear.

Terrell had thought to send the tape recorder with me, and so I sang the new little song onto tape. Driving down the treacherous mountains, the song kept playing in my head.

Back in Taos, I found Domenica and Ezra happily in love. Their happiness was contagious. Even the dogs seemed to pick up on it.

Ezra spent more and more time at our house, bringing a very welcome male presence to the table. There were nights when I could almost forget that Mark and I were in the throes of a divorce.

As divorces go, ours was civilized and brutally quick. With the help of my friend Ellen Longo, now a certified public accountant, we divvied up our meager assets. The intellectual properties were the hardest to divide. Mark wanted percentages on the writing I had done while we were married. Feeling that he had served as sounding board and muse, I agreed. We stepped before a casual blond-haired judge, who granted us a divorce in a matter of minutes. Afterward, I stood under a towering cottonwood, blinking back tears in the dazzling sunlight.

My Morning Pages continued to nudge me. "Go to London. You'll write beautiful music there," I was told. Incredulous, I told this to Domenica and Ezra over dinner. To my surprise, they took the idea seriously. Domenica was already heading to London with the Jenkinses for a West End theater tour. Ezra's mother had just come back and he had relatives there.

"Call my mother," Ezra suggested. "She knows somebody who rents flats."

I called Ezra's mother, who gave me the name and number of one Mr. Price. He rented London flats to visiting Americans. Now I was faced with something to really think about. Could I go to London? Tim was going back to London for the summer, so I would know at least one person there. Maybe it would do me good to get away from Taos, where I couldn't go uptown without passing Mark's apartment, always to stabbing grief. He was soon to move to Santa Fe, and from there to Los Angeles, but he hadn't done so yet. What he had done was move on from one young blond to an even younger one. He had loaned her my former pick-up truck, Louise. Taos has only one main street, and I seemed to pass the blonde and the truck every time I drove it.

"I will make exactly one phone call about this," I told Ezra and Domenica, who seemed to me to be exchanging knowing looks.

Allowing for the time difference, I made one phone call. I reached Mr. Price, who, in my mind's eye, must have been hovering near the phone. He had just what I needed, he explained. He described a charming flat, reasonably priced, mere blocks from Regent's Park in the very center of London.

"I'll take it," I heard myself say.

So now Domenica was going to London and so was I, but first she had to graduate. This meant that Martin would be coming to town and I would be playing gracious hostess to two former husbands, both of whom felt they had a large stake in Domenica's young life.

One more time Martin arrived in Taos, accompanied this time by his friend and archivist. They stayed again at the Taos Inn. We would go to the outdoor graduation and then all rendezvous for a celebratory dinner. I fretted that I had nothing suitable to wear, that all of my clothes were becoming "too Taos." I finally settled on a green silk creativity dress with a matching green hat. In the photographs I look delicate and eccentric. Martin looks proud but nervous. Mark looks the same, while Domenica smiles gamely, trying not to be overwhelmed either by the event or by her highly charged extended family.

Graduation was a festive affair—balloons and mortarboards in the air—with everyone present on their best behavior. I made dinner reservations for all of us at Lambert's, the toniest and most conservative restaurant in town. Even in Taos, Martin was famous, and even at Lambert's there was a little extra hoopla involved in the serving of the meal. In Taos, many of the artists work as waiters, and this was the case that night. We were served by Sambhu, a fine blues guitarist, who admired Martin and his work. Mark and Martin chatted with each other politely. Between courses, I told myself that soon I would be in London with all of this behind me. I had no appetite for dinner or for any social drama. I was still fasting more days than not, hoping for some elusive enlightenment. I needed sainthood just to swing dinner.

My flight for London left from Denver. Domenica's was to follow a week or so later. Packing a suitcase full of silk smocks and writing materials, I just made the flight. As the plane took off, I felt I was leaving my known life behind me. This was to be a great adventure. Except for Tim and actor Anthony Hopkins, a friend of friends, I knew no one and no one knew me. I would be anonymous, not a teacher, certainly not an ex-wife. I was free to be what at core I am—a writer, an artist.

Mine was an overnight flight. I was far too excited to sleep. Instead, I read and wrote my way across America, and then across the Atlantic. Just as the sun was rising over the British Isles, I thought I saw something slip past the wing, just out of the corner of my eye. When I looked to see what it was, I found myself staring at the first rays of a rosy dawn. "That was my old self, my known identity," I joked to myself.

Mr. Price, a tall, nervous, chestnut-haired man, met my flight and drove me the hour's drive into London. I tried to make polite conversation with him but found I was both too tired and too wired to do much coherent chatting. Besides, I told myself, he has seen jet lag before.

"It's a wonderful flat," he assured me, opening the door to the place I had rented sight unseen. My first impression was brown—everything from the walls to the rugs to the furniture was drab brown. My second realization was that everything was rather crooked. The floor sloped. The windows sloped. The furniture all but slid across the sloping floors. "Here we are!" Mr. Price added gaily.

I stepped inside, bitterly disappointed. "At least the windows are tall," I thought. "There will be enough light." I thanked Mr. Price and tried to pay attention to his last-minute instructions, the gist of which was to call him if I ran into any unforeseen difficulties.

With Mr. Price out the door, I surveyed my domain. Brown everywhere. Who could live in a place like this? I wondered. Then I hit on a bright idea. I had a suitcase full of delicate, colorful silk dresses. Finding a hammer and nails, I hung the dresses like paintings. The act seemed creative, not crazy. Next I checked the kitchen, which held some battered pots and pans, a small amount of silverware, and some ugly plates and bowls. The refrigerator was small but sturdy. I needed groceries and some sleep. Jet-lagged but determined to be grounded and sensible, I told myself groceries first—and then sleep.

I locked the door and went down the two flights to the street. I turned left toward a small fenced park. I knew I was somewhere close to Baker Street, but even Sherlock Holmes couldn't have found a grocery store. There were realty offices and copy shops, but the neighborhood I found myself in was short on groceries. I finally discovered a small green market and managed to buy coffee (expensive) and some vegetables for soup. I was still thinking in fast-like terms. What I bought were essentially the ingredients for gruel.

Back at the apartment, I sat on the crooked brown couch. That is when I heard the first strains of music. Clear as a bell, a man's voice started singing. I heard both lyrics and melody:

Life is a matter of mastery.
The mystery lies in that.
The spell lies in the knowledge.
The rabbit lives in the hat . . .

I grabbed for a notebook and wrote down the words. Lack of sleep had rendered me wide open. No sooner had I written down the first song than a female voice started singing:

In the center of your heart
Is a still, small part
Like a meadow in a forest made of green.

In the center of your heart
Is a still, small part
And that is where your soul must go to dream.

I remembered what the Morning Pages had said about a musical about Merlin. I remembered that I had been told that "radiant" songs would come to me in London. Now they were. I had imagined that if they did, they would wait a decent interval until I was settled, but that was evidently not the plan. Now a young girl's voice piped up with yet another melody:

I believe in mystery
And I believe in fate.

I believe in what I see
And what I contemplate!

Ready or not, I was evidently writing a musical. In rapid succession I heard from Merlin, the Lady of the Lake, and now a young priestess. Trying to write fast but legibly, I scribbled down the lyrics for each song as they came through, but I needed a way to capture melody. What if I forgot the lovely melodies? And I desperately needed some sleep. Sleep involved a crooked bed covered by a thin brown coverlet. I turned back the coverlet, crawled in, and hoped that the music would stop until I had more rest.

When I opened my eyes the next morning, I remembered the songs and my need for a way to record melody. I jotted a note to myself in my Morning Pages, and that's when it occurred to me to find an electronics store and buy a tiny keyboard, the kind children use in nursery school. With mounting excitement I hit on a plan. I could locate middle C and then use a Magic Marker to label each key up to G. I remembered the scale from six weeks of abortive piano lessons in the sixth grade. The lettered keys would allow me to write out the melodies using an alphabetic code.

I set out through the streets of London and eventually found my way to Tottenham Court Road. There I found a plethora of electronics stores. The third one I tried had tiny Casio keyboards. I bought one for seventeen pounds. In a stationery store I found markers. In a music shop I bought notation paper. Excited, I rushed back toward the apartment. Then I thought, "Wait! Get a tape recorder too!" I retraced my steps and purchased a small, cheap tape recorder, batteries, and tapes. Now I was ready to begin.

Back in my dull brown apartment, I set foot into the world of music. First I sang the songs into a tape recorder. Next, using my carefully lettered keyboard, I notated each song alphabetically. I used plus and minus signs to indicate above and below middle C. It was time to eat something, but another song reared its head. Once again, intricate rhymed lyrics came through with simultaneous melody. Once again, I sat on the crooked couch and raced to record what I was hearing. No sooner did I finish one song than another began. Then another. After a few hours, I realized it was long past time to eat. My legs and hand were cramped. I needed a walk. Hadn't the landlord said something about Regent's Park?

Food could wait, I decided, and taking the tape recorder with me just in case I was visited by another song, I set out down the stairs and to the right this time, away from the little square and the little business neighborhood, heading—I hoped—in the direction of the park. Sure enough, four blocks and two turns later, I found it. It was all I had hoped for and more: an oasis of green cross-hatched by canals on which floated ducks and what I would soon learn were called the Queen's Swans.

I entered the park and headed directly for the birds. I was not the only person so enchanted. The ducks were plump and well fed. Strolling elders offered them bread crusts. The swans were too dignified to beg. While the ducks clambered ashore, the swans glided serenely by, just out of reach. I crossed a small wooden bridge and found myself amid green playing fields. Youngsters whizzed by on in-line skates.

"I need some of those," I caught myself thinking.

Back at the apartment, I made myself a weak and unsatisfactory vegetable soup. I needed sleep, but the music seemed to need me. So I wrote on late into the night, listening and notating, thrilled that I was actually writing music, scared that as suddenly as it had come, the music might go away.

With sleep elusive and food of little interest, I found myself subject to obsessions. I wanted in-line skates. I had once roller-skated. How difficult could these be to navigate? I wanted to see Tim. I remembered his story of music coming to him first as a still, small voice and then in symphonic fullness, flooding him so completely that he wrote an entire album, *A Calmer Panorama*, overnight. Yes, Tim would have been flooded by music. Maybe he could help me to find my bearings and not feel so overwhelmed. I had a number for a woman in Cornwall. She kept track of his diverse affairs. I phoned her and learned that Tim was in London, set to do a large recording. Tracking him down, I arranged to meet him for a dinner.

When Tim entered the vegetarian restaurant he had chosen for us, I felt a wash of relief. He was just as I remembered him. From across the crowded room, he flashed me a welcoming smile. Once again I felt an intense sense of connection. Surely he would be able to make me feel more grounded about what was happening to me.

Hadn't he had the same experience?

When Tim settled in at the table, I had very little small talk to say. Instead, I told him what was happening to me, that I was hearing wave upon wave of music, that it was coming to me so quickly, I had trouble keeping up. Tim nodded and smiled sympathetically.

"The first time it happened to me," he said, "it was as if I had put my head inside a bowl of music. I heard the music both vertically and horizontally. It all came at once."

"And you lived to tell the tale," I joked.

"Yes. I did."

"I've never written music before. I know how to write words. With the music, I keep fearing that it will go away."

"Are you sleeping?"

"I am trying to."

"Well, just be sure to sleep and eat. That's the main thing."

"I am drinking an awful lot of water."

"Well, water is always good. Just eat."

I realized with embarrassment that I was picking at my meal, shoving it with my fork from one side of my plate to the other but making very little progress. Tim told me that he was in the studio with his friend Stuart Wilde and a young soprano protégée named Cecelia. He tended to be submerged in work when he was recording, he told me. He had a few photos of life in the recording studio. In them he looked frankly exhausted and a little loopy with fatigue.

"It must be a lot like shooting," I remarked, thinking of Martin's eighteen-hour days when nothing existed except the film.

"That it is," Tim agreed. He at least had an appetite for the food placed before us.

Dinner with Tim left me more reassured. I liked it that he was working in London, close at hand if unaccessible. It made me feel safer knowing that he knew what I was up to. He hadn't laughed at the news that I was now writing music. He wasn't skeptical or elitist with me. This went a long way to quiet my nerves. Now, if I could just sleep.

But sleep was elusive and my appetite was still off. I set a regime for myself involving long hours of notation and meandering, restorative walks in Regent's Park. I missed my dogs and I loved the number of dogs brought to the park by doting owners. Like my father who loved birds, I enjoyed the rowdy ducks and the serenely gliding swans. Walks were supposed to be time out from music, but I always carried the tape recorder "just in case." Very often, the walks seemed to catalyze songs, and I would sing quietly into the little machine.

Domenica arrived, full of youthful energy. I took her to the park to shake some of it out. I thought she would enjoy all the dogs and the birds, but she quickly stumbled upon a drama.

"Mom! Help me!" her frantic voice broke into my reverie. "Mom, quick! They're going to kill him!" She pointed to the ground nearby, where a young baby raven flopped awkwardly. As we watched, the little bird was dive-bombed by other birds. Domenica was hysterical. "Mom! Do something!" she screamed.

Without thinking, I dove for the little bird, scattering its attackers. Swooping the baby bird up in my arms, I clutched it tightly to my chest. It pecked and flapped. I clutched it tighter.

"Good, Mommy! Good!" piped up Domenica. "Now what?"

I didn't know "now what." I knew that Regent's Park had a small zoo, but I doubted they would be interested in the plight of one small bird. If I set the bird free, it was sure to be killed. If I kept it, it might die anyway. I could try to nurse it back to health, but its chances weren't good. Still, I could try.

Walking fast, with my jacket wrapped tightly around both me and the bird, I made it back to my flat. With no better idea, we set the little bird in the bathtub. It hopped around awkwardly but could not get out. We looked it over and it looked us over.

"What are you going to call it?" Domenica asked.

I looked at the little bird—not so little, actually, the size of a small crow. The bird looked back at me, fierce and feisty. It still had its baby feathers, and I imagined it trying, too soon, to fly—a bold move. "We'll call him Magellan," I said.

Magellan it was, but he couldn't live in the bathtub. I needed a birdcage for him and I needed to find out what he ate. Given time, his wings would grow strong. I wanted to give him time.

Domenica and I found a pet store after walking back through

the park on Camden High Street. We didn't know it, but it specialized in two species: birds and snakes. I am deathly afraid of snakes. When we entered the store, the first thing we saw was a row of glass cages featuring the big snakes. I remember in particular one startling butter-yellow python. The birds were in the next room and, yes, they did have a large, handsome cage that might do for a raven. Ravens, we learned, would do well on a diet of grubs, and so we bought a container full of the wriggling things. We bought the cage and were just paying for it, when a passing clerk dropped a container full of baby snakes. The snakelets went racing in all directions. We hurriedly hailed a taxi to drive us and the cage back to the flat. Magellan had a home and a square meal.

Domenica wanted to go to the theater. Theater was why she was in London. I was just the sidebar. And so, although I was beginning to feel strangely weak, she and I plunged into the streets, headed for the West End. We went through Piccadilly Circus, where I found myself feeling oddly frightened by the crowds and the bright lights.

"Mom, are you okay?" Domenica wanted to know.

"I feel a little weird."

"We're almost at the theater."

"Okay."

And so I pushed myself to just keep walking, although the noises of the cars and buses were making me more and more highstrung. At the theater we got our tickets and went inside to the blessed quiet and dark. "What's wrong with me?" I wondered.

Domenica stayed for several days, visiting me often from the Charles Dickens Hotel, where her tour group was bunkered. With her to focus on, and good theater to go to, I could ignore my mounting unease. I wasn't really eating and I wasn't really sleeping.

I fed Magellan at regular intervals but neglected to feed myself. I wasn't consciously fasting but I wasn't hungry.

"Mom, Mom, where are you?" Domenica would ask me, still towing me through the hectic nightlife. We went to see a harrowing show on Edith Piaf. We went to see *Miss Saigon* in a production complete with helicopter. I felt frightened and overwhelmed by the sound of the chopper blades, even though I knew they were not real. I wanted to get "home," back to the flat, as quickly as possible. I craved quiet and solitude, although whenever I was alone a song would come to me and I would need to grab my writing utensils and quickly take it down.

"Mom, you're too skinny. You're not eating," Domenica complained.

"I'm not very hungry," I answered.

I tried to tell Domenica about the musical I was writing, about the way the characters' songs kept coming to me. I had begun collecting images, postcards, and magazines that spoke to me of my project. I kept these images laid out wherever I could find space. I had Magellan in his cage in the center of the living room. The rest of the room was a fanciful panache of images. Like a mother bird, I was making a nest for myself amid scraps of paper. Domenica and her tour group were going off for a day trip to the ancient town of Glastonbury, in legend the home of Avalon, the Isle of Apples, about which I was writing.

"Bring me back some soil," I asked Domenica. I did not tell her I felt too weak and scared to travel far from my little nest.

"Soil of Glastonbury," Domenica announced proudly upon her return and, sure enough, she had brought me back a handful of dirt. I thanked her and placed the dirt in a little wooden box on the kitchen table. The table was more and more closely resembling an altar dedicated to the emerging musical. If Domenica thought it looked crazy, she didn't say so. She kept her worries to herself and then she was gone, headed back to Taos and then to New York for an extended summer's stay with her father.

With Domenica gone, I had nothing left to distract me from my obsession. The songs kept coming and I kept recording them, both on tape and on paper. I made a long trip to a Rollerblade shop on the northern outskirts of London and I came home the proud owner of a pair of blades. These I took to Regent's Park, where I put them on and tentatively glided past the ducks, swans, and dogs. I quickly learned that the rhythm of skating revved up my songwriting engine. It took a bit of careful balancing, but I carried the tape recorder with me because the songs that were coming through were long and intricate and insistent. I still have the tapes I made in those fevered days, and on them you can distinctly hear the "whir, whir" of the skates.

As a sober alcoholic, I had been carefully taught, "Don't get too hungry, angry, lonely, or tired." Well aware that I was in distinct violation of three out of the four categories, I sought out the company of other sober alcoholics, trying to ensure my sobriety. I found a sober actress, a sober writer, and a sober radio personality. I told them about what I was writing and described how the music seemed to be a never-ending flow. I sang them some of the songs. They were enchanted. *Avalon*, still in its birthing stages, was already attracting fans. I told them, too, about *The Artist's Way* and sent back to America for a box of books to share with them.

"Ordinarily, I would be teaching now," I explained.

"So teach us!" they responded.

For a nominal fee, I was able to rent a meeting room from a nearby convent. I convened a creativity class and began teaching, sharing both my tried-and-true tools and some new ones I found myself devising. I loved my little class, but it quickly multiplied like the loaves and fishes. One week I had three students, the next week six, and so on. The books arrived and I distributed them. Lit up by my own creative fire from working on *Avalon,* my little class caught fire and began to spread the tools to an ever-growing circle of others. Except for the teaching days, my days began to blur together. I would write and skate, skate and write. I was assembling quite a collection of songs, each one in a specific character.

"Is this the way it's done?" I wondered. "Shouldn't the play come first?" I felt like I was being given many brilliantly colored jigsaw-puzzle pieces but no schema of how to put them together. Still, it was wonderful—amazing—to be getting songs. Increasingly, I sang the songs to my class and to my sober alcoholic compadres. I discovered that my voice was a high, clear soprano. I sang and wrote. Wrote and sang. What I did not really do was eat.

I began to feel both more expanded and more powerful. As I felt physically weaker, I felt psychically stronger. I began to experience a strong inflow of exciting ideas, many related to *Avalon* and many not. I felt gregarious and loving. I wanted to reach out to people. If they didn't watch out, I would talk their ears off—or sing them off.

I called my brother Christopher, a pianist and composer. I told him a white lie, that I was working with a British composer. Then I sang him song after song, burning up the transatlantic wires. When I finally paused, my brother had a comment.

"This composer is good," he said. "Are you sleeping with him?"

"No," I answered.

"So who is he?" my brother wanted to know.

I took a deep breath and then I confessed, "Christopher, I wrote all those songs myself."

My brother took a deep breath while he absorbed the idea that his nonmusical sister was actually writing music.

Christopher liked my music! At least, he liked a lot of it until faced with the fact that it was mine. In view of the family mythology stating "Julie is nonmusical," I thought that was doing pretty well. I got off the phone giddy with glee.

Magellan required fresh food every few days. That meant a long trek across the full breadth of Regent's Park to the snake-and-bird store, as I thought of it. Increasingly, I found the trek hard to make. It was not only that I was scared of the snakes, I was beginning to be scared of the walk itself. Instead of an adventure, it seemed to me to be a venturing too far from home. Increasingly, the apartment did resemble a giant bird's nest with scraps of paper and images everywhere: on the walls, on the tables, on the floor, and on the furniture. I was making a giant collage of *Avalon* and in moments of clarity I saw that the apartment looked like a madwoman's house. I say "like" because I was only beginning to be frightened. As long as I stuck to my little routine, I felt safe. But safe was about to be capsized. The phone rang. It startled me. No one knew my number.

The caller was my landlord, Mr. Price. Did I remember that when I took the flat he told me there would be two days when I had to be elsewhere? The days were coming up. Did I need a ride to my other lodgings?

What other lodgings? I had completely forgotten that I was about to be unhoused. What about Magellan? What about the enormous collage in which I was living? For that matter, where could I go? I remembered the name of Domenica's hotel. I got the number and called. Yes, they had a single room available. I was in luck. Luckier still, I found someone to take charge of Magellan.

All that remained was for me to take my dresses down from the walls and carefully fold and pack my myriad papers.

As I began dismantling my live-in collage, a sword of fear passed through me. I made myself a cup of tea—coffee had by then proved hard to find, hard to get, and unduly expensive—and I sat down on the crooked brown couch in the crooked brown living room. Suddenly I felt alone, utterly alone. I didn't know how much more music was still to come through, and I was frightened of somehow losing the songs I had already written. I packed them all into a large duffel bag that I would take with me to the hotel. It all seemed safe enough, but something felt terribly wrong. I didn't know it, but I was becoming paranoid.

For six weeks now I had been under-eating and under-sleeping. That, coupled with my relentless skating routine, had taken its toll. I had gone from thin to far thinner. My little silk smocks hung from my shoulders. I looked and felt rickety. It was all I could do to get my suitcases down the stairs and into Mr. Price's waiting car. He seemed to notice nothing amiss, keeping up a stream of mindless chatter. Greater London passed me by in a blur. We were headed "not far," just over to Hyde Park, but it seemed like a tiring journey to me. At the hotel, they led me through a warren of halls and finally deposited me and my bags in a sparsely furnished room. By then I was truly frightened. To me the room looked not like a safe haven but like the perfect setting for an alcoholic binge. How close was I to drinking? Going over my HALT checklist, I realized I was hungry, angry, lonely, and tired—all four.

I had no appetite to deal with hungry. I was angry at being un-housed, but that was a fait accompli. I needed sleep but felt too high-strung to get it. That left lonely. I decided to try to find Tim, by then in my imagination a mythical figure of safety and security, the one who "understood." I called the woman's number out in Cornwall. She said that Mr. Wheater was in the studio with Mr. Wilde, but that she had a number to call for emergencies. Was this an emergency? she wondered. I must have sounded shaky.

"Yes, I guess it is," I said reluctantly. The woman—a kindly old soul named Olive—carefully spelled out the number for me to call. I got off the phone from her and dialed. A woman's voice answered and I asked for Tim. After a moment, he came on the line sounding annoyed.

"Hello? This is Tim Wheater. Who is this?"

"It's Julia Cameron."

"Ah. I am afraid I am in the studio, working."

"I am sorry to disturb you."

"What is it, then?"

Frantically, I fished for something sufficient to interrupt his work, no mere personal emergency. Finally, I remembered. The little toning tape I had made for him was selling very well through the Ark bookstore in Santa Fe. In fact, it was their number-one seller. I told Tim that.

"So do I owe you any money?" he asked, to my ear harshly.

"No, no. You don't owe me anything. I thought you would be pleased."

"I am pleased, but I am working and can't really think about other things right now."

"I'm so sorry." I heard my voice take on a placating feminine tone.

"Yes, well—they need me back."

And with that we hung up. So much for my fantasies of understanding and rescue. It was understandable, I told myself sternly. I had interrupted him in the midst of his work. He just needed to get to the business bottom line. He certainly didn't mean to be cruel, but the call left me reeling. If I had been lonely before, now I felt utterly alone. Panicked, I searched for the number of another sober alcoholic.

"I think I'm in trouble," I began the call—and then went on to describe the abrupt and painful phone call.

"This man sounds bad for you," came the verdict from the other end of the phone.

"No. I don't think he is, not really. It's just that I had hoped—"

"You can say whatever you want. I've got my opinion. Sometimes we don't like to hear the truth."

I tried to explain that there was a much larger truth to consider. I was beginning to realize that I was in very dangerous waters. When had I last eaten? When had I had a real night's sleep? I didn't want to drink—not yet—but I knew that I was in jeopardy.

I stayed at the hotel for two full days. I tried to work but couldn't settle down. On the other hand, I couldn't really sleep either. The little hotel room became my cell. I stared at the walls and waited to be released. Finally, the time ticked by and I was able to go "home."

Back at the flat, I collected Magellan from the woman who had cared for him. She wanted to keep him—"I've always wanted a raven"—but I wouldn't hear of it. My plan was to nurse him back to his eventual freedom, and he seemed to be growing stronger daily. He beat his wings more and more fiercely when I reached into his cage to change his food and water. His baby feathers were being replaced by the real thing. Soon he would be ready for a return to the wild—or the relative wild of Regent's Park.

"Don't worry. You'll have your freedom," I promised him.

In response to my mothering, Magellan simply cawed.

I laid out my elaborate collages again. I remade the tabletop altar with the dirt of Glastonbury as its centerpiece. When I finally sat down on the couch and listened for music, I was rewarded with a long, intricate song. I worked late into the night, taking it down. Back in my little nest, I felt safe again, but I also sensed that this was an illusion. Trying to sound "normal," I called my literary agent, Susan Schulman. One more time when I had a willing ear, I launched into song. I sang her a "demo" of the songs I was hearing.

"I love them," Susan said. "But are you okay?"

I was not okay and to those who knew me well this was evident. It wasn't just a case of Mr. Wrong—a great deal was wrong beyond that. For one thing, I started to be uncomfortable even in my flat. I found myself longing for green grass and trees. And when I got to them, after a few blocks of walking on concrete, I found that the trees seemed to shimmer and murmur. They seemed hyperalive. I would lean against them as though they, not people, were the comforting elders. I felt myself falling into a sort of swoon. People and events seemed to float past me. It was pleasant but alarming. I felt myself entering a fantasy world. I began to see everything as symbolic. Colors pulsated. Cars seemed to swim through the streets like fish.

I decided the time had come to release Magellan back to his natural habitat. I enlisted the help of a young student. Ceremonially, we marched the birdcage through the London streets. I insisted we carry it all the way into the park to the very spot where Magellan had fallen.

"Like the ark of the covenant," I told the girl. "Like we're carrying the ark of the covenant."

We carried the cage into the park with Magellan alert and wary inside it. Finally we got to a grove of small trees, and there I knelt on the ground and opened the cage. "C'mon," I coaxed, "you're free now." Magellan hopped from the cage. He crossed over to where I was kneeling and gave my hand a last fond farewell peck. Then he flapped his healed wings and landed in the lowest branches of the smallest tree. He would be safe, I decided tearfully. I wept to see him go.

"You're scaring me," announced the girl whose help I had enlisted. "What's wrong with you? He's just a bird, for God's sake."

"He still seems so young," I managed to say, but by then the girl was leaving, hurrying away without a backward glance. Once she was gone, I positioned the cage in some reeds along one of the canals. Then I made my way through the glowing, shimmering park toward home.

"I am really losing it," I declared to myself—although the process of losing it was actually quite pleasant. One day I simply decided not to wear my contact lenses. With Magellan gone and nothing and no one to care for, who needed to see clearly? Things were more pleasant slightly blurred. It was in this fuzzy, woozy state that I telephoned Sonia Choquette, picking out her number with difficulty. After listening to me for a few minutes, she interrupted me with a diagnosis.

"You're not grounded," she told me. "You need some strong coffee and some red meat and you need it right away. How long has it been since you had any protein or caffeine?"

I confessed that it had been weeks.

"You need to eat and you need to sleep. I am going to pray for you. I am lighting a candle right now, but you do what I tell you—red meat and coffee. I mean it."

I heard Sonia's alarm, and a part of me knew that she was very right. Another part of me was too far gone to really listen. I placed another phone call, this time to my daughter in New York.

"Mommy, are you okay?" she wanted to know.

"I don't know," I told her. "Sonia says I need red meat and coffee. She says I am not grounded."

"You don't sound very grounded."

"Maybe not."

Like Sonia, my daughter was alarmed. She wanted me to eat and sleep. I told her that I found sleeping difficult. I kept waking at odd intervals, feeling a compulsion to do yoga asanas. I would do the asanas until I was exhausted from them, then drift off to sleep until the compulsion would hit again. "This is not normal," I told myself. "This is a compulsion." I felt frightened.

I passed another difficult night, and as dawn came up, I dressed and wandered out of the apartment, all of my money in a little purse. I was going to get some help for myself somehow. First I went to a Catholic church, where I knocked on the door and asked to see the pastor. He opened the door to a thin, wild-eyed woman—me.

"I need help," I told him. "I'm not grounded—and why are all the doors to your church locked? How can anyone get inside to pray? You're wrong to lock your church up like that." I switched gears from needy to confrontational. The priest took my measure and ushered me to the door—I was simply a crazy lady, someone whom he could not really minister to. He showed me out the foyer and to the street. As the door closed behind me, I fought down panic.

Next I walked to the convent where I was teaching. One more time I found it locked and I rang the front bell. A slender young nun came to the door. She looked me up and down. She didn't like what she saw: a rumpled, stained dress and wild hair.

"I teach here," I said. "I'd like to come in." I tried to sound saner than I looked.

"I am afraid that's not possible."

"I think I am in trouble."

"Mother Superior isn't here."

"Please, can't I just come in?"

"No."

With that, the young nun shut the door. She clearly had her orders. I stood disoriented in the street. Now what? Then I remembered that my friend Sambhu had given me the name of some very spiritual people he knew and loved. I dug in my purse for their number.

"I think I am in trouble," I told the man when he answered. "I am a friend of Sambhu's. Can I please come over?"

I was given an address in St. John's Wood. I managed to flag down a cab. A few minutes later, we arrived at the door of Sambhu's friends. The cab pulled over. "We're here, lady." But I had trouble counting out the right money for the fare. I simply handed over my purse and told the driver to take some.

Sambhu's friends were a husband and wife. He was tall and lean and ascetic looking. She was round and plump. "I think I am in trouble," I repeated. Looking me up and down, they thought the same thing. The wife hurried to the kitchen to fix me a plate of food. The husband tried to talk to me, but I was too disoriented to carry on a real conversation. It was decided that they would call their guru and ask for advice about how to handle me. I clearly took "handling."

"Feed her bananas and honey and heavy cream. Wrap her in yellow silk and tell her to sleep," the guru advised them. It might have worked, too, but I heard the wife muttering to her husband, "What is she doing here with us? I don't like it!"

Very quietly, I simply slipped from the house. I had moved past panic into a quiet despair. At the end of their street, I spotted a welcoming park. I walked toward the park. The trees were as talkative as I wished them to be. They seemed to offer a place of safety and advice. I almost didn't notice the men who looked up as I entered the park. I was focused on the green grass and the serenity of the gardens. One of the men came after me and took me gently by the arm. I felt a faint distant alarm, but the man seemed harmless enough and oddly familiar.

"Are you a nice girl?" he asked me. He led me off the path. He patted a spot on the grass and motioned me to sit down. Now I had it: he reminded me a little of my Taos friend John Nichols. He must be all right, I reasoned.

"He's going to help me," I thought. Then I realized, as from a great distance, that he was not. I started weeping. He simply ignored my tears.

"Easy now," he said. "You just lie back down. Are you a nice girl?" He pulled up my smock and pulled down my underwear. The next thing I knew he was unzipping his pants and thrusting himself into me. It was a rape but it was a very gentle rape, more of a molestation.

"Are you a nice girl?" he kept repeating. I didn't know what to say. I didn't answer him. I lay on the ground quietly weeping and trying to make sense of what was happening to me. I felt my mind and my feelings split apart. "It's part of *Avalon*," I told myself. "It's a ritual, like Beltane. I am just a symbol. This is just symbolic."

"You are a nice girl," the man said as he ejaculated. He seemed suddenly distressed by my tears. "You are a nice girl," he repeated. He again seemed like a kindly man, and when he was finished with me, he simply got to his feet and walked away.

I do not know how long I lay there, but eventually I got to my feet and made my way out of the park. One more time I flagged a taxi. I gave my home address. When we got there, the taxi driver followed me up the stairs.

"What do you want?" I asked him when we were inside the flat. Again, as from a great distance, I sensed I was in danger. I handed over my purse. "Take all of it," I told him. "Just go away."

"I don't want your money," he said.

"Please go, then," I said. I stared at the man and the man stared at me. Suddenly I had an inspiration. "You get out of here now!" I ordered sternly in the lowest voice I could muster. Abruptly, the man turned and ran.

Now I was alone. I was safely back in the flat. The familiar images of *Avalon* were all around me. I was all right, I told myself. I was all right. Then came the pounding at the door.

"Who is it?" I didn't open the door.

The pounding came again and then the demand, "Open your door. We are the police."

Reluctantly, I opened the door to a woman and two young men.

"Are you Julia Cameron?" the woman asked me.

"I am."

"We've come to take you to the hospital. Do you think you need to go to the hospital?"

Suddenly I was frightened, very frightened. I bolted to the far side of the room. The young policemen stepped toward me. They each grabbed me by an arm.

"I am a writer," I told them. "I am writing a musical about Avalon. That's what all the papers are about. Do you want to hear a little?" I started singing the beautiful ethereal songs I had been given. The young policemen seemed to soften for a moment, enchanted by the music.

"She seems okay," one of them said. I felt suddenly lucid and back in control.

"No. She's not okay. Look at all of this," said the other, shaking off the music's spell and tightening his grip on my arm. "We don't get calls about people who are okay."

"I am a sober alcoholic," I blurted out. I tried twisting my arm to get free. Suddenly I became determined to fight them, but they had an easy time of it. I was far too weak.

"Who called you?" I demanded to know.

"Your husband from America."

"I don't have a husband. I mean, I had two husbands. I mean—"

The woman spoke up calmly and gently. "I think you had better come with us. We're not going to arrest you. We're going to take you to a hospital to get some help."

They did not put me in handcuffs or wrap me in a straitjacket, as in the movies. They did take me firmly by each arm and lead me to a waiting paddy wagon. I do not remember much of the ride or much of what happened once I was at the hospital. I do not remember all of the rigmarole that must have accompanied admission. What I do remember is someone saying, "Now, then. We are just going to give you this injection."

"Please! No drugs! I am a sober alcoholic!" I pleaded. I felt utterly hopeless.

"It's for your own good," someone responded as a needle

pricked my haunch and I instantly began to drift out of touch. I would later learn I had been given thirty times the minimum dose of Haldol.

When I came to, I was lying in a bed near another bed, which held a young, terrified black woman. I began to talk to her about creativity, about the way that even when there was nothing else left, that was left. Up near the ceiling, far above our heads, I began to see silver, a shimmering double helix. "You see," I said, pointing. The girl's wide eyes widened further still—either she saw what I was seeing or there was nothing up there to be seen and that frightened her.

"Walt Disney understood about creativity," I told her. "And I think the Dalai Lama understands—maybe. Steven Spielberg understands."

The next memory I have is of Mark leaning over my bed, softly speaking my name in a voice of infinite, gentle concern. "Julia," he said. "Julia?"

I came around long enough then to speak to him. To try to tell him that they had shot me full of drugs, that I was doped up and disoriented. Mark listened carefully.

"You needed the drugs," he told me. "You were pretty far out there." He sat quietly by my bed and held my hand. "You're pretty skinny," he added.

Mark met with my doctor and told him of my mother's history of depression and my father's history of manic-depression. Based on what Mark said, I was tentatively diagnosed as manic-depressive as well.

I don't remember Mark leaving, but he left. I do remember that the hospital seemed to be made up entirely of tiny winding corridors and intricate small staircases. I remember being led up and down those staircases, through those tricky halls, into a large room where they were serving dinner. I didn't want to eat, but a kindly nurse with a lilting Jamaican accent told me that I was much too thin and that food would be good for me.

The food probably was good for me. Maybe, too, the drugs, which they doled out in pill form three times a day. I slept a lot and spoke several times to a kindly doctor who had been assigned my case. I don't remember what I told him. The calm-inducing drugs erased my memory.

My daughter, Domenica, arrived unexpectedly. Her entry made me cry.

"I didn't want you to know. I didn't want you to see me like this," I told her.

"Oh, Mommy," she answered.

Domenica sat by the side of the bed and gently told me that it was she who had called Mark and Mark who had called the police. Their concern had been to get me safely off the streets. I didn't tell Domenica that they had caught up with me too late. Even on drugs, I had some residual parental concern. I didn't want to scare her even worse than she was already. She seemed so brave and so adult, patting my hand, murmuring that I would be all right

Soon after Domenica arrived, so did my college friend Gerard.

"Hey, good-lookin'," Gerard said, entering. A tall, thin, formal man, he, too, sat by the bed. Like Mark, he thought I looked a little rickety. I didn't know it then, but it was Martin who was paying to keep me in a nice private hospital. Everyone had rallied, financially and personally. Everyone wanted me to get better. Gerard and Domenica met with my doctor. They wanted to take me back to America, back to New Mexico, to "home."

"They want to take you home," the doctor told me.

"Is that good?" I asked.

"We think so," said the doctor.

And so, with a month's supply of Haldol and his concerned best wishes, the kindly doctor released me to Gerard and Domenica's care. There was my apartment to pack up and then a day's wait before our ten-hour flight back to Los Angeles, and then from Los Angeles to Albuquerque, where a shuttle bus would drive us three more hours up the steep mountains into Taos. The trip sounded daunting, but packing up my apartment was daunting enough. I was afraid to have Domenica see it.

"Mom," she insisted, "I will be fine."

I turned the key in the lock and opened the door to my tiny kingdom. Floor to ceiling, on every available surface, I had made a collage. The room looked like sheer madness. I was worried it would frighten Domenica, but Gerard stepped forward brusquely, saying, "Well now, where do we begin?"

"I don't want to throw anything away!" I burst out. "It's all important. It's all *Avalon.*"

"Well then, we'll just pack it all," Gerard said brightly.

Pack it we did—into suitcases and duffel bags. We took every scrap—all the magazine images, all the postcards, all the carefully recorded tapes, all the overflowing notebooks, and all the accumulated books—fifty plus—that I had managed to purchase in three months' time. It took us a full day to dismantle the apartment. At the end of it, we had thirteen tightly packed bags—an entire caravan.

"I can't afford to lose anything," I kept repeating. "It's all *Avalon.*"

"You can put it back together again when you get to Taos," Gerard said comfortingly.

That night we went to see Barbara Cook in concert. Gerard was determined that we behave as normally as possible, and so we sat in orchestra seats listening to the great singer go through her considerable paces. The following morning we drove to Heathrow, where we caught our flight. What I remember of that transatlantic flight is that I spent most of it standing up in the galley. Despite all the medication, I was too high-strung to sleep—or even sit down.

Gerard got us as far as Los Angeles, where Domenica and I assured him that we could get safely home to Taos. I do not remember the flight from Los Angeles to Albuquerque. Domenica tells me that I spent it clinging tightly to her hand. I do remember the long drive up the mountains to Taos. Our bus broke down twice. We arrived home fragile and exhausted.

7.

Home looked a little the worse for wear. The gardens needed weeding. The lawn begged to be cut. And there was bad news. During my time in London, Calla Lily, our senior white standard poodle, had been hit by a car and killed. Sambhu, house-sitting for me, had not wanted to convey the bad news long distance. The other dogs were wild with glee at our arrival. We lined them up in a row in the kitchen, and when they were all sitting quietly, we gave them each a celebratory dog treat. We were officially "home."

"Mom, are you okay?" Domenica wanted to know.

"I am not sure," I answered her. "I don't like being on drugs. I'd like to come off them."

"I think you'd better ask the doctor," Domenica said carefully.

"You're probably right. I guess I better find myself a doctor."

"I think that would be great." Domenica tried to sound upbeat.

Domenica was worried about me, but she tried to mask her concern with an adult demeanor. I was worried about me, too, but I tried to hide my concerns as well. I wanted Domenica to feel safe with me. I did not want to have her repeat the same terrifying experiences I had had with my own fragile mother. There had been times when my mother had been too disoriented to know me. At least I still knew who Domenica was.

I began my search for a doctor, but Taos is a small mountain community and doctors are few. There was one small mental health clinic, and it specialized in substance abuse. I heard of a woman therapist who was said to be compassionate and good, but when I met with her, her eyes looked clouded to me and that frightened me.

She seemed spacey and ethereal.

"I am not sure you are grounded enough to help me," I told her, probably a case of it takes one to know one. I later learned that I was accurate; she had a drinking problem. In the meanwhile, I was without skilled medical help. Left to my own devices, I decided to come off the Haldol. I didn't know about stepping down a notch at a time, taking a little less of the drug each day until I had tapered off. Instead, I quit the drug cold turkey. This sent me flying. Fortunately, Domenica had gone back to New York to finish out the summer at her father's.

The symptoms that had begun in London resumed at home in New Mexico. Once again nature became compelling to me. Trees and the earth itself seemed to talk to me. Barefoot, I walked my property lines over and over again. When friends stopped by, I invited them to walk with me. One more time I had a fevered charisma. Friends tell me still that we had great conversations.

I was uncomfortable indoors. I set up camp outside under an apple tree. Inside the house, electricity bothered me. I switched off the power so that the whole house was quiet and dark. At night I slept outside under the bright New Mexico stars. One morning, as I woke, I experienced the strong, strange energy of a kundalini awakening. A "serpent" of energy coursed through my body. Looking toward the east, I saw a great egg where the rising sun would be.

Sambhu and Ezra's mother, Bee, thought that I was having a breakthrough and not a breakdown. As they saw it, my nervous condition was actually a spiritual experience. Veterans of ashram life, they were prepared to walk me through the months it might take me to integrate all that I was experiencing. Appointing themselves my caretakers and guardians, they were willing to live by candlelight until I became less sensitive to electricity. Power lines now hummed for me, and I could feel them from a distance as an unpleasant tingling on my skin. It felt like an allergy. I began to tell people I was allergic to electricity. My skin reacted equally strongly to certain colors. I began to be attracted to plain white. That is what I started to dress in.

They say a fool and his money are soon parted, and I began to spend money foolishly. Like the fool from the tarot deck, I was stepping off the edge and into space. I bought an entire trousseau of white clothes. I bought an unneeded and largely uninhabitable house trailer.

Taos is a small town, and tales of my eccentricity began to spread. Some people, like my friend Rhonda, the metaphysician, seemed to take it in stride. She began paying me a daily visit, willing to listen to my insights and fantasies. No matter how far out I got, Rhonda seemed to keep pace with me. Hers was a therapeutic presence.

Not everyone was willing to allow me such freedom. A friend's daughter decided that I was simply too crazy and that she would take me to the emergency room. Dutifully, I got in the car with her as ordered, but when we pulled up at the hospital, the emergency room was blazing with electric lights. I bolted in panic, running away from my captor, heading overland across the great sage fields. Barefoot and weeping, I ran through a huge electrical storm that left me drenched and shaking. It took me hours to make it home.

Someone decided to call Mark. I was acting crazy, they told him. Worried, he decided to investigate, and when he got to the dark and quiet house, he did not like what he found.

"What's wrong with the electricity?" he wanted to know. "Let's get some lights on in here."

"Julia feels she is allergic to electricity," Sambhu and Bee told him. "She wants the house dark."

"Allergic to electricity? That's ridiculous. In fact, that's crazy. Where is she?"

Mark was shown outside to my favored spot under the apple tree. He took one look and that was enough for him. I had a teaching tour scheduled in ten days and I clearly couldn't teach if I were crazy. What I needed, he decided, was help—and fast. To his eye I was sicker and more frightening than I had been in London with Haldol in my system. He was alarmed to learn I had come off the Haldol without a doctor's supervision. The entire situation struck Mark as precarious and dangerous. He had no patience with Sambhu and Bee and their spiritual theories. As far as he was concerned, this was a case for modern medicine.

"I am taking her to Santa Fe to a hospital," he announced. "Julia, you are coming with me."

"I don't want to go. I think I am going to be okay. I am learning a lot."

"What do you mean, you're learning a lot?" Mark was incredulous at my defense.

"I mean I am realizing a lot of things. Here, listen to this." With that, I began to softly sing. It was a little alphabet song that I had devised to help students to focus.

"That's the alphabet!" Mark exclaimed. "And you certainly didn't invent it. Come on. You're coming with me and we're going to get you some real help."

By "real help" Mark meant modern, state-of-the-art Western medicine. To wit: drugs. He had no patience with Taos and its New Age chatter. To him, such talk was dangerous self-indulgence. What I needed was medicine, and I needed it fast.

"If I am going with you, I need Bee to go with me," I counteroffered.

"Fine," Mark said, closing the deal. "I am going to make a few phone calls. You get your things together. Pack."

I do not remember what things I packed. Packing was too much for me. In the end Mark put a few changes of clothing in a small suitcase and then he ushered me and Bee to the car. We faced a two-hour drive with Mark grim and tight-lipped behind the wheel. Santa Fe was seventy-five miles away through the twisting canyons. Mark still remembers the nightmare ride to the hospital. I sang most of the way, urging Bee to join in. To Mark's ear, both of us were crazy and Bee's humoring me was dangerous. He wanted me back solid and sane. To his ear, my little alphabet teaching songs were gibberish.

"Mark, I can feel the electricity!" I told him, frightened, whenever a high-power cable ran alongside the highway.

"You can't feel the electricity," Mark would answer firmly.

I do not remember the check-in at the hospital. I do remember that the hallways featured fluorescent lights for which I felt a particular horror. If electricity frightened me, this form of electricity frightened me most of all. There was no escaping the lights. I felt as if I were inside a microwave oven with the heat turned on. I was only too glad to get to my room, which was small and dark.

"No drugs!" I kept saying to anyone and everyone who would listen. "I can't take drugs. I am a sober alcoholic."

The next thing I remember clearly is the soft, island-accented voice of my doctor, Arnold Jones. He sat calmly at my bedside. Patiently and carefully, he explained to me that I needed to take drugs, that drugs would help me to think soberly, that they were not a slip but a necessity. I was very reluctant to do as he suggested, but he was gentle with me, firm and quiet.

"Let's try it," he suggested. "Let's see if you don't feel better." He held out a little paper cup and some pills.

"You're sure I'll still be sober?" I asked him again.

"You'll be sober," he assured me. "I promise you that you'll still be sober."

And so I took the pills that he offered me. They hit my system very hard, sending me plummeting into much-needed sleep. I lay facedown on my bed with my world whirling around me.

Dr. Jones was right about the drugs. My fear of electricity receded. I found myself turning back into a coherent person, able to visit with Mark and talk over what we needed to do. *Avalon*, all of the songs and the story I was trying to write, was part of a life Mark did not share with me. His concern was our teaching, the many years I had put into *The Artist's Way*, and the fact that the book was now taking off and needed my support. To Mark's eye, my breakdown couldn't have had worse timing. It threatened to dismantle all the work we had done together. He believed in me as a teacher and he wanted that part of me back. He wanted me to be solid again and respectable. He knew I could do it if I tried.

What I remember of the next week is largely Mark's pep talks and Dr. Jones's cautious agreement that perhaps it would be good for me to try doing something I had done many, many times before, namely, teaching.

"You're a great teacher," Mark assured me. "It will be good for you to teach. There are a lot of students waiting for you. You don't want to let them down."

Mark was determined that we not cancel our teaching tour. He felt that with the security of his presence and the help of the drugs I was on, I should be able to teach and teach effectively. All that was necessary was for me to reiterate the central teachings of *The Artist's Way*. He could help me break the classes into clusters and lead the students through exercises. With a little determination— of which he had plenty—it could be done.

And so I was released from the hospital into Mark's care. We would teach for a week in California and then I would come back to New Mexico, where Dr. Jones would oversee my recovery. I would commute from Taos once weekly to consult with him. I would continue on drugs until further notice.

My next memory is of a hotel room in San Diego. I am lying on the bed, frightened, and Mark is sitting by my side, urging me to believe that I was safe and that the lectures were going fine. I next remember standing in front of a large group of people. I am teaching them the principles of *The Artist's Way*. Mark stands by my side.

My memories now unfurl like a newsreel. Somehow we have traveled from San Diego to Los Angeles, the second stop on our teaching tour. We are seated in a window booth at the Hamburger

Hamlet on Doheny Drive. Outside, it is a bright and sunny day. Inside, in the cool dark, I am sitting with Mark and with a concerned Jeremy Tarcher. The drugs I am taking create an illusion of distance. I watch us as through a telescope. They are talking about the fate of my book, the fact that it needs support if it is to continue to rise.

"I can teach for her while she's recovering," Mark tells Jeremy. "I know the material."

"They'll want Julia herself, the author," Jeremy answers.

"Maybe we could add my name in the new printings," Mark ventures.

"That might work," Jeremy concurs.

"But won't people think that Mark wrote it, then?" I ask.

Faced with commercial suicide, I allow the two men to brush aside my authorly concerns. They feel we have bigger fish to fry. It is decided that Mark's byline will be added to the book. In that way, he will be able to be advertised as "coauthor," and the book will have the public support it needs if it is to continue to grow. I do not like this decision, but I tell myself that I am being paranoid about its possible repercussions. We order a large slice of chocolate cake and then the memory blinks out. I do not remember the rest of the tour.

What I do remember clearly is the time that lay ahead of me in Taos.

My first thought was for Domenica. I had been hospitalized the same week she had begun college. She had had no parental send-off, either from me or from Mark. Our troubles had absorbed us, and so she had started her college life with little sense of ongoing security.

"I am so so sorry," I told her over the long-distance wires.

"Oh, Mommy. It's okay," she bravely answered me. She was doing fine, she assured me. Her classes were good and so was she.

"I'm fine too," I told her reassuringly. "I am on the mend."

As always, I wanted Domenica to think of me as a source of strength, stability, and consistency. I didn't want to be fragile and erratic. I didn't want to be "crazy." But "crazy" was how I had seemed to Mark and perhaps also to Jeremy. Sambhu, who continued to stay at the house with me, did not think I was crazy. He listened carefully to the many intricate songs from *Avalon*. Quietly and with humor, he urged me to seek out spiritual explanations for my breakdown. I began a voracious course of reading.

With Domenica away at college, I co-opted her pale lilac bedroom as my writing room. With the dogs ranged on the floor around me, I would lie on her bed and read for hours. Beginning with Stan and Christina Grof's book *Spiritual Emergency*, I tried to explore the idea that my breakdown might actually be—as Sambhu and Bee had claimed—a breakthrough. I read many books on shamanism and spiritual awakenings. Had my time in London actually been a sort of initiation? I had the many songs of *Avalon* to show for it. The songs were coherent and very lovely. I began to sense how their many fragments could fit together into a cohesive whole. If *Avalon* could be made whole, couldn't I? And wasn't I perhaps already whole enough to tackle *Avalon*? A compulsion came over me. I needed to go back to London and finish the work I had begun there. I told this plan to Dr. Jones, who was understandably wary of my proposed agenda. "This time will be different," I told him. "I have medicine. I'll be careful to eat and sleep. I'll take Ezra with me so I have a sense of safety. I will be fine. You'll see."

There was no stopping me. I was bound and determined to get back to London and back to work on *Avalon*. I called a British writer I knew, Jill Robinson, author of *Perdido*, a marvelous novel about Los Angeles. Could I rent a room from her? I asked. I could.

This time I had all my notebooks and tape-recording equipment close at hand. I set up shop in the basement room that Jill rented me, and I prayed for the songs of *Avalon* to please come back.

At first, I did not think my prayer was heard. I had set up a writing table in my room and I sketched out the shape of the story as far as I knew it. Then, one fine fall day, I began to hear music again. With relief, I took the notation down. The autumn days were short in London, although my workdays felt long. At twilight I would set out a few short blocks to meet Ezra for dinner. We would share a meal of Thai food—alternating red, yellow, and green curry—and he would ask me how *Avalon* was unfolding.

"You are the prototype for the little wizard," I would tell him. "Domenica is who I see in my mind's eye for the little priestess. I am getting songs for you both."

Ezra was in London not only to help me but also to study film, and he was filled with enthusiasm. It was a joy to me to see his excitement as I tried to focus on my own creative adventure. This proved hard to do. While I began to see the shape that *Avalon* should take, I also began to become edgy and depressed from my days of basement living. I felt like a mole, burrowing down deep below the city of London. I missed light and air—eventually, I admitted it, I missed Taos. But could I go back without a draft of *Avalon* in hand? Wasn't *Avalon* a product of London and the environment there? I was torn between homesickness and a sense of duty. Duty won.

Feeling that I was playing beat the clock, I rushed to finish a draft of *Avalon* before my optimism ran out. I copied down song after song, looking up only to notice the feet that passed by my basement window. For his part, Ezra was concerned with my teetering moods. He wanted me to be well and he began to be convinced that London and life in a basement were too much for me. He began to lobby for me to go home to Taos. I hated to hear what he was saying, but a part of me knew he was right.

Reluctantly, telling myself that *Avalon* would one more time survive the transplant, I headed home to Taos. Ezra remained behind in London. Sambhu awaited me at home. Twenty years a veteran on a spiritual path, he lived monklike in a large spare room at the back of the house. I depended on his quiet companionship. He was a musician of the first water, and I felt his company was good for both me and *Avalon*. In Taos, a town filled with eccentric characters, Sambhu and I became the newest odd couple. Never romantically involved, we nonetheless lived together. I felt Sambhu anchored me to the earth, and I needed that anchoring.

One day a letter arrived from Chester, Connecticut. "Dear Julia," the letter ran. "Are you my dear Julia?" The writer was Max Showalter. He had encountered *The Artist's Way* and wondered if the author was the same woman he had sheltered during her terrible divorce and fragile early sobriety. He enclosed a phone number and I dialed it immediately. His long-ago familiar voice came over the wire.

"Max, is that really you?" I asked him tearfully.

"It's me, sweetheart," he assured me. He had sold his Hollywood Boulevard houses and retired to charming Chester, Connecticut, where he one more time had half an acre's garden and a rambling old stone house. He was deeply involved with the Goodspeed Musicals and the Ivoryton Playhouse. He enjoyed mentoring young people just entering the theater and had settled happily into his role as a creative elder.

Did I enjoy my teaching? he wanted to know. Would it bring me to visit him in Connecticut? I promised him it would. I told him about my work on *Avalon*, the way that music had come to me suddenly and unexpectedly. Max laughed with delight. He himself was multitalented. He acted, wrote, painted, and composed. He saw all of it as the Great Creator working through us. It was our job to cooperate, he believed. He was glad to hear that I was cooperating. I got off the phone feeling heartened and inspired. Max was eighty and full of plans. Couldn't I rally with some plans of my own?

It was time for a second creativity book from me, and I was determined that it should be a good one. I wanted it to take students further than I had with *The Artist's Way*. I wanted them to dig deeper and discover a reliable and personal spiritual taproot. My own spiritual practices began to deepen. Daily, I wrote my Morning Pages, seeking to make conscious contact with my creative source. Daily, I took the dogs for long walks through the fields of sagebrush. Daily, I worked with affirmative prayers, stayed sober, and continued my contact with other sober alcoholics. Weekly, I drove to visit with Dr. Jones.

"It's very unusual, your having stayed sober through the events that happened to you in London," Dr. Jones told me on one of my weekly visits. A kindly yet formal man, he spoke with calm detachment.

"What do you mean?" I asked him.

"Most people drink as a way to self-medicate," he explained. "You didn't do that."

"It never occurred to me that a drink would make anything better," I told him.

"You were right. It wouldn't have."

Nor would a drink improve the times I was in since my return. I didn't like taking medication. It made me feel as if I were living underneath an anvil. My moods were flat and slow and harsh. I missed the quicksilver wit of *Avalon* as it had first appeared to me. London and the days of singing seemed far behind me. Despite my rough draft, I despaired of ever reconstructing *Avalon*. I feared that on medication I simply was unable to reach where I needed to go. (This fear would prove groundless.)

Meanwhile, Dr. Jones seemed to feel that I was doing well. He was glad I was reading and writing. He thought my walks were a fine idea. He was particularly pleased that I continued to seek out other sober alcoholics. He seemed to be relying heavily on a notion to which I only gave lip service: "This, too, shall pass." I wrote my father that I was stable but fighting depression.

My days felt dronelike and unending. Each day was a long march. I felt no levity, no humor, no joy. On my walks, I moved with leaden steps. "Please guide me, please help me," I begged. Meanwhile, snowy clouds moved across the face of the mountain. Often—almost daily—I wrote to my father. On the page, I tried to make optimistic sense of the passage I was going through. "Julie B, just hang in there. It will get better," my father wrote back to me.

"Mom, are you okay?" Domenica would ask me long distance from Connecticut, where she was in school.

"Domenica, are you okay?" I would ask back. I missed her physical presence in my realm. Long-distance mothering was difficult.

Although she did her best to reassure me, Domenica was not okay. She was overtired and overworked, throwing herself into her projects and activities with a feverish energy that was, perhaps, intended to block the pain of her tumultuous summer. And then I got the call that she was in the clinic. Her burnout had turned into a bad case of mononucleosis. She needed rest.

"Honey, you are not okay," our calls now went.

"No, Mommy. I am not." She sounded little and lost.

While I toiled through my heavy days in Taos, Mark toured the country teaching and speaking. His name was now on *The Artist's Way*, and it served him well. He was booked into many prestigious venues. His gregarious personality lent itself to teaching. He seemed to teach everywhere. When Domenica fell sick, he invited me to join him for an East Coast tour that would feature a visit to Domenica in Connecticut. We arrived to find her still too thin and overtired. When she gave us the tour of her campus, I worried that she belonged squarely back in bed, but no, she insisted, she was fine, much better than she had been. In that case, how bad had she been? I wondered. Certain that her stress was psychological as well as physical, I lobbied for her to seek out a therapist. "I already have one," she confessed. To her credit, Domenica had sought out a gifted older therapist who was able to do for her what I could not: give her a sense of stability and safety.

Our literary agent, Susan Schulman, had a country home in Litchfield, Connecticut. She and her husband, Shelly, invited Mark, Domenica, and me to spend Thanksgiving with their family. Seated around the dining room table, trying to make bright conversation, I found myself haunted by the fact that although we were together, we were no longer really a family. This holiday togetherness was an oddity, not a cherished ritual. Domenica later reported that she, too, had felt sad, haunted by the ghost of what once had been.

With the holiday over, I returned to Taos while Mark went to his new home in Santa Fe. Domenica stayed on in Connecticut. Although she and I talked daily on the phone, our contact left me longing for more proximity. We felt scattered to the winds. Our family days were officially over. I wrote to my father about my grief and he wrote back simply that I should try to hold a steady course. I tried.

I continued to read and to work on the book that would become *The Vein of Gold*. I had an idea that I wanted to explore creativity a kingdom at a time, leading people through the magical realms I had myself experienced. Despite the heavy medication, the embers of *Avalon* were beginning to stir. In London I had written down many melody lines complete with lyrics. What I needed now was someone who could arrange suitable harmonies. Sambhu thought he knew a man who might be able to help me. We worked on several songs before I discovered that he wanted to co-opt the work, not just serve it. Finally, in desperation, I called Tim's colleague, Michael Hoppe. I explained to him what I was seeking: someone who could serve the songs without wanting to steal them; someone who would be willing to do arrangements for hire. I was willing to pay well for the help.

"I do think I know somebody," Hoppe responded after a few moments' thought. "His name is Tommy Eyres. He is one of the most genuinely musical people I know. You may know his wife, Scarlett Rivera. She was Bob Dylan's fiddle player. Tommy worked with Lionel Bart on *Oliver!* He might just be your man."

Hoppe gave me a number for Eyres, who lived in the San Fernando Valley. Screwing my courage to the sticking point, I phoned him and outlined the job I had to offer. My weekly visits to Dr. Jones and my careful regime of medication meant traveling was out for me. "I would need to have you come to Taos. I would pay for your hotel and meals. I would pay you to work with me on arrangements." I tried to make Taos sound glamorous. I mentioned the ancient pueblo and the lively arts scene. I spoke of the spectacular scenery. Taos did hold a mystique. Dennis Hopper had lived there for many years. D. H. Lawrence was buried in Taos. The pueblo was the oldest continually inhabited dwelling on the continent of North America. Eyres was at first intrigued and then willing. He and his wife would come.

When Eyres arrived, I found him to be a kindly and lively mentor. We began a song at a time and he quickly fell under the spell of *Avalon*. We worked swiftly and efficiently, finding that our musical tastes were compatible, as Hoppe had hoped they might be. Eyres had grown up around British musical halls. His arrangements for *Avalon* were rowdy and infectious and perhaps not as delicate as the songs they served. Still, the songs could now be played. *Avalon* was coming into recognizable form. I was willing to pay whatever it took to bring the songs to fruition. My royalties on *The Artist's Way* were being poured straight into *Avalon*. This struck Mark as spendthrift. I felt I had no choice but to try to bring to life the work that so compelled me.

"There's a hell of a lot of music," Eyres observed rightly.

"We're doing fine," I would encourage him. I was hoping I could get him to stay until the show was completed.

After two weeks we had the show half finished. In my living room we threw an impromptu concert for my friends. The concert was encouraging, but Eyres was restless to get back to Los Angeles, where he made a handsome living as a studio musician. It wasn't ideal, but we thought the work could continue long distance. "Or you can come to me next time," Eyres insisted. If I'd had my way,

I'd have kept Eyres hostage, but that was not to be. Eyres and his wife said their good-byes and left me alone one more time with my dreams.

Once again, with my company gone, I settled into my lonely days of writing and walking. I hadn't planned on being solitary and celibate, but that was the order of the day. I was laying a great deal of track in my daily writing stints, and I began to be optimistic that *The Vein of Gold* might turn out well. It was a complex book with many sources, and I was trying somehow to honor all those tributaries while keeping the book readable and accessible. It was a difficult and complicated job, and I realized, with alarm, that I once more needed help, which I again might not be able to find in Taos.

When Domenica came home for Christmas, I told her that I thought I needed to temporarily relocate to California. I had gotten sober in Los Angeles, and my work had gotten sober there as well. Feeling crippled by my medications and by the psychological fallout of having had a breakdown, I thought it was best if I go back to my roots and see if I could find the stability there to execute the work I so badly wanted to turn out well. There was an oceanfront hotel called the Shangri-La that I liked very much. An old art deco glory, it featured plain square rooms with views out over the palm trees to the vast Pacific rolling beyond. If I stayed there for a while, I might be able to quickly and efficiently finish my book. I would have the help of my longtime friend Bill LaVallee. An expert typist, he was so good that he functioned as a copy editor as well. Besides, Jeremy Tarcher lived in Los Angeles, and he would be editing the final book. Not to mention that both my musical mentors, Eyres and Hoppe, would be accessible to me as moral support for finishing *Avalon*. Yes, Los Angeles seemed to beckon.

"Do what you need to do, Mommy," Domenica said to me. "I am in Connecticut anyhow. I don't need you to stay home for me."

And so, bidding Dr. Jones a cautious good-bye, thanking him for the help he had given me, I moved myself and my work out to Los Angeles, where I set up camp in a sunny suite on the second floor of the Shangri-La. Just outside my window, the Pacific stretched blue and seamless to the horizon. Close at hand, the palm trees scraped against my windows. I set up a typewriter and office in what was intended to be the suite's kitchen. As I had in Taos, I devised a daily schedule of hours spent writing and hours spent walking. Additionally, I found a coffee shop where sober alcoholics gathered daily for early morning cappuccinos and conversation. With my structure firmly in place, I felt safe. I wrote my father that I was doing well and he should not worry.

For the first time in many years, I was physically close to the people I had gotten sober with. I met with them almost daily. I found their presence and continued sobriety greatly reassuring. I was not the first sober alcoholic to have suffered a breakdown or a divorce. "Just don't drink." "One day at a time." "This, too, shall pass," they told me.

It was probably the combination of solitude and safety that set the stage for what happened next. Nearly a year had passed since my trip to London and my bout of fragility there. Now I was settled in a safe little nest. I was working productively on a new, if difficult, book, and I was feeling replenished in my sobriety. All was well with me, if a little jerry-rigged. It was then that I learned Tim Wheater was passing through town and that he wanted to see me. The news rattled me, but I felt a need to face down my demons, and my memory of Tim and London was one of them. I accepted a dinner date.

Tim arrived in my rooms at the Shangri-La looking thin and ashen. I was frightened to see him after our last harsh call, but I was also curious as to why he would want to see me. After the debacle with the toning tape, it seemed that our business with each other was really over and that a rift yawned between us that might not be easily healed. Surely whatever goodwill existed between us was now eroded.

The sun was setting over the Pacific when Tim entered my suite. He was as uneasy and overwrought as I was. Our hellos were strained. A very uncomfortable duo, we set out for dinner. Tim chose a posh restaurant this time, and as we picked our way through a costly meal, he told me of the difficult year he had just finished passing, a year characterized for him by heartbreak and loss. He had fallen in love with a terribly unsuitable partner. The alliance had cost him his art and nearly, he said, his equilibrium. I didn't doubt him. He seemed a shell of the man I had known. Just looking at him, it occurred to me that "femme fatale" was a literal phrase.

We finished dinner and I offered to drive him back to where he was staying. When we reached his destination, he suddenly turned to me. "I am so sorry," he said. "I am so sorry I wasn't able to be there for you in London. I am so sorry for what you went through. Please forgive me."

I was stunned by his apology, realizing that Hoppe must have filled him in on my breakdown and the difficult year that had followed. "It's okay," I told him. "Thank you for your apology, but do not worry. My breakdown was not your fault. There were many other variables involved."

With a solemn hug we parted company. I watched as Tim trudged up the street to his lodgings. "What an odd, lovable man,"

I thought. Over dinner I had gotten a glimpse of the depth of his calling to make art. I hoped that he would one more time find peace and equanimity. I hoped that soon he would find himself happy again and writing music. His music, I remembered abruptly, had catalyzed my own. Little did I realize, it would again. A shy and highly strung man, never my lover or even a conventional friend, Tim remained for me a very powerful muse. He was for me a "fuselighter," firing me with creative possibility.

I fell asleep that night to the sound of the ocean. I woke the next morning to discover that one more time my world had changed utterly. Gone were the drudgelike days of working on my book. Just as in London, I woke with a head filled with music. This time I heard a beautiful soprano voice and the lament of a sailor's wife, keening for her long-absent mate.

The first birds of spring have come home to the shore.
The winds off Africa are laden with flowers.
The birds on the wing sing their songs of the showers.
Seasons change. Tides rearrange. Are you returning?

By my bedside I had a book about Magellan, picked up on a whim at a travel bookshop. "Oh my God," I thought to myself suddenly, "it's Magellan's wife I am hearing!" The woman's voice sang on as I grabbed for a notebook to take the song down. I was only two blocks away from a shopping mall, and so I raced out with cash in hand to buy myself a small tape recorder and keyboard. This time, I thought to myself, I do know what to do. I will not have a breakdown. I will keep eating and sleeping. I will capture the music rather than let the music capture me.

But the music did capture me. It came in great rolling waves. I heard the ocean singing and Magellan singing. I heard sailors at their tasks. I heard the creak and groan of the ship's rigging. Music woke me every morning. Music sang me to sleep. My lingering depression lifted as I began singing out the songs I was hearing. I tried to remind myself to stay grounded, but there was no denying the tide of music that swept me along with it. If *Avalon* was lovely, *Magellan* was tragic and majestic. The soprano arias soared. I found my own voice stretching to encompass them. I was thrilled by the high, pure notes that I could hit. I was flattered when Maria, one of the maids, asked me if she could have a tape of the songs she heard me singing.

Determined not to repeat London, I tried to keep myself and the music in a routine. I still met daily with my sober alcoholic friends. I wrote. I walked. I visited with friends, but the music was inexorable. Whenever I was alone, the music pumped through me. Once, when I went out to eat, a song interrupted my meal. I sang it into a tape recorder. I wrote it out as alphabetic code. Magellan and his story, the story of his abandoned wife, began to claim the forefront of my consciousness. Nothing else seemed as vivid or as compelling. Just as I had in London, I raced to take it all down.

One of my friends—I have never been able to determine just who—must have begun to worry about me. I was having another breakdown, they feared. So they called Mark. Once more Mark came rushing to my side. This time he came to my hotel. He knocked on my door and announced sternly, "Julia. It's me, Mark. You must let me in."

I opened the door to him and another man, a sober alcoholic Mark thought I might listen to with respect. They stood in the living room, arms sternly folded across their chests. What they had in mind was an intervention and perhaps another trip to the hospital.

"I hear you are writing music again," Mark began.

"I am."

"Are you eating? Are you sleeping?"

"I am."

"We don't want a repeat of London."

"Oh, Mark, I am fine. The songs are beautiful. It's not a breakdown. It's just music. Listen." With that, I grabbed Mark and his colleague by the hands. I seated them on the long couch that looked out the window to the vast Pacific. They weren't expecting this, and they sat uncomfortably, keyed up and ready for any form of erratic behavior.

"Just listen," I begged them, and I began to sing. I sang the song of Magellan's wife yearning for her husband long at sea. Next I sang a song of the sailors. Next a song of Magellan himself.

Despite themselves, the men began to relax. The music was beautiful, and it had its way with them.

"I am all right," I reassured Mark. "I don't want to be locked up. I don't want more medicine. It's just music. I am very lucky that it came to me again."

"I just want you to be safe," Mark insisted.

"I am safe," I told him, the same thing that I was telling myself.

"Well, if you are certain." And with that Mark and his compatriot left. I felt I had had a very close call with hospitalization. Panicked, I called Dr. Jones, who assured me that I was stable, more stable than I realized. He added that he was able to practice in California and that he would not allow me to be hospitalized as I feared.

Hotel life was expensive, and I began to think that I needed a real Los Angeles apartment. I contracted for a small, charming cliffside house that stared out over the Pacific. Contractors were at work on the house and thought they would be finished "soon," but a contractor's "soon" is never soon enough, and costly months passed as work on the house went uncompleted. I began to feel I was running through my money.

"I have a loft you could rent," a woman I knew offered. "There is just one thing. Margaux Hemingway died in it."

I went to look at the loft, thinking that a death by overdose was something I had narrowly escaped in my twenties and something it didn't hurt me to be reminded of. The loft was a large, sunny room that looked due west through the palm fronds to the blue Pacific. The part of me that was writing *Magellan* craved the sea, and so I took it. I found that the space felt oddly peaceful. I wondered sometimes, as I lay down to sleep, what thoughts had eddied through Hemingway's consciousness. The loft seemed a lovely place to live, filled with light and air. It seemed like an incongruous place to die.

Death, meanwhile, was coming for my beloved father. He had moved off his sailboat to live again in Libertyville, Illinois, near my older sister Connie. He had at first been situated in an old people's home, but he found himself claustrophobic and malcontent and instead rented himself a small cabin on an isolated lagoon. The drive to the cabin passed along waterways. Everyone in the family worried that Dad and his little dog would go plunging into the waters, but Dad was determined to live out his days amid beauty, and the cabin was surrounded by birds and other wildlife. I flew in repeatedly to visit with him. I found I loved his little cabin and its wild surroundings. He set up a cot not far from where he slept. In the mornings we watched the birds together. He kept his little dog carefully tethered lest he go too near the waters.

My father had suffered multiple breakdowns and he was concerned about me, not wanting me to go through the hell he had re-peatedly experienced. He had been diagnosed manic-depressive, and his medicines had been at first Lithium and then a new drug called Depakote—which I took while misdiagnosed. The drugs my father took rendered him carefully sane, a little gentler and more spacey than his true nature. He was content to spend his long, waning days reading Dick Francis mysteries and watching the birds. He had a love for all birds but particularly cardinals and scarlet tanagers. We would watch for them from his deck.

Visiting my father, which I did often, I tried to reassure him that I was okay. He was saddened by my divorce from Mark but felt that it was really for the best. Our value systems had differed, he felt. He approved of my writing and was proud of my books. He was pleased that I had a royalty flow and that I was being of-fered more substantial advances. He wished me as long and as fruitful a career as his had been. I found myself confiding in him my concerns and my reservations about the ever more public path I seemed to be on. I was increasingly in demand as a teacher. I felt conflicted about this, always worrying that it would take too much time and energy away from my life as an artist. My father assured me that with careful focus I could have it all.

I did not want my father to know how unsettled I really felt. I had uprooted myself from Taos to Los Angeles, where I felt more secure in my sobriety. Every morning in Los Angeles, I would walk to the small, dingy coffee shop where sober alcoholics gathered to begin their day. I would drink a cappuccino, or perhaps two, and I would listen to the trials and travails that others were suffering through. After all, I told myself, wasn't I really lucky? I just needed to stay sober. I just needed to keep writing, slowly and steadily. I just needed to keep teaching.

Throughout this time there was teaching work enough for both me and Mark to be out on what I came to call the circuit. We were sought after by human-potential centers such as Esalen and Omega. There was a steady call to teach at Unity churches. There were secular gigs as well, for places as diverse as the Smithsonian and *The New York Times*. I was repeatedly invited to appear on *Oprah*. I did so despite my fragility. My star was on the rise.

With the help of Bill LaVallee, I finished my manuscript for *The Vein of Gold*. As I had foreseen, the book was divided into creative kingdoms. Immersed in it, the reader passed from realm to realm, ever deepening his creative experience. At book's end, there was a careful and extensive bibliography, a discography, a filmography, and a "pop"ography. I was excited about the book and began teaching its tools well in advance of its publication date. With the book finished, I found myself restless in Los Angeles, yearning one more time for the mountains and sagebrush of Taos. I headed "home."

Back in Taos, I discovered a discontent John Newland. If Newland was frustrated by Martin's stance on Domenica, he was equally frustrated to find himself in Taos with time on his hands. Restless by temperament, a born worker, he had busied himself with directing his college acting class and some community theater productions, all to great success. But Taos was a small pond for such a big, old fish. Newland missed the limelight of Los Angeles. In Taos I was as close to a Hollywood person as he could get.

"What about your own work?" Newland abruptly wanted to know. "I'd like to see some of your plays. I've heard you're good."

"I can give you some of my plays, but what I am focused on right now is something called *Avalon*. It's a musical. Do you do musicals?"

"I began in vaudeville. I'd like to look at your musical."

"I wrote it in England."

"I've worked a lot in England."

"What I'd really like is an English production."

"Well, let's start by having me read. Get me your plays."

And so I went home to round up some plays for Newland's scrutiny. Almost as I had with Martin, I felt a heightened sense of anticipation and excitement. Directors carry a charge of personal magnetism, and Newland was no exception. I was eager to work with him, hoping that something from my body of work would catch fire. For openers I gave him my first play, *Public Lives*. He read it immediately and said he liked it. He added that his wife, Areta, had liked it, too, and that she was a real litmus test. Next I passed him two more plays, *The Animal in the Trees* and *Four Roses*. Again he liked them both. He wanted to put them up immediately. I was thrilled—but I wanted him to see *Avalon*, a much more ambitious work. We sat together on my porch, looking out at Taos Mountain. "What are we doing here?" Newland asked me as he often asked himself.

"We should have met sooner," he griped. We had lived a half-mile apart on Hollywood Boulevard twenty years earlier. I had walked past his Nichols Canyon home nearly every day. "We could have done so much together—but we'll see what we can do now. Show me *Avalon*." I gave Newland *Avalon* to read.

In the interim, I had teaching to do and the winter had not yet spent itself. It was on a snowy and hazardous night that Mark and I flew together into Denver. We were slated to teach a workshop in Colorado Springs, normally a twenty-minute drive from the airport. We drove a rented four-wheel-drive vehicle through a foot-plus of snow. It took us hours to travel the twenty miles.

"Who will come out in this to see us?" we ruefully asked each other. "Where was it written that we should risk our lives to teach?"

The day of the workshop dawned with snow still driving hard. Eighteen inches had accumulated and more was still on the way. Even in Colorado, they were officially calling the storm a blizzard. Blizzard or not, the workshop was scheduled to go on. More than a hundred people trekked through the snow to attend.

What I remember about that workshop was a frisson of tension between Mark and myself. We had been teaching separately for a while, and when we came back together, sparks flew. Our banter had more of an edge to it than usual. We differed in our pacing. We had trouble laughing at each other's jokes. It did not help Mark that there was a bald, genial, and charismatic man sitting in the front row. He beamed approval whenever I took over the microphone. He asked excellent questions and threw himself enthusiastically into the group activities we devised. Who was he? I wondered.

After the workshop finished, I watched the bald man don a bright red beret and make his way out of the venue. Outside the plate glass windows, I saw him stop, turn on his heel, and retrace his steps. Now he approached me.

"I am James Nave," he announced. "What are you doing for dinner?"

I didn't know at first if this was a romantic advance or a professional one. Mark bristled at the thought of either one. I told Nave that there was already a dinner planned, but that he was welcome to join us. He did join us, and all through a long sushi dinner he plied me with questions. I fired a few of my own back and learned that he was the cofounder of something called Poetry Alive, which took teams of poets across the country, performing live in grammar schools and high schools. In this pursuit, Nave himself drove 150,000 miles a year. In the decade that the enterprise had been under way, many teams had crisscrossed the country; more than a million students had been reached.

"So you're a teacher too," I told Nave. I did not tell him that since Mark and I were now divorced, I was looking for a male teaching partner, preferably someone both charismatic and experienced. He fit the bill.

"Come to Asheville sometime and see me teach," Nave invited. "I will take you for a ride in my convertible and you can see the mountains in spring."

After Nave left, Mark had a few pointed questions for me. Just who was that man, he wanted to know. "A teacher and a poet," I told him. I explained about Poetry Alive, and despite himself Mark was impressed.

Back in Taos, I received a note from Nave in the mail. One more time he asked me to come watch him teach. He didn't know it, but he was auditioning. I phoned him in Asheville and arranged to fly in for a visit. In Asheville it was already spring. I landed in a fairyland of dogwood and blossoming fruit trees. As promised, Nave drove a sporty little convertible. A few charming stories and it didn't take long to determine that he was a potential lady-killer. Maybe teaching is part seduction, I found myself thinking. We quickly clarified that our intentions were strictly business.

"I am teaching about three hours from here," Nave told me. To him, driving long distances was no issue. And so we set out on curving mountain roads for a school in rural North Carolina. Once there, I watched with interest as Nave mesmerized his young audience. He was a born storyteller and soon had the youngsters' rapt attention. He was particularly good dealing with tricky teens. Watching him work, I thought, yes, I would like to try teaching with him. Finding such a colleague was a cause for celebration, but my joy was cut short by an emergency phone call. My father was visibly weakening. I needed to go home.

As his health deteriorated, my father had moved from his little house on the lagoon to share my sister Connie's farm with her. The farm had a duck pond, and one more time my father gravitated toward the water. Although he knew he was terminally ill, he set out to build himself a small house on my sister's pond. Setting an example of resilient creativity, my sister and father worked all fall and winter to design it. The house would have a modest foundation and large windows. It would overlook his beloved birds and bear a striking resemblance to a large sailboat. Despite delays from the architect, the house was now nearly ready to move into. It had been for my father a grand project, a glorious act of creative defiance. The lovely little house would live on after he was gone. When I pulled into the driveway at my sister's, the first thing I saw was the upward thrust of my father's roofline.

"I thought you might be showing up right about now," my father greeted me. He was propped up in a tall chair in my sister's kitchen. Normally a small man, he was now also visibly frail. His cancer had taken his appetite but not his humor, his body but not his mind. Still, he looked too fragile to live much longer. I decided to call Domenica to Connie's farm, and she arrived the next day, by which point my father had retired to bed.

"Hello, Domenica," he greeted her, then lapsed back amid his pillows. Although he seemed lucid and in good spirits, we knew he was in considerable pain. The doctors had prescribed something called Brompton's cocktail, a mixture of morphine and cocaine.

This concoction kept him alert and focused while it eased the pain of his disease. Just outside his bedside window, a lilac bush was budding.

Very soon after Domenica's arrival, my father slipped from ordinary consciousness. He was drifting in and out now, with one foot on each shore, the living and the dying. My sister Connie hovered protectively. She told me that the day before I arrived, they had carried my father the short distance to his little house. They had taken him inside, but he was too weak and in pain to really savor his accomplishment. I found the story heartbreaking.

"C'mon, Domenica," I said. "Let's go for a run in the forest preserve." Donning runner's garb, we entered the woods just across the road from my sister's farm. The running trail looped for several miles, past ponds and marshes. The woods were filled with bird-calls and the first flowering bushes. We ran for perhaps a mile, when suddenly a scarlet tanager darted out in front of us. It was one of my father's favorite birds, and I took it to be a sign.

"Let's get back now," I told Domenica.

We arrived at the house to discover my father quietly dying. My sister lifted his little black Scottie onto the bed. My father was too weak to greet him, but Blue gave a final lick to his master's hand. Next my sister, Domenica, and I took up places by my father's bedside. The room was filled with a quiet, even afternoon light. Time seemed to slow and then to vanish. My father drew a few wispy, shallow breaths and then he simply breathed no more. Peacefully and gracefully, he was gone.

My father, like my mother before him, donated his body to science. There would be no wake, no funeral service. His body was taken away, and that was that. There would be no official closure, no ceremony to send him on his way. I was scheduled to do a

Canadian teaching tour starting the day after his death, and so I simply went. In Toronto a woman approached me after I spoke. "I just want you to know your father is fine," she told me. "I see lots of angels surrounding him. He is at peace."

My own peace was more elusive. Back in Taos after the teaching tour, I went for long daily walks with my dogs. We would cross a small creek bed where, regular as clockwork, I would keenly miss my father. I took to singing a very plain and sad little song. Its only words were "I miss my dad. I miss my dad. I miss my dad. I miss my dad."

Walking through the sagebrush, gazing up at the cloud-wreathed summit of Taos Mountain, I would pray for my father, although I, too, had the sense that he was "fine." What was not fine was life without him. For years I had written him several letters a week. When it was possible, I faxed him daily. These regular missives were just about life as it was unfolding. My father was both my confidant and my adviser. His gentle yet rueful wisdom had walked me through my divorce and my first year alone. I treasured his infrequent notes to me. "Just a thought," he would scrawl in his distinctive hand.

I missed my father's humor and I missed his hardheaded guidance. A few words from him could often straighten me right out. With him gone and Mark gone, I found myself missing male counsel and company. I saw Dr. Jones once a week and often spoke to him about my quest for a grounded male teaching partner, my belief that a male-female teaching team was actually the healthiest way for my material to be taught.

Left to my own devices, I could appear to be what Mark called "airy-fairy" or "woo-woo." There was the keynote address I gave at the A.B.A. NAPRA convention, sharing a platform with Carolyn Myss, who was very serious and lectured upon "lessons." I arrived, roller skates in hand, to sing to the audience and urge them to remember the "play" in the "play of ideas."

In my vintage-style suit with my Rita Hayworth hair, I quickly encountered Myss's disapproval. Looking me up and down, she hissed with exasperation, "Why can't you dress like the rest of us?" I had no answer for her. I couldn't really defend my apparel. Compared to her short-cropped hair and dress-for-success business suit, it was too Hollywood, too Lucy-in-search-of-Desi. Mark would have had me in crisp navy blue, dressed appropriately for the spotlight. A reluctant public figure, I dressed like a girl rather than like an authority figure.

Furthermore, I felt high-strung in the limelight. From my years with Martin, I knew too well the costs of fame and career velocity. As the sales of my books continued to mount, I was increasingly asked—and expected—to both teach and speak. Jetting around the country was disorienting to me. Out on the road, I longed to be home in Taos. Couldn't I make the road somehow more appealing? More a part of my own artist's life? I prayed for guidance. Once back in Taos, I got it.

Walking daily through the sagebrush, I found myself thinking again about Tim Wheater and how effortlessly we had taught together. If only I could get him to come back to America! The thought became an obsession. Couldn't two do far better what I was trying to do alone? I believed so. I remembered my Chicago teaching days with Mark. Didn't a male-female teaching team really serve students best? I thought it did. Once Nave finished up his current commitments and became more familiar with *The*

Artist's Way, I could perhaps begin to teach with him, but in the meantime Tim was already a compatible teaching partner. I was determined to convince Tim to work with me.

While in Los Angeles, I had met a man named Richard Cole. Tall, thin, silver-haired, and suntanned, Richard exuded cool mystery. This was a man with a past. Sure enough, he had been the road manager of Led Zeppelin at the height of their fame and fortune— British country houses, exotic cars, and private jets—and he was expert at dealing with musicians' problems and egos. Thinking about Tim, I found myself thinking about Richard Cole. Perhaps he could help me enlist Tim? I called Cole and asked him if he would fly with me to London. I explained that my aim was to get Tim Wheater to commit to some U.S. touring with me. Although it was certainly small potatoes compared to Led Zeppelin, to my delight Cole was game. I did not think he was a man to be argued with.

Meeting at LAX, we flew from Los Angeles to London. In London I settled into a small tony hotel where I asked Tim to meet me. He entered my suite warily. This was a man who'd had recent, bitter experience with a conniving woman.

"I want you to come to America," I told him. "I want to tour my book *The Vein of Gold* and I would like you to come with me and demonstrate toning. We could sell my books and your albums. It would be good American exposure." Despite himself, Tim was interested. "This is strictly a business proposal," I added. "Richard Cole will be booking our tour." Cole was my rabbit's foot, and I thought Tim seemed intrigued at the mention of his name.

"We would do combination book signings and concerts," I laid out my idea. "We would teach workshops as we traveled." Surely the publicity would be good for his work?

"Let me think about it," Tim countered.

I repeated that I was now working with Richard Cole—yes, "the" Richard Cole—who would be booking our tour for us. Despite himself, Tim seemed impressed. He knew of Richard Cole from his own days with the Eurythmics.

"I'll need to know soon," I pressed. Putnam, my publisher, was interested in the idea of a mixed-media tour, but they needed to know that it would pay for itself and not be some expensive, ego-serving debacle. I needed Tim's commitment so that Richard Cole and I could plan our itinerary, booking teaching engagements to match our book signings.

"I am staying in London a few more days," I finally offered. "Can you let me know before I leave?"

I spent an uncomfortable few days twiddling my thumbs and hoping. Hours before I was to leave for the airport, Tim's call finally came. It was short, to the point, and good news.

"Count me in," Tim said.

8.

I plotted out an intricate itinerary that began with a swank book party in New York and looped from there up through Connecticut and then across the country, hitting some ten cities in twenty days. It would be a real whirlwind.

Living in Taos, with the rest of the world at one remove, it was easy to plan bold adventures. My daily life, waiting for the tour to launch, was really quite tame. I seemed to live either at my writing desk working or on the phone trying to console my daughter Domenica, who was now in Dublin for her junior year abroad and finding it tough going.

"It's so drunk here, Mommy," she complained.

"I'll come see you soon," I promised her. "Just as soon as my book tour is over."

With Tim slated to accompany me, the book tour loomed ahead as a great adventure instead of a grueling chore. Daily, I put myself to the page, took my unwilling self out on a longish walk, and then hurried back to the phone one more time to say, "Hang in there, Domenica. It will get better. You will make some friends. You'll see."

"But, Mommy, they all drink here!" Domenica complained, knowing exactly what would worry me the most. "It's an alcoholic culture," she continued. "Every date ends up at the pub."

"I promise. I'll come see you soon."

My phone calls with Domenica left me drained and heartbroken for her. Martin generously paid for our transatlantic contact. Meanwhile, my book tour was launching. Tim had confirmed that he would report for duty at the book party and then be mine for the duration of the tour. I arrived at the party to find him already there, impeccably clad in black Armani, and ready to entertain our guests. Michael Hoppe was slated to perform with him. I made a few remarks and then turned the stage over to Tim and Michael. They played a half-hour set, wowing the crowd, which was not used to live entertainment at a book party.

Early the next day Tim and I set out by hired car to Connecticut. We were teaching for the nuns at Wisdom House Retreat Center in Litchfield. The good sisters had gathered a crowd of stalwart New Englanders. Their dour countenances made teaching a test, and then, out of the blue, one of the students, a pudgy fifty-plus woman, leapt forward and threw my skirt up over my head. Nothing in my teaching experience up to that point had prepared me for such an occasion. I tried to make the best of it.

"If you really can't hear me teach without looking at my legs, I might as well show them to you," I announced, and having said so, I unzipped my skirt, folded it, and placed it on a chair. Now I was teaching in fishnet stockings and high heels. ("Mommy, you have legs like Tina Turner," Domenica loyally announced when I told her about the incident.)

To his credit, Tim appeared to take this event in stride. It was only when the class ended and he hissed to me, "Let's get out of here!" that I realized he had found the event as unnerving as I had.

Back into the rented limo and off to New York. Alone together, with a month of such time looming ahead of us, we made awkward conversation until I realized that I had with me a packet of poems. "Here!" I said. "Try reading these aloud to me. You have a beautiful voice!"

Tim launched into my poetry, and it was quickly apparent that my words and his voice were a perfect match. "I tell you what," he exclaimed excitedly. "Let's make an album together! Do you think you can write an album's worth of new material while we're out on tour?"

The answer to that question was yes, and I began to write like a woman on fire. The highly pressured book tour began to play second fiddle to our making some art. At every stop, whenever I had a moment to myself, I had pen to page. Tim and I would meet for meals and I would say, "Here! Try this!" and thrust a new poem across the table. We began trying out the poems at our book signings. The poems caught our audience by surprise and they loved them. When we reached tour's end, we were in Colorado. I knew an excellent studio high in the Rockies. We went there to record. On our first night of recording, we were visited by a mountain lion. We took it as a good-luck omen. Our album would be fierce.

In three days flat we laid down an entire album of poetry, *This Earth.* We took one day to record the thirty-odd poems and two more days for Tim to lay down an accompanying score. The resultant album was beautiful and passionate. It would go on to win an award, Best Original Score, from *Publishers Weekly.*

"You see," I had always told crowds when I taught, "I am actually the floor sample of my own tool kit." I now had the album to show for it. It wasn't difficult, sharing artist to artist. Touring with Tim, my artist self felt both seen and heard. We taught joyfully and effectively. It was a pleasure to share our work with audiences. Clearly, we were catalytic for each other. Both of us were filled with innovative ideas for the other's creative trajectory. Tim and I agreed to reconvene for more teaching after his winter's stay in Australia. I, meanwhile, had a daughter to visit in Ireland. I couldn't wait to see her.

When I stepped onto Irish soil, Domenica was there to greet me. We traveled by cab through the green countryside back to Dublin, where she showed me the romantic gates of Trinity College and then stopped at her own dormitory, a terrible concrete-block bunker. Far worse than I had imagined it, her room was a tiny cubicle with one window looking out over a pub. I began to see why alcohol dominated her impression of the city.

"Come on," I said. "Let's go shopping and see if we can't find some posters to spruce this place up." By day's end, we had transformed her little bunker with posters and wall hangings. She took me out to meet her tiny group of Dublin friends.

While I came to Dublin knowing little about the city, Dublin already knew about me. *The Artist's Way* had preceded me, and it seemed that everywhere we went, Domenica and I ran across grateful artists who had used my book to good effect. One such artist was a tall, black-haired young man named Fiuchna—"Raven" in Gaelic. He was a singer-songwriter with a hot band, the Hothouse Tulips, and he promptly proposed that we try our hand at writing tunes together. I was delighted by this adventure and found him easy and pleasant to work with. We hammered out half a dozen songs during my stay with Domenica, and she seemed very proud that her mother was so unexpectedly hip.

The hotel I was staying at was far north of Dublin, on the sea. Every day I took long walks along the sand, enjoying the dogs that gamboled there. "Please guide me," I prayed. Although it was exciting to teach with Tim, it was also unsettling. He was a peripatetic world traveler who thought nothing of jetting off to New Zealand for a few days' vacation. Our times together were intense, and then, when we were finished, he was gone, pffft! Incommunicado until we rendezvoused again. Tim was my friend but not my boyfriend. If anything, we were mutual muses in love with each other's art. Because I traveled so much to teach, my personal life was subsumed by my work and this left me with a quiet ache of longing. I began to yearn for a sense of roots and some more steady companionship.

Returning to Taos, I faced down a debilitating bout of loneliness. I had the sagebrush. I had the mountains. I had my work. None of it seemed to me to be enough.

I walked daily, always saying the same prayer, "Please guide me." I was probably hoping to be led to a happy love match. No such luck. What happened as a result of those prayers was a flowering in my work. At Tim's suggestion, I wrote two children's books, *Prayers for the Little Ones* and *Prayers for the Nature Spirits*. Next, talking to my publisher, Joel Fotinos, I told him of my yearning for a spiritual mentor, how much I missed my father and his wise advice.

"Have you tried reading Ernest Holmes?" Joel asked.

Holmes was a mentor indeed. Composer Billy May had given me Holmes to read when I was newly sober. I had been reading him ever since.

"Yes," I told Joel. "I love his book *Creative Ideas* and I read it all the time."

"Well, then you know the power of affirmative prayer. Why don't you try writing a prayer book of your own?" Joel's thought seemed bold, even a little heretical. True, I prayed a lot personally, but could I write prayers for others? Wasn't I too secular and sinful for that? I was a lapsed Catholic and twice divorced. I longed for wisdom, far from feeling I embodied it.

"Me? I hardly think of myself as saintly enough to write prayers."

"Why not you?" This time the question was a publishing directive. Joel wanted me to try my hand at a book of prayers. He was adamant. "Just a little book of prayers," he coaxed.

And so I now turned my hand to prayers. To my surprise, the prayers seemed second nature to me. I wrote them quickly and easily. I would sit at my typewriter in Domenica's lilac-hued room and look east to the Sangre de Cristo Mountains and the rising sun. Weren't you supposed to pray facing east? I did.

When I read some of the prayers over the phone to Joel, he chuckled with satisfied delight, "Good prayers!"

"You think so?"

"I think so."

"Oh, good!"

I realized next that I could record the prayers with Tim. They would be beautiful set to music and soon we did exactly that. In rapid succession, three small prayer books flew from my pen, *Heart Steps*, *Blessings*, and *Transitions*. We recorded audiobooks with original scores to accompany them all. This work was deeply satisfying to me. As baffled as I felt about my personal life, I felt professionally blessed.

Throughout this year, Tim commuted to America to work with me and Michael Hoppe, while I commuted to Ireland to visit Domenica and to study music. Just outside of Dublin, I had found a composer who volunteered to give me a crash course in harmony. In retrospect, the course was an expensive folly. Harmony cannot be successfully crammed—or at least not by me. I spent thousands of dollars learning what a children's music course could have taught me in a few inexpensive months. What I learned chiefly was that I was a sitting duck for opportunists, particularly musical ones. With *The Artist's Way* sales steadily mounting, I had a cash flow that I didn't know how to handle wisely. I was impulsive, too daredevil for my own financial good. With my father alive, I made fewer mistakes. With my father gone, I promptly undertook an ill-considered adventure.

Taos is a town that attracts travelers from far and wide. It is a known destination for spiritual seekers, and so it should have come as no surprise to me that it attracted travelers from Glastonbury, England, most notably a woman who claimed to be a high priestess. She towered six feet tall and dressed in flowing robes. She certainly looked like a high priestess.

"I wrote a musical about Avalon," I told her.

"You must let me see it. We could put it up in Glastonbury. I would love to help you. I could work with you just as soon as I go back."

A high priestess to help us! (She was nothing if not persuasive.) Avalon in Glastonbury! This was an enticing, albeit wildly impractical, idea. Where would we live? How would we gather the necessary cast and crew? The priestess said she could provide lodging for both me and Newland, as well as introduce us to an excellent musical director who she was sure would be thrilled to work on our material.

"I like it," Newland got back to me about *Avalon.*

"I like it," echoed the high priestess.

"How would you like to go to England to put it up?" I asked Newland.

"I'd love to go to England. When do we leave?"

"Spring."

"Spring in England! I haven't done it in years. Let's go."

And so it was decided that Newland and I would travel to England to put up a workshop production of *Avalon* in Glastonbury. From the very outset, this expedition was fraught with signs that there were better ways to spend our time and money.

Flying into Gatwick, we were met by an amiable and slightly stoned young man, who drove us through meandering back roads for the better part of a day. We arrived in Glastonbury just as the sun was setting. It glinted off the many crystals that hung in shopwindows. Glastonbury was a New Age center, and like Taos featured lots of crystals, candles, and incense, many forms of alternative healing and very little of anything else. Newland was to stay in the town's single creditable hotel while I was to have a room in a commodious house.

I arrived at the house to find the refrigerator squarely off-limits. The household was vegan and no meats or dairy of any kind would be tolerated. This did not bode well. My luxurious room turned out to be large enough, but directly above the room was one that belonged to a young monk who rose every morning at five to chant and meditate. Since I am a light sleeper, this meant I would be rising at five as well. Added to this strict "spiritual" atmosphere was an omnipresent pitcher of what I later learned was "hashish wine"—a staple among the inhabitants. After many years clean and sober, it was a shock to live among people who were at best hazy and at worst seriously stoned.

Across town, lanky six-foot-four Newland was trying to fit his frame into a room the size of a generous closet. The bed was big enough for most of him, if he didn't mind sleeping with his feet in midair. The room's single window opened to a view of a carport. For the first week we were in town, Newland didn't breathe a word to me about his accommodations. He was determined to rough it. As he put it, he had "seen worse."

Back home in Taos, we were accustomed to a certain mañana attitude, but it never extended to Newland's work. There, in the theater, he was the boss and his cast and crew gave him the courtesy of punctuality. Not so in Glastonbury. We would schedule a meeting, only to be left waiting for hours until our patience was gone. We soon realized that we were on "Glastonbury time" and that the normal clock did not apply. Nor did the normal standards for casting. *Avalon* required a small, bright cast. We kept auditioning stoners. Finally, there was one too many a whiff of marijuana for Newland to tolerate any longer. He was no priss—he had taken part in early LSD experiments—but he didn't feel drugs had a place onstage.

"Let's leave," he proposed simply as we sat cooling our heels, waiting for another scheduled audition. We had been in town all of two weeks.

"You mean leave leave?" I asked. It was one of the better ideas I had ever heard.

"Yes. Let's get out of here. The show will never be any good. We might as well cut our losses."

"I am with you."

And just like that we decided to head back to America. The high priestess was saddened but not surprised to see us go.

"It's the hashish wine, isn't it?" she asked.

"Something like that," Newland replied.

One more time we drove through the meandering back roads to

for a Peeping Tom and, they added, that was what we were probably dealing with. There had been similar complaints from the pretty young woman who lived just across the field from us. We should stay away from the windows, the police warned—but there was no way to stay away from the windows in a house like ours.

"Come sleep by me," I told Domenica when the police finally left. We called together our dogs and retreated to my bedroom. My bed was more than large enough for two. The dogs slept nestled at our feet. They did not bark again until morning.

In the morning I set out to discover what I could. What I found out was frightening. There was a prowler on the loose. Young women Domenica's age were targeted. There had been a veritable siege of complaints, and instead of being discouraged by all the uproar, the prowler seemed to be getting bolder. The young girl who was our neighbor had come home to find that her house had been broken into and her underwear drawer pawed through.

Many people in Taos keep guns. My friend Crawford Tall kept a small arsenal. I had no gun and didn't want one. It was enough, I thought, to have the dogs. Perhaps what we needed was another dog, a real watchdog, not a pet. Driving into town, I spotted a sign advertising rottweilers for sale. As luck would have it, there was one young female left. She was very beautiful, sleek, and sinister. I took to her immediately, paid a fairly exorbitant price for her, and loaded her in the car to take home to Domenica. It was a loving but misguided gesture. The puppy was far from a trained watchdog.

"She's such a lady!" Domenica exclaimed as the young dog froze in the presence of our other, older dogs.

"That's it, then. We'll call her Lady," I responded.

And so, Lady was added to our already large menagerie. By day

Gatwick. This time we checked into the Hilton there, willing to pay exorbitant prices to acquire two American-size rooms with a view of the hotel's parking lot. Settled into our rooms, we met for lunch in the downstairs café and discovered, to our amusement, that the specialty of the house was southwestern fare. Over guacamole and quesadillas, Newland startled me by proposing, "What the hell. I say we put the show up in Taos."

"In Taos?" I was at first resistant. What a letdown after the romantic idea of Glastonbury.

"Yes. We'll rent the community auditorium and run for a few weeks. It will give you a good idea of what you've got. What do you say? Are you in?"

My mind ticked over the variables. No producers would have seen the show in Glastonbury and no producers would probably see the show in Taos. Still, we would see it and that was a start. A Taos production would be like a good workshop. With Newland at the helm, the show could shake out its kinks. It wasn't a giant step forward, but it was a step, and a step was better than nothing.

"I am in," I told Newland.

Settled into my seat, jetting back to America, I could practically hear my father scolding me through the ether. "That was a quick way to blow fifteen thousand dollars." I resolved to be better about money, better in general. Still smarting over the folly of the trip to Glastonbury, I nonetheless was beginning to be excited about this new prospect. If we put the show up in Taos, I might just be able to get Domenica to play the young priestess, a role I had crafted with her in mind.

"I think you should let me offer her the role," Newland correctly proposed. "I am the director and it's important that the offer come from me and not from Mommy." And so, upon our arrival in Taos, he phoned Domenica and asked her if she would have any interest in doing a musical during her summer break.

"I'll get back to you on that," Domenica coolly told him. I was proud of her professionalism but worried that she wouldn't take the role.

Meanwhile, Newland set about lining up the auditorium rental and finding a set designer, costume designer, and musical director. We hadn't been home a week before he had the crew assembled and announced that he was ready to hold auditions. We needed an older priestess and an older wizard. There was a young actor who Newland felt was perfect for the young wizard, although, like Domenica, he wanted time to consider the role. I began to get more nervous. Without a strong young wizard and a strong young priestess, I felt it was pointless to put up the show.

"They'll do it," Newland assured me. "They're just acting like actors do."

Sure enough, Domenica phoned Newland to say that her hat was in the ring. I made arrangements for her to work with a physical trainer, as the role of the young priestess required peekaboo costuming, a bare midriff, and a sleek physique.

Now that I was back from England, I resumed once a week driving to Santa Fe to meet with Dr. Jones. He was now convinced that I had been originally misdiagnosed in England and that I was not a manic-depressive after all. The diagnosis had been made largely based on my family history. After observing me over time, he was convinced that it was wrong. I had had no further manic episodes.

"I want you to just forget that diagnosis," he told me. "Pretend you never heard it. It has nothing to do with you or your psyche. I am taking you off Depakote. I'd like you to use a very low dose of Navane."

I was relieved to be moving to a lighter dosage of a less i[n]sive medication. I still had difficulty taking medicine at all. I [needed] to be constantly reminded that the medicine was not a slip, th[at I] wasn't taking it to get high. I needed to be repeatedly persuaded t[hat] the medicine in fact helped me. With the show going up, I want[ed] to think soberly. I wanted to see what I had and what I didn't. I w[as] excited but scared. Taos is a small town, but it is heavily laden with critics. Both Newland and I qualified as high-profile in our small town, and we did not know if we should expect to be treated kindly. For Domenica, too, working in front of the Taos community was a challenge. While she loved to sing, she didn't really think of herself as a singer, and the role required that she sing very well. Our music director, Bea McTighe, a persnickety perfectionist, put her on a program of rigorous coaching. In between her physical workouts and her vocal ones, Domenica was soon working harder than she had at Trinity.

Because I had co-opted her small bedroom as a writing room, I gave Domenica a large studio room at the back of the house. It featured plate-glass windows to assure good painting light, and it was through one of those large windows that one night she caught a prowler spying on her as she changed into her nightgown.

"Mom! Help!" Domenica screamed in a voice that was truly unhinged by terror. I raced from my end of the house to hers. The dogs set up a racket, lunging against the windows, barking excitedly. "There was somebody out there watching me, Mom!"

I squinted out into the night but the intruder was gone. Domenica described a man of medium height and weight wearing a hooded parka. She was shaking. We phoned the police and two young officers arrived quickly. Looking over our house with its large windows, they warned us that we—two attractive women—were sitting ducks

Domenica would go off to rehearsal with Newland and his cast of actors. Nerves atingle, even in broad daylight, I would settle in at the desk, writing a new book about writing, *The Right to Write*.

Once more, this book was a brainchild born of a conversation between Joel Fotinos and myself. Quieter and more self-contained than John, Martin, Mark, Tim, or Jeremy—the other muses I had encountered—Joel was proving to be as catalytic as any. Once again I found the book that he had proposed racing off my pen. I wrote long days while Domenica rehearsed. At night we huddled with our dogs, hypervigilant to any sound. Both of us were overworked and overtired. We had nerves about the opening and nerves, period.

The week that *Avalon* opened, *The Taos News* did an in-depth story on Newland and his cast. Domenica and Arron Shiver, as the young priestess and the young wizard, were pictured on the front page. It was rare for an original musical to play Taos; more often we saw revivals of tried-and-true vehicles like *Fiddler on the Roof* or *Jesus Christ Superstar*. The flyers for the show trumpeted, "World Premiere!" It was a modest premiere, but I was very edgy nonetheless.

Opening night I sat in the back of the theater feeling that the music was bumpy and erratic, rushed where it should be slow, slow where it should have hurried. I could not separate the music itself from the performance it was getting. Sometimes the songs soared. Other times they strained. Even with Newland's able direction, we were still working with amateurs, and the result was uneven. I sat in the back of the theater trying to take it all in. I alternated between bliss and despair—leaning more toward despair.

After the show I was called upon to take an author's bow. As I did so, I caught sight of a beautiful young woman with spiky platinum blond hair. She and a small cadre of others were applauding wildly. I didn't recognize her as being from Taos, and I wondered where she could have come from. When she introduced herself, I found out.

"I am Emma Lively," she told me. "I am studying at the Taos School of Music." She named the small and prestigious summer music school located in the Taos Ski Valley. She introduced me to her friends, violists and violinists all. Young classical musicians with a great, even overweening, respect for composers, they were filled with glowing compliments. I took in their words, but in my heart I was still feeling discouraged. The music had not sounded right to me. I had heard it full and perfect in my imagination. In performance it was flawed, and the flaws were what I focused on. Above all else, what I had heard very clearly was that *Avalon* needed new arrangements. Those Tommy Eyres had done for me were serviceable but nothing more. Where would I ever find an arranger? I wondered.

August came to Taos Valley, and with it the first hints of an early fall. High on the mountain slopes, aspen were turning gold. Chamisa bushes flared brightly across the valley floor. The glory of the days was equaled only by the terror of the nights. The prowler was becoming bolder. Mark heard of our difficulties and insisted we install an electronic alarm system. Even with the alarms in place, Domenica and I did not feel safe. Friends warned us that they had seen an unrecognized man in a hooded sweatshirt feeding tidbits to our dogs. One day I came home from town to discover that the lightbulbs had been unscrewed on all of our outdoor lighting. Domenica was terrified and I was not much better. Every night we slept in my bedroom with our pack of dogs gathered on the floor around the bed. Nearly every day we heard of some new sighting of the prowler. One of our neighbors found footprints in the mud below her bedroom window. No, we did not feel safe.

Domenica was slated to return to Wesleyan for her senior year. To my eye, she was returning underweight and shaky. I worried that she would have a relapse of mononucleosis. I worried, period, and Domenica conveyed my worries to her own doctor, who in turn referred me to a psychiatrist in Manhattan. Dr. Jones had newly retired and I missed him. Without his help, without another competent doctor, I felt isolated and scared in Taos. I spoke with the Manhattan doctor long distance.

"You cannot live the way you are living, holed up in one room of your house, terrified by every sound," the doctor told me. "You will never feel safe in that house again. I think you should sell it."

This was radical advice, but the Taos police showed no signs of catching the prowler. More and more reports of break-ins made the gossip circuit. If anything, the prowler—and now it was believed there were some copycats as well—was growing ever bolder. I spoke with a retired policeman, who told me he was worried by the prowler's escalation. He thought that his voyeurism was a mere prelude to actual sexual violence. "Would you like me to teach you how to shoot a gun?" he asked me. And then a woman reported that a knife-wielding stranger had broken into her house and that she had narrowly escaped with her life.

Enough!

I flew to Manhattan for some publishing meetings and, while I was there, I stayed at an old hotel I liked, the Hotel Olcott, where I had lived for a few days during the filming of *Taxi Driver*. Now as then, the Olcott was a mixture of hotel and apartment building. One day, officially on a whim, I asked to see the apartments they had available. There was a corner two-bedroom in my price range. It was bright, sunny, and safe. I rented it, telling myself it would be good for Domenica to have a pied-à-terre in Manhattan, since she would undoubtably be moving to the city after graduation and would need to have her feet underneath her then. I did not tell myself that I was moving back to New York. I thought of the rental as something to help my daughter—but my first night's sleep there told me that I was also helping myself.

My apartment in the Olcott was on the eleventh floor. It felt like a little bird's nest, looking out at the city. Despite the sirens and the racket of the city, I slept soundly. The doctor had been right that my nerves were overwrought in Taos. While I romantically thought of Taos as a retreat or a haven, it was actually more of a pressure cooker. I painted the New York apartment a sunny Taos yellow, nearly the color of chamisa. I bought myself some cozy Victorian furniture and began to write. I set up a desk in front of a large window and put in my hours there daily, just as I had in Taos.

I loved being close to Domenica and, just as I had hoped, she began coming to the city to visit me. Interested by writing as well as acting, she signed up for a playwriting course with Tina Howe of *Painting Churches* fame, and soon her excursions into Manhattan were a regular part of my life. She was directing short films at Wesleyan and she found the Manhattan movie scene to be both lively and friendly. To my eye, she seemed destined to live life as a hyphenate: writer-actor-director. The apple had not fallen far from the family tree.

If I felt that I had amputated my beloved Taos, I tried to make it up to myself by counting all of the blessings of being in New York. There were theater and movies and concerts and ballet and opera. There was the romance of Central Park. The glamour of the skyline. The excitement of Times Square. The charm of the Village. Why, I could buy fresh flowers at the corner Korean markets. In addition to tulips, roses, and daffodils—ordinary blooms—they had both orchids and pussy willows, two of my more exotic favorites. Yes, there was much to love about New York. And, too, there was my hunger to be near Domenica, to give her again the sense of safety and security that had eluded her last stay in Taos.

Starting with long weekends, she began to spend half of each week in Manhattan, drawn by the excitement and energy of the city. She would come in for a play or a movie or simply to visit with me or her father. I loved having her stay with me. I felt I was being a good mother again, helping her acclimatize to her future.

A writer's day is built on ritual. I would get up every morning and take myself to the page, longhand. Then I would go to my desk and put in a couple of hours at the typewriter before it was time for lunch. Lunch meant a trip downstairs and out into the world. I loved a café called the City Grill and I was fond of a coffee spot called Timothy's. Fueled by a rare hamburger and an iced cappuccino, I would head back upstairs to write, telling myself that I was making good progress and that progress should be proof against loneliness.

But every day at four, just like an attack of low blood sugar, loneliness would strike. What was I doing in Manhattan? Why wasn't I home in Taos? What kind of chicken was I to think of selling my house there? True, it was good to be sleeping and sleeping soundly, but wouldn't they catch the prowler sooner or later? Maybe I could just stay in Manhattan "until."

And so—until—I settled in to write. I was still writing *The Right to Write* and the city seemed to lend itself seductively to the venture. I wrote about shiny cafés. I wrote about U2 concerts. I wrote about anything and everything that crossed my path—and, meanwhile, I tried not to miss the seasons ticking past in New Mexico.

Missing a place creates a slow and constant ache. The body goes into mourning as if it had lost a lover. And to me Taos was like a lover—a romantic place, not a mere dot on the western map. It had captured my imagination, and if my love for it had already cost me my marriage to Mark, it seemed strange that I could now voluntarily part from it. "Just keep writing," I urged myself, battling homesickness and loneliness with my time at the page.

Longing for an anchor—and still trying to be one—I made the trip to Connecticut for Domenica's graduation. The speaker was Oprah Winfrey. She talked about the difficulty of being a public figure, always on the go. It didn't seem to have much to do with Domenica's graduation, but I ruefully identified. Rootless and restless, I was too much on the go. I missed my beloved connections. Gerard had made the trip up from Manhattan to watch Domenica receive her diploma. All day I searched for him in vain amid the throngs of parents. We never found each other, and the missed connection with him seemed to me to be hauntingly symbolic. If I was losing touch with Gerard, my life was going too fast for me. Nonetheless, I kissed Domenica congratulations and returned to New York.

Headed out for lunch one crisp and snappy day, I ran directly into Emma Lively, the young platinum blond I had met at the *Avalon* premiere. Despite the coolish weather, she was wearing shorts and a T-shirt and looked to my eye impossibly young and fit, more mountain climber than Manhattanite.

"How are you, Julia?" she wanted to know. "How is it going with your music? What has happened with *Avalon*?"

Emma did not know it, but she could not have contrived a more painful set of questions. I was miserable over the current fate of *Avalon*. I was miserable over music in general. Both *Avalon* and *Ma-*

gellan were packed away "until such time." And now did not seem to me to be the moment. When Emma inquired about my music, it was as if she were lightly tapping someplace where I was badly bruised.

"I am fine," I tried to shrug her off. "I am writing a lot. I have a new book I like that's taking my time and attention. I am not doing much music these days. . . ." My answer trailed off.

"That's too bad," Emma kept on relentlessly. "I really liked your music. It would be a shame if it just—" She broke off, afraid of being tactless. She could tell from my expression that I was dismayed by our conversation. Maybe, she thought, I just hated to have my anonymity shattered. After all, I had moved to New York, hadn't I?

Running into Emma and her sunny hellos and inquiries about my music began to be a daily occurrence. I ran into her at Timothy's getting coffee. I ran into her at the City Grill buying a burger. Walking in Central Park, enjoying the spring blooms, I ran into her again. Always, she asked me about my music. She was the voice of my creative conscience speaking.

"Where do you live?" I finally asked her. She gave an address on Seventy-third Street. I realized that her building was the one that lay just beneath my windows. If I dropped a flowerpot, it would land right on her roof. I began to look forward to crossing paths. Maybe it was good to know someone in New York, particularly someone so optimistic and so kindly inclined toward my art.

Clinging to the idea that I still really lived in Taos, I kept a Taos mailing address and employed a young woman named Erin Greenberg to run my office there. One afternoon when I made my ritual call back home, Erin said she thought I needed to face facts: I lived in New York and I needed to get a New York assistant and do business from New York, not New Mexico. "I love working for you," Erin said, "But I am thinking you should really phase me out."

With Erin's voice in my ear, I took a break from my writing and went downstairs to Timothy's for my usual iced cappuccino. It was there that I ran directly into Emma Lively. By then we greeted each other like old friends.

"How are you? How's the music?" Emma asked.

"Would you like to have lunch?" I countered.

"Sure. I would love to," Emma answered, and so we walked the twenty or so feet to the City Grill, where Steve, the manager, ushered us to a window table for two.

"What's your day job?" I asked next.

"I graduate in one week with my master's in viola performance. I actually need a day job," Emma answered.

"How would you like to work for me? I need a literary assistant and there are two musicals that I need help with."

"That sounds great."

As simply as that, it was settled that Emma would start working with me. At the time I thought I was hiring an assistant, not acquiring a new and significant collaborator. I do not remember asking her about the musicals, but she swears that I did, remembering that for her, wanting to work on the musicals was a large part of why she took the job.

From the start Emma seemed to be a good-luck charm. One afternoon the phone rang and it was Susan Schulman calling with good news. My Elliot Mayo novel that I had written five years before had at last been bought and was finally to be published! The press in question was small but excellent, Carroll and Graf. My proposed editor, Kent Carroll, phoned and I liked him immediately. Nonetheless, I was struck by a bad case of writerly whim-whams.

The Dark Room was nothing if not dark. It dealt with child molestation and grisly murders. It was not what my reading public might be expecting from me. While it made sense for someone who had once written for *Rolling Stone* and *Miami Vice*, those credits were long behind me. Would the book be accepted on its own merits? I wondered. Or would it fail because I had been typecast as a creativity guru? I was afraid to find out.

I well remembered the long days of writing in Taos and then Chicago. Although it hadn't occurred to me at the time, it was now clear to me that the book had been grounded in the sordid details of the world inhabited by my college friend Tray Mongue. Dying of AIDS, he had sent me a packet with a sketch of his sexual past. "Perhaps you can make something of this," he had written. "I have never been able to." The "this" Tray had been referring to was the underbelly of a sexual netherworld mired in pornography and S and M. It was a far cry from the spiritual principles of *The Artist's Way* or the hopeful world of my more recent prayer books. Still, I had been called to write it and now I was very glad that I would have a published novel to my credit, since I was also publishing a writing book and wanted to show that I could practice what I preached.

"This book is terrifying!" Emma was quick to report to me. One of her jobs as my assistant was to help me go over my galleys. "I read it and I was up all night! You're worse than Stephen King!"

Delighted by the compliment, I more willingly kept my nose to the writerly grindstone. My final draft of *The Right to Write* was due, and I was dealing with Jeremy Tarcher's many provocative questions. One more time, answering his queries, I nearly doubled the size of my book. One more time, I felt blessed by his catalytic intelligence. At his instigation, I wrote about Mood, Drama, Specificity, Loneliness, and Witness. I debunked many a writer's myth. I argued, persuasively I hoped, that we all had "the right to write." I certainly was exercising mine.

I have found that in writing, my appetite for writing increases. I have also found that for me writing is a potent painkiller, and in painful times I take even more often to the page. Missing Taos, trying to love New York, these were painful times. "Maybe Taos is an obsession for you like drinking," one friend tried to warn me. I wasn't ready to hear it.

Trying to put some levity into my life, I began working with my sister Libby on what would become a series of cartoon books. We did cartoons about creativity, cartoons about spirituality, cartoons about blocked creativity. It was a delight to work with my sister, who seemed boundlessly inventive. The more we worked on humor, the more we acquired some—and this came as a welcome relief. The loss of Taos haunted me.

Summer came to New York early that year. By mid-May we were enjoying sun-drenched days, and Emma and I often built a longish walk in Central Park into our workday. While it was not the same as walking through the sagebrush wilds, the beauty of the park still seemed to lubricate my writing gears. Emma and I would walk and talk or I would walk alone and pray.

I prayed my usual "Please guide me," but I missed what had always seemed to me to be the listening presence of Taos Mountain. "Please grant me the serenity to accept the things I cannot change, the courage to change the things I can, and the wisdom to know the difference," I prayed. The skyline did not seem to answer me like the mountain did, and yet, increasingly, it felt like the psychiatrist was right and I should put the Taos house up for sale. The thought sickened and saddened me. I pushed it aside. At the advice of my sober mentors, I was trying very hard to live one day at a time. I would know, they told me, when I was ready to sell. Meanwhile, I focused on each day's gentle routine. Every day I took my own emotional temperature. How was I doing? Was I close to another breakdown or safely normal? Normal, it seemed.

My apartment had two bedrooms, and one of them, painted a deep delphinium blue, was set aside for Tim Wheater, who was to stay with me while I helped him to write his musical memoirs. He arrived ready to work, and I soon found myself taking dictation as he unspooled his colorful life events onto the waiting page. His was an eventful life—and a difficult one. He'd had a fragile mother and, due to divorce, an absent father. During his early teens he had been responsible for putting bread on the table, making a life for himself and his mother by wheeling and dealing in antiques. He still had an eye for a bargain, and when we would take writing breaks, we often headed out to the local thrift shop, eyeing what was there to be had.

Working with Tim gave me a vicarious satisfaction, the same I had experienced working with Martin on *Taxi Driver* and *New York, New York* and working with Mark, first during our courtship on *The Light Rangers* and later on his book *The Prodigal Father.* My friends have sometimes told me that I am too generous with men, but I have always found a genuine joy in service to art that has nothing to do with the men. There is joy in being a believing mirror for someone else. I have served as such a presence on several of Sonia Choquette's books. The process always brings me joy.

I was pleased to work with Tim and I was doubly pleased at the way our pages were mounting up. The book was to be called *Sound-*

tracks, and the adventure of Wheater's musical explorations enthralled me. As a character and an artist, Tim himself enthralled me, and it was with some rue that I learned that, since our last time together, he had fallen deeply in love. The transatlantic phone lines burned daily with calls from the woman he had left behind. I began to feel guilty to have caused their separation. Our work was exciting and satisfying, but it was no substitute for true love. Writing long hours together daily, Tim and I began to feel claustrophobic. He was pleased and so was I when a neighboring apartment opened up and we both had our own space again. I found myself hungry to write and burning the candle at both ends so that I could do my own writing during the evenings, since Tim and I were spending our days on his.

In the midst of my collaboration with Tim, Mark phoned to say that he was ready to write a new book. "We can call it *The Artist's Way at Work*," he exclaimed, chomping at the bit, eager to get started. True to his dreams, he had taken a year and done graduate work at Harvard, receiving a master's degree. He had discovered a great deal there and was eager to share it with me and with our readers. He had already shared much of his knowledge with the viewers of *Oprah*, where he was a regular for two seasons, part of Oprah's team of experts to heal America. He had attracted her attention with his work on absentee fathers. Mark had a knack for knowing a great idea, and he was certain that *The Artist's Way at Work* would find a large and willing audience.

One more time my feminist friends expressed their alarm for me. What, they wanted to know, was I doing collaborating with an ex-husband? I told them what I told myself: we had always worked well together, and here was a worthy piece of work waiting to be done. Mark did not like waiting for me to finish up with Tim. He considered my work with him a detour. I disagreed.

If Martin had embodied moviemaking and my enchantment with film, Tim embodied musicality for me and my enchantment with music itself. Even if I wasn't writing my own music at the time, I spent happy hours writing my book while Tim practiced his flute in an adjoining room. To Mark, my musical explorations were a diversion, a sidebar to what he considered the real work. Couldn't I hurry up? he wondered. No, I could not.

Central Park in summer is a leafy emerald haven. Emma and I began taking in-line skating expeditions. Soon Tim, too, wanted to learn, and the three of us began making daily sorties, skating our way past the Belvedere Fountain and along the stretch known as Poet's Walk. We weren't fancy skaters, far from it, but we loved it. It was a good summer's adventure, compensating us for being in the city by at least getting us out of doors. Then, too, the work we were doing was intense, and we needed to blow off steam. Many of Tim's memories were volatile, and the work to excavate them was delicate. I felt as much like a midwife as a muse.

By August, Tim had used up his window of available time and needed to head back to England, where he had a full slate of festivals to play. I was scheduled to go to London to teach with him once, but after several years of intense collaborative work, it was becoming clear that we were heading in differing directions. Tim was heading into an extended domestic idyll with the woman he loved. For my part, I was starting to get itchy to head back into music myself.

9.

I t's time we go to work on *Avalon*," I told an unsuspecting
Emma one bright September day. We began by hauling out
the boxes into which the show had been haphazardly packed
after its Taos premiere. Opening the boxes to find the mess within,
I kicked out suddenly and viciously in my frustration, sending one
box flying across the room.

"I need all new arrangements!" I exclaimed in exasperation.
"The whole show has to be redone, top to bottom." I kicked another of the offending boxes, scooting it all the way across the
room. In my mind and heart, *Avalon* was so beautiful. In real life
Avalon was still botched. Emma was startled to see my temper and
the depth of my frustration. Suddenly I turned to her. "You
arrange it," I proclaimed.

"But I have no experience! I am a classical violist," Emma

protested. Her protests fell on deaf ears. I suddenly "knew" that she was my arranger.

"I have no sympathy for you," I told her. "I wrote all the melodies and I had no musical training. You have years of playing harmony to fall back on."

"But—" Emma was indignant. Just who did I think I was, some creativity expert, ordering her around?

"But nothing!" And with that I stormed out, swung shut the door, and locked it behind me. "Start!" I called back over my shoulder.

Locked alone in a room with a piano and a seemingly impossible task in front of her, Emma abruptly began to hear music. She thought of a melody line from *Avalon* and found herself flooded with harmony. Although she had never told me, writing music was a childhood dream of hers. The chance to arrange was a dream come true. No wonder she was seized with terror. Just as I had been, she was afraid that the music would go away. She grabbed for some paper and a pencil. Hurriedly, she began to sketch in the shape of what she was hearing. Outside the room I could hear her harmonies from beneath the door. I hugged myself in excitement. It sounded perfect to me. Over Emma's protests, our collaboration was born.

Summer turned to fall. The trees in Central Park blazed with color. Mark arrived, bringing with him an editor and a researcher. He moved into an apartment two floors beneath me. We began creating *The Artist's Way at Work*, passing chapters up and down the stairwells at the Olcott. For Mark it was a difficult birth. He had so many ideas, so much to say. He wanted to say all of it, and a book can hold only so much. I sat in my apartment, writing longhand, racing to keep up with him and his ideas. There was so much he wanted me to be excited about. He foresaw a whole new audience for *The Artist's Way.*

As always, it was haunting to be with Mark. There was so much right between us—and so much wrong. Mark enjoyed the intellectual sparks that flew between us, but I was not domesticated enough to suit him. I was too headstrong, too temperamental, too volatile—and I was all of those things as we hammered the book into shape. For my part, I was accustomed now to writing books on my own, working at my own pace, without much interference or input until Jeremy Tarcher stepped in with his guiding intelligence. We had no Jeremy Tarcher on this book, no overview memo to work from. The entirety of the book was in Mark's head, and his many ideas jostled and fought with one another as they came to the page. Add to this a bottled-up sexual attraction, and the recipe for tension was clear.

"Why is it," I asked him, "that you always have all the right material just in the wrong order?" I found that often all I needed to do for a cohesive rewrite was to number the paragraphs so that his ideas played out in a more orderly fashion.

"I am not the writer you are," Mark would answer. "I build a book more than write it."

"Now you tell me!"

Despite my protestations, despite the stress and the many heated confrontations, the book did get "built." Mark, on the whole, seemed to be pleased with it. For my part, I was pleased when Mark and his helpful entourage one more time vacated the Olcott and left me to myself. "Maybe I am turning into a spinster," I thought.

As fall turned the corner into winter, I found myself again

missing the wide western skies of Taos. Was this denial? Was Taos really a dangerous and unhappy obsession? Was craving Taos really like craving a drink? The prowler or prowlers still eluded capture, and I began to seriously consider that I should sell my house. I could always buy another one, I told myself. And a new house would not hold memories of Mark.

"Let go. Move on," I lectured myself. "Let go and let God," my sober mentors advised. I finally found the courage to put my house on the market. Mercifully, within days, I had a buyer who pleased me. I sold my house to friends of mine from Los Angeles. I knew they would take delight in it, and I was glad to think it had moved on to such happy owners.

"So now you live in New York!" Domenica crowed with delight.

"Maybe," I told her guardedly.

Still craving horses and "country," I took the money from the house and invested it in a small horse farm in rural Virginia. It was a good market to buy into, and I needed an escape from Manhattan. While they weren't Taos and the Sangre de Cristos, the Blue Ridge Mountains were beautiful.

"Dear Dad, please guide me," I would pray often. "Please help me to hold on to my money." Without my father to advise me, I was wary of my own judgment. I wanted to keep my money bound up in real estate, because then I couldn't spend it foolishly. Virginia was like a savings account for me. If it didn't capture my imagination, it at least kept my assets safely frozen.

My emotions were safely frozen as well—at least that is what I told myself. Focused on my writing, I was safely single and working in my prime. Excited by the simultaneous publication of *The Right to Write* and *The Dark Room*, I abruptly realized that I was living out my childhood dream. I was a writer, a New York writer. Riding in a limousine on my way to a *Dark Room* book signing, I thought, "This is probably as good as it gets." Enjoying the crowds at book signings, I basked to fine reviews—with the notable exception of one clunker in *The New York Times*, which disliked my "Jungian" detective Elliot Mayo.

The morning of the *Times* review I felt I should go outside on the Manhattan streets wearing sackcloth and ashes and a big sign: "Writer shamed." It was astounding to me how one negative review could emotionally outweigh twenty positive ones. Then I told myself that I had joined a distinguished club: those who had survived a bad *Times* review. As I often did, I reminded myself that pain was a part of the creative territory, that few artists escaped unscathed. I called to mind some difficult reviews Martin had suffered. If he could survive them, so could I, I told myself firmly. Still, wasn't there supposed to be more to life than "my brilliant career"?

Having asked that question, enter Peter.

We met through friends. Our affair began innocently enough with a dinner date. Peter liked sushi and so did I. Manhattan is crammed with sushi restaurants. We picked one in my neighborhood and settled down to get to know each other. Like me, Peter was a writer, although he specialized in advertising copywriting and comedy. His droll humor was irresistible—at least to me. Filled with wry, self-deprecating stories, Peter was a born raconteur. By the time we ordered dessert, he had made a conquest. Back at my house, he asked me, "What? Do I have to lawyer you into bed? You're going to say yes sooner or later."

Sooner seemed fine. It had been years since I'd had a lover, and Peter was both funny and ardent, a charming combination. He was filled with tales of his wild past—a past now safely behind him, he assured me. We quickly fell into a routine of several dinner dates a week.

"I am cash short," Peter told me one night over dinner. "I'm behind on my mortgage and it looks bad. I don't suppose you could float me a short-term loan, could you?" He named a sum. It was a handsome sum but one I knew he could afford to pay back and one I myself could afford to lose if it came to that. Because Peter made me laugh, because I liked his company, and because, without my father's savvy, I was an easy mark, I loaned him the money. My newly acquired conservative accountants were appalled. So was Emma.

"You what?" she exclaimed. Emma found Peter a little slick, and now her doubts about his character were confirmed.

"He's just a little short."

"I'll say. When is he supposed to pay you back?"

"Soon."

Now that he owed me money, Peter became suddenly volatile. His good humor wore thin. He acted like I was a loan shark dogging his heels. I didn't like this turn of events. For that matter, I no longer liked Peter. What I needed, I decided, was to put time and space between us. I suggested to Emma that we take a trip out to Taos, "just to clear my emotional palette."

"I need a vacation," I told her.

Taos was beautiful, more beautiful than I'd remembered it. The high mountains were still blanketed with snow. The spring nights were cool, but the days were warm and balmy. Emma and I stayed at my favorite haunt, the El Pueblo. We took many long walks out west of town on Valverde, the high road that overlooked a large meadow and bordered a small, beautiful cemetery. My friend

Larry Lonergan lived on Valverde. When I told him I was homesick, he suggested that we look at rentals. Emma and I found a charming house right on Valverde, within walking distance to Larry and to town.

"It's better than spending more money on Peter," I told Emma as we paid the rent. Peter and I were talking on the phone, but the last conversation had gone badly. Peter confessed that he was back on cocaine and asked if he could one more time borrow money. This time I resisted.

"No," I said.

"I won't spend it on drugs, if that's what you're afraid of."

"No, Peter. Once burned, twice shy."

"Be that way."

With matters soured between Peter and me, I had little impulse to go back to Manhattan. With its great beauty, Taos still spoke to me. I loved the daily walks, the closeness to Larry and my other friends. "I don't belong in the city," I told myself, and in my final phone call to Peter, I told him the same thing.

"I am not coming back."

"You're just gone?"

"I'm just gone."

And I was "just gone." Officially on vacation, I had less and less inclination to go back. From Manhattan I had been talking to John Newland. Dissatisfied with Taos, he and Areta had moved back to Los Angeles. He wanted me to come to Los Angeles and do theater with him there. "It would be great," he promised. The play he had in mind was my alcoholism play, *Four Roses*. He thought he could get excellent casting, and with any luck we would be reviewed by *Variety* and *The Hollywood Reporter*. Who knew where a few good reviews might lead us?

To me, Newland was the Pied Piper. I still had access to a studio apartment on the beach in Venice. I could live there while we worked. To make it even more enticing, there was a wonderful role for Domenica, who was working to make her way as an actress. It would be good for her to get some Los Angeles exposure. It would be good for me to get another thorough dousing in Los Angeles sobriety, sometimes jokingly referred to as the "Harvard of the recovery movement." Yes, I decided, I would go.

But before I could join Newland in Los Angeles, I had a month of teaching commitments in Taos. For the better part of a year, I was now working with Nave instead of Tim, and Nave and I had planned a very special creativity camp.

Our creative elder was to be Max Showalter. Max, at eighty-two, was flying in from Connecticut to share his experience, strength, and hope with our students. I would teach mornings. A wide panoply of classes would occupy the afternoons. Many of my Taos friends would participate. Dori Vinella would be the official hostess. There would be a field trip to painter Paul Pascarella's studio, a hands-on art class with designer Jo Dean Tipton, a drumming workshop with Rosario Carelli. Nave would teach performance poetry and Max would cap it all with a live concert. We were expecting both Larry Lonergan and Rhonda Flemming to offer participants spiritual readings. Sambhu Vaughan would provide musical evenings.

Taos seemed to me to be an ideal place to teach. Students fell in love with the beauty of the community and many went home laden with southwestern art treasures. The pueblo was nearby for anyone who cared to explore Native American culture, and the local restaurants featured savory New Mexican cuisine. My little rented house on Valverde was convenient to the campus and felt to me like another safe and lovely nest. The prowler and my former house seemed distant memories—until a burglar struck.

We came home from a day's teaching to find that our new little house had been ransacked. Emma's bag and wallet were missing. Clothes were awry, drawers gaped open. When we called the police, they arrived with bad news. Now Taos was undergoing a siege of robberies. "Kids on drugs" were the suspected culprits.

"It's not safe here," Emma declared. She had heard my stories of the sexual prowler and she didn't like passing in front of a window at night. When the police left, she circled the house on foot, trying to gauge how easily each of our windows could be jimmied open. The news wasn't good. Our house was long on charm and short on security. Walking the neighborhood after the robbery, we came upon Emma's empty purse, tossed in the trash at the community library. "I don't like it here," Emma announced.

Even without Emma's warnings I found myself uneasy in the little rental house. The prowler had never been caught, and now there was the robber to contend with as well. The police seemed casual at best. Hoping to forestall further catastrophe, I made a decision to let go of the rental and leave Taos as soon as creativity camp was over. I asked Erin Greenberg to pack the house for me while Emma went back to oversee our affairs in New York.

Looking for elusive stability, I was actually on the run. My life seemed to be lived anywhere and everywhere. I promised Newland that I would come to California at least for the duration of a production. I arrived in California just as spring was turning to summer. The little apartment on Venice Beach featured a small balcony and a good sea breeze. I was mere blocks from the welcoming coffee shop where sober alcoholics gathered. I was even closer than that to the shoreline and the blue Pacific waters where dolphins danced. I should have felt peaceful, but instead I lay in bed at night with my head spinning. I felt disoriented and adrift. I tried to connect with all that was familiar but I did not feel at home. I hoped that seeing Newland would make me feel more grounded. We shared a passion for work and that had always been centering for me.

For his part, John Newland was happy to have me in California. To his eye, Taos was a romantic dead end, "not a destination for healthy people." Los Angeles, by way of contrast, had been his home for forty years. He knew where the restaurants were and didn't mind driving his white Chevy Blazer to get to them. My apartment was a block from the Rose Café. It was there that Newland first suggested we rendezvous.

"Good to see you, John!" I exclaimed, taking in his tall and still-handsome person.

"Good to be seen!" he answered back, bending down to give me a welcoming peck. "Well, what are we going to do? I found a little playhouse over in Westwood that looks perfect for us. I thought we could start there by putting up *Four Roses.*" Newland was gathering a head of persuasive steam. "I think your idea that I work with your friend Rosemary Welden is a super idea. She's a good casting agent and we've got six great women's roles—five, actually, since we know we want Domenica for the young junkie. We do, don't we?"

Getting down to business began with casting. True to her reputation, Rosemary Welden had a deluge of actresses for us to meet. Newland picked through them like a gourmet in a bonbon factory. Watching him put them through their paces, I saw again how powerful his charisma was. At eighty-two! One particularly beautiful actress took me aside and hissed to me, "I'd do him in a minute. You know what I mean?" I knew what she meant. Without much difficulty, we filled out an excellent cast. We found that Newland's reputation was a lure and so was my own. Half of our cast had worked *The Artist's Way*. The chance to work with us was a chance to say thank you.

Domenica decided that she would undertake the role of the young junkie. While I was pleased by her decision, it also meant that at rehearsals I was daily exposed to a Domenica I didn't know—an angry, rebellious, sexualized teen. Newland took her transformation in stride. With six highly trained, highly strung actresses to work with, he was in his element. He wanted big, edgy performances from them, and that was what he was getting. By opening night he had brewed a highly combustible cocktail. Audiences were moved. The critics approved. Domenica received good notices and was immediately offered casting in another production. I felt shrewd that I had been able to help her take a step forward. Maybe we both belonged in L.A.?

More than critical approval, I enjoyed the chance to put some work up in front of my longtime friends like Julianna McCarthy and Ed Towle. Over the years they had cheered me on long distance, and now here we were all reunited again. It was very satisfying to watch them watch the proceedings onstage. They had bet on me, and now I felt their bets were paying off. Emma came out from New York to catch the play's end. She, too, pronounced it a success.

All too soon the play's run drew to a close. Newland wanted to move on immediately into another production.

"I am not ready, John," I told him.

"What do you mean, you're not ready?"

"I'm thinking about film," I stalled.

"Ah."

Newland was disappointed in me. He knew that at his age he was unlikely to be chosen to direct a feature film. If he wanted to direct—and he did—then he would need to turn his energies toward theater. Why couldn't I see it his way?

Looking back, I wonder if I didn't have a failure of nerve. It had been hard putting work up to intense critical scrutiny. We had survived it. We had even prevailed. But it was difficult. Newland was both older and tougher than I was. I begged him to understand my hesitancy. He had no patience with it. More to the point, he had no time for it. While to me he seemed vital and ageless, he knew he wasn't getting any younger. He found my hesitation frustrating and uncharacteristic. Was I all right? he wondered. No, I was not.

Without the routine of a production to anchor my days, I found myself feeling aimless and ill at ease. When I talked on the phone to Emma, New York seemed impossibly far away to me. How, I wondered, could I ever have imagined that I could live there? I loved the flora and fauna in Los Angeles. I loved the gentle, balmy days. I began to think that I belonged in Los Angeles, that it was good for my sobriety to be around old friends and new ideas. Newland had an idea of teaching a monologue class, could he interest me in that? he wondered. One more time I begged off. I was feeling restless and unable to focus. What I was really feeling was rootless. I had been transplanted one time too many. Although I didn't yet see it, I wasn't stable.

Venice Beach is named for its canals, and there is a tiny, picturesque area known as "walk streets," where there are no cars, only walkways. It was to one such street that I found myself pulled repeatedly, and there, on a telephone pole, I saw advertised a rental cottage. I took down the number and called the landlady. I liked her immediately, and I liked the little cottage she had to show me.

The street was serene and pastoral. Parrots flocked in the trees. The neighborhood seemed charming and gentle, drawn to a comforting miniature scale. "I'll take it," I said.

It remained to break the news to Emma. She was halfway done with arranging *Avalon*, and the even larger piece *Magellan* still lay ahead. Could she pack up New York and join me in Los Angeles? Our work would be the same. She would continue to focus on *Avalon* and I would return to writing books. We might do the occasional play. With any luck, I could one more time sell a movie. New York was too hard. There weren't enough trees. Wouldn't she please join me? Emma says that when I asked her, she experienced a distinct shudder of foreboding. Nonetheless, game and plucky, she agreed to move west.

To the casual eye, Nowita Place looked like paradise. It was a neighborhood of gardeners, and climbing roses overhung the walk. Lawns were immaculately kept and houses were freshly painted. Life looked very good to the observer. Moving into Nowita Place, anticipating a gentle life to match my environment, I quickly found myself slipping into trouble. As it had in London, nature began to be luminous for me. I would walk the length of our tiny street, passing by garden after garden, and each bower of flowers seemed to speak to me. One more time, as it had in Taos, electricity began to bother me. I doused the power in my little cottage and lit candles for every room. I was sliding into eccentricity, but in a setting so idyllic that I didn't notice my slippage with any concern.

It fell to Emma to see the situation clearly. To her eye, I was one more time growing fragile, and even though she had missed the London breakdown, she knew the story and she began to grow alarmed. Reaching out for help, I called my friend Rosemary Welden. She came to the little cottage and listened gravely. "You're becoming oversensitive," she concluded. "That's why they call people like you sensitives." She thought what I needed was just what Nowita Place had to offer: rest and quiet. Next I called Jeremy Tarcher. He met me for lunch and pronounced, "Darling, you are not well." Finally I called Newland. He listened acutely and then offered his bottom line: "Don't they have some pill you can take to get back on the ground?"

The truth was that I was trying to avoid taking pills. I probably needed Navane again, but with Dr. Jones retired, I was reluctant to put drugs into my system. Unsupervised, I was perversely proud of the time I was racking up without the need for medication. I still wasn't convinced that in some cases drugs could make me more sober, not less. Listening to Newland's concern, I began to have doubts about my position. "I think I need a doctor," I told Emma.

The doctor we found was a Jungian referred to us by trusted friends. He found my case fascinating and was particularly impressed by my continuous creativity. He listened to me say I was afraid of electrical power and that I was starting to be afraid to drive the car. Instead of telling me my sensitivity to electricity was a delusion, he was fascinated by the altered states I seemed to be experiencing. After a few sessions, he confessed to me that he often took drugs in order to arrive at the states of consciousness that I seemed to be arriving at naturally. He explained that he was interested by shamanic experiences. He wondered if I had experimented with a certain exotic South American drug. He and his wife had used it to approximate the very condition I was in. When I said I had not tried it, he seemed disappointed.

"I think I need a different doctor," I told Emma. By then I was experiencing myself as increasingly ungrounded. Days ran into nights. Weeks ran into months. Everything blurred. It was all I could do to walk daily and to write. My Nowita Place neighbors began to think me eccentric. They had noticed that I seemed to live by candlelight. Meanwhile, I fought for normalcy. It was getting harder and harder to drive. This meant it was difficult to meet with my sober alcoholic friends. I tried to rely on the phone, but soon even that seemed "too electric" for me. I was becoming as isolated as I had in London. Even my relationship with my daughter suffered.

Domenica had rented a place in nearby Venice Beach. I was worried about her safety. Her charming little apartment was too close to the boardwalk. She called me in the middle of the night to say she was afraid to step over a vagrant who had found shelter in her doorway. I lobbied for Domenica to move to safer quarters. I worried about what her father would say if he knew of her dangerous circumstances. He was protective of Domenica, but she loved the beauty of the beach, and the bawdiness of her neighborhood appealed to her. "It's like the Village," she would try to reassure me. I was not reassured. Instead, I grew ever more apprehensive. What if something happened to her?

"She's old enough to make her own choices," friends told me.

"I'm sure you're right, but I still think of her as my little girl."

"Well, she's not. Try having some faith."

But faith was elusive—and genuine detachment seemed impossible. All that I could do was voice my concerns and try to stick faithfully to a sane routine. I set up a writing desk in my music room and, at the suggestion of Bernice Hill, a Jungian analyst, started each day by writing a small "animal" song. That done, I would get up from the piano, cross to the desk, and begin to write on the two books I was working on simultaneously, *God Is No Laughing Matter* and *Supplies*. I contracted my sister Libby to work as illustrator, and we sent her the essays as they unfolded.

I was working on an IBM Selectric typewriter and I loved the comforting sound of the keys trotting along. I kept separate folders for each book, and I would finish one essay and go straight to another. Sometimes I would write an essay that seemed to belong in both books. Despite my sense of disorientation, my writing seemed clear, just a little more hard-edged than usual. I didn't recognize myself in its tone.

"Do I seem okay?" I would ask Emma and Domenica.

"Not really," they would answer.

One more time, through friends, we located someone who thought she could help me. This time we were dealing with a New Age healer who did intuitive counseling long distance and then prescribed herbal remedies. Based in Sedona, Arizona, she consulted with me by phone. My system needed to be detoxed, she told me, as did Emma's, and so we embarked on a cleansing fast that left us reeling with dizziness. Flat on the couch with the room spinning, I would say to Emma, "Are you sure this is helping us?" Domenica was becoming increasingly alarmed. I tried to reassure her, but I wasn't reassured myself. Ezra came to visit me, and he was very worried by what he found. In retrospect, I would say I was having another breakdown. At the time, I was writing so productively that I didn't think in terms of breakdowns—although my friends were beginning to use that word.

Newland was officially worried about me, as were Jeremy Tarcher and Ed Towle. Unwilling to leave my little neighborhood, I met each of these men for lunch and grew cross with them when they questioned my regime, some twenty herbal remedies prescribed by the Sedona healer. By now Emma and I had added in long daily bike rides. Our days were productive both musically and in terms of literary output. They were just terrifying emotionally.

Accustomed to a network of close friends, Emma was uncomfortable in Los Angeles. She did not feel that she fit in. My sober mentors began to express alarm at my increasingly dramatic thinking. I was sober long years, but I was standing too near the abyss.

"Just don't drink," I lectured myself. "Just hang in one day at a time." And one day at a time I did hang in, writing music, writing essays, and fearing more and more for my sanity. All I could manage was my little routine. My friends were near, but they seemed very far away.

"Just take a pill, for God's sake," Newland would chide me.

Instead of taking a pill to feel better, I impulsively acquired two small puppies, a cocker spaniel and a West Highland terrier. We set up little runs for them and would sit on the lawn in the sunshine, watching their antics. Nature remained preternaturally seductive to me. The gardens of Nowita Place changed seasons, and I gloried in their beauty. Parrots flocked in the trees overhead. A raven set up sentinel on a neighboring A-frame.

"Let's have a dinner party," I suggested to a startled Emma, who was used to my just getting by day by day.

"We could do that," she answered cautiously.

And so we invited a small group of friends that included the playwright George Firth, whose longtime lover had recently, suddenly died. As we sat around chatting after dinner, George asked me what I was working on next. I told him I had an idea of writing a musical about ghosts in Manhattan.

"That's a great idea!" he burst out. His enthusiasm was contagious.

Waking early the next morning, I found I had a head full of music. All feelings of being shaky were swept aside by its imperious flow. A beautiful song began to unfurl itself. I raced to keep up, grabbing for notebook and tape recorder.

"Emma!" I told her excitedly. "Listen to this!"

I no sooner finished with one song than a second was waiting in the wings. Now I was on familiar territory. I knew how to just take dictation and let the music move through me. And this music was so enjoyable! Rollicking comic songs played in my head. Beautiful ballads woke me. George Firth had set off a tempest of music with his enthusiasm. Driving Emma to her viola lesson, navigating five lanes of fast-moving traffic, I suddenly "heard" an intricately rhymed comic aria. "Quick!" I said to Emma. "Take this down!" I sang it to her, and she did.

If music has charms to soothe the savage beast, it also had charms to soothe me. Rosemary Welden loved the new songs, and her enjoyment triggered still more of them. The more music I wrote, the more normal I felt. Just as Bernice Hill had predicted, my writing seemed to smooth out again. Its tone became less harsh and agitated. Good humor reappeared. Even better, a small publishing company contacted me about publishing my book of short stories, *Popcorn: Hollywood Stories.* Several of the stories were selected for a reading series, and I looked forward to hearing them done by good actors. Life seemed to be taking a turn toward the sunny side. Reality was stabilizing again—and then it all went tilt.

Without warning John Newland was hospitalized, the victim of a sudden savage stroke. His wife wanted him to have no visitors. And so we watched and waited, waited and watched, praying for his recovery—but he did not recover. Instead, he suffered a second, even more severe stroke, and then he died. I got the phone call just as I was leaving for the reading of *Popcorn.* My immediate sense was not of his absence but of his presence. John was with me, I felt, as we drove over the mountains to the theater in the valley where the reading was being held.

"You will always be able to reach me," I remembered John promising me once when we had talked about the difference in our ages and the fact that he would in all probability die first. "Just remember that you will always be able to reach me," he had assured me.

In the days following John's death, I did try to reach him. I simply could not accept that he was gone. I played and replayed our last lunch together, angry with myself that we hadn't started a new project. How could I have been so blind? Why didn't I realize how truly old he was? I called a famed medium and asked if she could make contact. She tried, and there was John's voice coming through. "Hello, baby," he said clear as a bell through the ether. "Was he in show business?" the medium asked.

Areta did not want a funeral or a memorial. It fell to me to organize a small gathering for John at my house on Nowita Place. It was a crystalline evening with the January air as clear as a goblet. We sat in a circle and spoke of what John had meant to us. Everyone missed him acutely. He had seemed to us all to be larger than life, and it was difficult to picture life going on without him. "Without him" loomed so huge.

10.

As John had so keenly known, without work to do, Los Angeles was a beautiful hell. In the weeks that followed, Emma and I both felt displaced. I had my old friends, but they had lives of their own and their careers were well established. Missing her close friendships in New York, Emma was lonely in Los Angeles and often complained that she felt invisible there. I felt visible only as a name brand, the *Artist's Way* author. Without John to help me, I did not feel visible as an artist. I felt I had lost me as well as him. Our relationship had been an important part of my artistic identity. He believed in me as a playwright. Now I wondered who I really was. Life without John felt both foreign and undoable.

But life did go on—and it sometimes seemed John still had a ghostly hand in it. Shortly after John's death, Emma and I were contacted by Marcus Kettles, a New York producer, who listened to the ghost songs and wondered if we wanted a New York reading for our work. By then we were calling the show *The Medium at Large*, and we were delighted to be offered an opportunity to move it forward. Kettles offered to produce a reading for us in the fall. The reading was back in Manhattan, which we had so recently left behind. Emma was exultant. Manhattan! At least there we had an artistic identity.

The call from Kettles threw me into conflict. Los Angeles felt like a dead end to me. It held my past but not my future. What was I doing there? I fretted. Despite my sober friends, despite the presence of Jeremy Tarcher, my editor, I simply didn't feel I belonged there without John. He was symbolic to me of both safety and opportunity. Now I missed them both. The reading Kettles offered was a tantalizing carrot. The world we had left behind seemed to loom once again in our future. Maybe I had been wrong to leave New York. As the days wore on, as John's absence grew more and more real, Los Angeles seemed ever less a fit.

Meanwhile, Emma and I went through our paces daily, writing words and music, but there was no place to land the work once it was done. Los Angeles is a hard town for theater, especially musical theater, and John Newland was a hard act to follow. Increasingly, Emma missed New York and I again, stubbornly, missed New Mexico. She yearned for anonymity and crowds. I yearned for familiarity and wide open spaces. Increasingly, both of us felt alienated from Los Angeles. Although it prides itself on having diverse culture—and more than before, now it does—Los Angeles remains a one-industry town and we were not "in the business." Instead of feeling "a part of," we felt our noses were pressed to the candy store window. We were outsiders without John to mount productions, and every day that felt more clear.

As we became less and less comfortable in Los Angeles as a

whole, the coziness of the little Nowita Place neighborhood felt nosy and intrusive to us. For our comfortable neighbors, we were the object of gossip and disapproval. Burnt-out and burned up, we decided to take the dogs and drive to Taos for a vacation. We left Los Angeles on April Fools' Day.

It is two short days or one long one from Los Angeles to Taos, and Emma and I chose to drive slowly. We were both thrilled to leave Los Angeles behind us. Although we were not yet quite admitting it, our transplant there had failed. We were eager to be back in the West again instead of on the coast. Halfway to Taos, we pulled into a barbecue restaurant. Cowboys slouched against the bar. The jukebox played country and western.

"It's not L.A.!" we told each other gleefully.

No, Taos was not L.A. It was Taos, and this time Emma and I stayed at my familiar and beloved El Pueblo. This time we had the dogs with us, and the El Pueblo gave us what passed for a penthouse, an A-frame condominium looking out at Taos Mountain. I set up a writing table facing the mountain and was dimly aware that I was imitating my earlier self. Nearly twenty years before, Morning Pages had begun at a similar table facing the same mountain.

Emma and I quickly settled in to a Taos routine. It involved long and beautiful walks and long and fruitful days at the page. I was ecstatic to be back in Taos, amid my friends. And yet, if I had missed John in Los Angeles, I missed him even more back home in Taos. I kept expecting to see his white Blazer. I thought I would spot him turning a corner. I phoned his good friend Nancy Jenkins and together we commiserated over missing him. "There's just no one else like him, is there?" Nancy asked me. No, there was not.

Taos did, however, have some newcomers who were a welcome addition to the mix. Two of director John Huston's children, Tony and Allegra, had recently taken up residency. I met them with eagerness, happy that Taos had more filmmakers. Out of all the world, I could understand why they had settled there. They had grown up in Ireland, and Taos shared with Ireland a poetic, even mythic, beauty.

As the days ticked past, I found myself reluctant to leave. I was due back in Los Angeles for a large book event, but I didn't want to go back, and I particularly didn't want to go back to public appearances and speeches. My mental health was more tenuous than I cared to admit. Just picturing the long drive back to Los Angeles brought this home to me. Nearly daily I spoke with the Sedona healer. Did she really think I was getting better? She prescribed more and more potions, but I was feeling worse.

"Cancel it," I told Emma. "Tell them that I simply cannot come."

My words turned out to be prophetic. I had a telephone radio tour to do, and after fourteen hours on the phone, talking with a dozen different interviewers, I was exhausted and shaking. Catching sight of myself in the mirror, I looked both pale and frail. This was something worse than mere fatigue. With growing apprehension I toted up my symptoms. One more time I found myself feeling increased sensitivity to electricity. One more time nature began to glow and speak. I felt inexplicably weak and my appetite one more time disappeared. I didn't call what was happening to me a breakdown, but I was breaking down and Emma knew it. Our escape to Taos had merely masked my condition.

"You need a doctor," Emma told me.

"What good are they?" I asked. "If I'm going to be sick, let me be sick here in Taos. Here is beautiful."

"Beautiful" was the consolation prize. Officially a best-selling author and at least a semipublic figure, I privately felt that public life was too much for me. Let me live simply and simply write, I told myself. I told Emma the same thing. We would still work on music, I promised her. Telling herself that was enough, telling herself I needed her, Emma soldiered on—but she was worried. Trying to lift my spirits, she kept her worries to herself.

My friend Dori wanted to sell her old adobe house and move into town. Dori's house was five miles outside Taos in Arroyo Seco, a tiny, picturesque village. The house featured views of the Sacred Mountain and a tiny old campos santos. Huge willow trees graced the property and lilacs guarded the drive. It was a retreat in the best sense of the word. I had always loved Dori's house, and I re solved to buy it. Without bickering, we quickly settled on a price. If I sold the Virginia farm, I could just swing it.

Thrilled that I would have a Taos home again, and one I loved, I arranged to have a sober alcoholic friend pack up my Nowita Place cottage and ship all of my and Emma's belongings straight to Taos. When the truck arrived, all of our furniture fit into place as if it had been bought to fill the house. With two separate wings, one for Emma and one for me, the house felt both spacious and cozy. From my little crimson writing room, I could watch a field full of Arabian horses grazing. Like my fragile father, I took consolation and joy in nature's creatures.

If I felt at home in Arroyo Seco, Emma felt more at home when the Taos School of Music reconvened atop the ski valley. There were concerts two nights a week, and Emma's favorite teacher, a concert pianist named Robert McDonald, was back in residence. Emma and I invited him for dinner. He was tall, thin, lively, and engaging. After dinner he stayed on until midnight, merrily chasing the conversation wherever it galloped.

"That man is very attractive," I told Emma when he left.

"I thought you two would get along," she said smugly.

With his crystalline playing and ready wit, McDonald became for me an immediate muse. When he played, I felt I could hear the actual architecture of the music he was playing. "I've been told that," he remarked mildly. He instantly catalyzed my music to pour forth.

"That man is like Magic Johnson at the keys," Nave commented. I agreed. I wrote a series of songs I called simply, *The Bob McDonald Songs.* They were beautiful and structurally more complex than anything else I had yet attempted. "I wish I could speak music," the lyric to one of them ran. Trying to speak music to McDonald, I wrote song after song. Every morning I would now write a "flower song." Every afternoon Emma would harmonize and arrange the morning's work. Ours was a productive household.

After lunch it was time to take the dogs for their walk, and the walks were now more adventurous than mere rambles through the sagebrush. A small river came crashing down the mountain from the Taos Ski Valley. Every afternoon the dogs and I would wade up that river. "Trout hunting," I called it, and we often surprised foot-long beauties at their ease. Looking back, it was dangerous, venturing out into the forest with just the little dogs for company. The wilderness held both bears and coyotes. Then, too, there was the constant danger of snakes. I saw no rattlesnakes on our walks that summer, although I saw more than my fair share of garter snakes and little water snakes enjoying the river. The dogs weren't afraid of snakes, and I had to call to them to stay away.

One of the graces of being back in New Mexico was being within driving distance of my friend Elberta Honstein. Once a week, more often if we could swing it, Emma and I loaded the dogs into my little Honda SUV and drove down the twisting canyon to Espanola, home of the Honsteins' Roy-El Morgan Farm.

Once there, Elberta would greet us with homemade green chili stew and freshly baked pie. She would watch patiently as Emma learned the rudiments of riding. I would sit in her calming presence and feel myself drawing back from the brink. Elberta embodied an optimistic faith. I tried to emulate her. Sometimes I would tell her of my worries.

"I am scared, Elberta," I would begin.

"You've got everything within you to meet whatever challenges you face," she would answer me back. I wanted to believe it.

June and July swept past. Emma made a whirlwind trip to New York to consult with Marcus Kettles and to visit with Max Showalter, sadly failing at his home in Connecticut. I felt too shaky to go. Still plucky and upbeat with only two more weeks to live, Max had pointed Emma toward some signed mementos to him from Richard Rodgers and Oscar Hammerstein II. As a young man, he had been Hammerstein's protégé.

"Always ask them for help," Max gravely advised Emma. He told her that he himself often sought the guidance of his famous friends who had passed over. "Meet me at dawn," he would often tell them before he slept at night. In the morning he would get up to write, feeling their inspirational companionship. Emma returned to Taos strengthened by his spiritual beliefs.

Suddenly it was August and time for Bob McDonald to return to New York. We watched his final concert with regret. He had been such good company that we felt suddenly bereft. Taos, after all, was a small town and we had big-city dreams. Even with each other and our work for company, we often felt lonely there. Late in the afternoon the loneliness would hit, and we would clamber into the car and drive uptown to visit our friend Larry Lonergan, the medium.

"You know we're writing a show about you," we would kid him. "It goes up for a reading in New York this fall. It's too bad you can't come."

"Yes, but you had better go," Larry would reply. He didn't foresee much future for us in Taos.

"We are going to New York just for the reading," we told him. "But first we have an entire book tour to accomplish. We're going to miss the dogs."

"Yes, and they'll miss you, but they'll be fine. You've got business to take care of in New York." Larry faithfully pointed us toward True North. Although he loved having us in Taos, he did not necessarily believe we belonged there. Faced with my recurrent fragility, he wondered—as Sonia did—if the energy of a big city didn't help me to stay on track. Emma, too, longed for New York—specifically, New York doctors. She was growing leery of New Age practitioners and what she considered their exotic formulas.

With the cottonwoods turning yellow and the aspen turning gold, Emma and I faced time on the road. Ten cities loomed ahead of us with New York at the very end. We were excited to rendezvous there with Bob McDonald and also with our new mentor and friend, Bruce Pomahac, music director of the Rodgers and Hammerstein Organization. Bruce had entered our life through Max, who had listened to our rough recording of *Avalon* and then phoned Bruce in excitement. "You've got to help these girls, Bruce," Max had said. Bruce in his turn had listened to *Avalon* and agreed, saying of one song, "This could earn you girls an Oscar." We clung to these compliments like talismans of our future. But first we had to tour.

I worried about the tour: airplanes and airports; crowds and questions and hotel rooms. And yet I was excited to go. Due to

Emma's steadfast company and my actual love of teaching, I have often found book tours to be as rewarding as they are difficult. Nervous as I was, this tour proved to be no exception. A city at a time, a crowd at a time, we made our way cross-country.

It takes resilience to survive a book tour, and Emma and I arrived in New York a little tattered and worn. We were offered refuge at Bruce Pomahac's house, and we took him up on it for a week. Bruce lives in the heart of the theater district, and just being there with him made our dreams feel more real. After a week we moved to our old favorite, the Hotel Olcott. It was time to rehearse for our reading of *The Medium at Large*, and the Upper West Side was convenient for the actors and music director.

They say that it takes seven years to shape a musical. Emma and I were in our second year of work on the show, and it was time to hear what we had. All plays play differently than they read but none more so than musicals. We could have something or nothing at all. By doing a reading in New York, using real Broadway talent, we would have the chance to evaluate what we had.

The reading went very well. Our score was tuneful and catchy. The ballads were lovely. The book was funny. "You've got something, girls," the verdict came back to us, which led us to our very next question: Now what? In the wake of the reading, Emma and I soon realized what Larry had been suggesting to us all along: that we could not go back to New Mexico. There was no future for our show there. At best we might swing a workshop production, but where would that get us? No, our time in New Mexico had led us squarely back to New York. We decided to get an apartment and try our luck. In the meantime, we camped out at the Olcott. "I wish we could just stay here," I would say to Emma, but the Olcott did not take dogs, and Emma and I missed ours.

Few things are as harrowing as searching for an apartment in Manhattan. Emma and I knew we wanted to stay on the Upper West Side, with its density of musicians and performers—not to mention parks for walking. Emma wanted to do advanced studies in conducting and orchestration at Juilliard, and it, too, was in the neighborhood. We looked at apartments that were lovely but in dangerous areas. We looked at apartments that weren't lovely at all. Finally, our broker told us we could look at a two-year sublease in a building on Riverside Drive. We walked in, saw the large windows overlooking the river and Riverside Park, and thought that for two years at least, we were "home." The very first thing we did upon moving in was to purchase a good piano. If we were going to work on musicals, we needed a real piano. We bought a fifty-two-inch Petrof upright at the recommendation of Bob McDonald's piano technician. It had a large, beautiful voice.

Another large, beautiful voice floated through our windows. There was an opera singer in our building, and she rehearsed and taught for hours daily. Far from being annoying, the sound of her voice was inspirational. "What are you doing about your art today?" it asked.

Emma and I were busy with our art indeed. First of all there was *Avalon,* now ready to go up for sale with all-new arrangements by Emma and a matching demo disk. Next there was *The Medium at Large,* with which we were constantly tinkering, ready for another reading and needing the sure hand of a wonderful director this time. Then there was *Magellan,* next up to bat and probably the most beautiful of all. Closer to an opera than a musical, it owed more to *La Bohème* than it did to *The Fantasticks.* As we settled into Riverside Drive, it seemed I couldn't stop writing music. Bob McDonald was one of our neighbors and again a muse. Emma raced to keep up. One more time the music seemed to be good for me. My fears of another breakdown receded.

"New York is good for you," Sonia said.

"Music is good for you," Bernice, my silver-headed Jungian friend, said. Like my aunt by the same name, Bernice believed in creativity, especially music, as a cure. Even if I weren't cured, I was certainly better. In between New York and the music, I managed to find elusive stability.

Emma found opera singers and a pianist, and we recorded rough drafts of *Magellan*. If I felt like an amateur and a musical pretender, the work still sounded glorious. The melodies were beautiful, and in professional hands they were beautiful indeed. Whenever I would say, "I don't know what I am doing," Bernice with her eyes twinkling would say, "So do music anyway." I tried to follow her advice.

Every morning we began our day with dog walking and Morning Pages. After that it was time to sit quietly and ask for guidance. As eccentric as it may sound, we sought daily guidance just as suggested by Max Showalter: we asked for help from him and from his friends Richard Rodgers and Oscar Hammerstein II. Sitting quietly, we would take down what we heard and then we would act on it. Very often the advice seemed wiser than anything we could come to on our own.

"Just get to the piano, Julia," Richard Rodgers repeatedly advised me from the ether. Knowing his own prodigious work habits, such advice seemed likely. Cranky and unwilling, I would go to the piano, only to find a beautiful melody waiting for me. I would take down the melody line and then call to Emma, "Emma, come here! Listen to this one!" Very often "this one" would suit Emma as well.

Tutored by Bruce Pomahac, we began to know something of

the history of the American musical. Among many other books, I read *Musical Stages,* Richard Rodgers's autobiography. It was clear from his account that what mattered to him first and foremost was the work. Emma and I tried to follow his example. He wrote daily and so did we. From both Rodgers and Hammerstein we learned the value of setting a regular schedule. I would work on music and then, at morning's end, I would cross to my writing desk, where I was working on a new creativity book, *Walking in This World.* I would try to write one short essay a day. I tried to hew to the advice of my early sobriety: let God take care of the quality; let me take care of the quantity. The quantity was three daily pages.

By midafternoon Emma and I would be ready for a breather, and Riverside Park lay just outside our front door. "Girls, would you like to take a walk?" we would ask the dogs, and they would come bounding to our sides, tails wagging. We either walked or ran, putting in an hour's exercise as the sun set through the trees and the river took on its twilight magic. From our windows we could watch boats making their way up and down the Hudson. We could look across the river's waters to America. For me it was easy to pretend that we were not too far away from Taos, that it lay just to the west, beyond our sight but always there and always waiting for our return.

Emma had no eagerness to return to Taos. She remembered it as lonely and isolated, except for the Taos School of Music, and that convened only eight weeks a year. "I just don't fit in there," she would tell me, but I would mention our work and say that we always got vast swaths of it done in the quiet Taos atmosphere.

"I can work anywhere," Emma would retort.

"We could probably finish the whole rough draft of *Magellan,*" I would coax her.

"You and Taos," Emma would snort. "I just don't get it."

Nonetheless, I yearned for Taos, and as winter turned to spring and the trees in Riverside Park filled to a bouffant fullness, we decided to spend the summer in Taos, work feverishly on *Magellan*, and return to New York for the fall. It was mid-May when we set out, the little Honda SUV filled to brimming with all our work, our clothes, and, of course, the dogs. The drive to Taos took five days and was both a respite and a test. It was wonderful to be away from telephones and business. It was scary, wondering on each day's drive if we would find safe lodging that night for us and the dogs.

Pulling into Taos, crossing the little wooden bridge to our property, was like pulling into another world. The old adobe house stood welcoming us at the end of the drive. The giant willows made green curtains in the air. The lilacs were just budding as we arrived. It was spring, but the nights were still cold and the mornings chill. I was happy to be back in Taos, happy to have the horses grazing outside my window. I was so happy that at first I didn't realize anything was wrong.

It began as a creeping apprehension that came upon me as I wrote. "I am scared," I would tell Emma, but I could not tell her what frightened me. When Domenica phoned from L.A., I learned with relief that she was finally moving to a safer building in a safer neighborhood. She was also renting a safe and cozy place in the West Village. Her acting career demanded she be increasingly bicoastal. Talking to her, I tried to sound normal.

"Are you doing okay, Mommy?" Domenica wondered, antennae at the alert.

"I'm okay," I assured her—as I tried to assure myself.

And then something very frightening did happen. My favorite aunt, Bernice, my mother's older sister, was murdered by her own son, my cousin Jimmy. It was a cocaine-and-alcohol-fueled argument. He shot her point-blank.

I was scheduled to teach creativity camp with Nave, and Aunt Bernice had been slated to attend. She was looking forward to her trip to Taos. She wanted to explore the pueblo. At eighty, she was still lively—and interested in pursuing her creativity. Since my mother's death, my aunt Bernice had been a mother figure to me— a feisty, funny woman with whom I kept up a lively exchange of letters and books. A daredevil herself, she had been a chemist and pilot during World War II. She had encouraged me in all of my adventures. She remained full of daring. I could not believe she was dead. I still had her voice among my messages.

"Aunt Bernice has been murdered," I told Emma numbly. From my siblings I learned more and more grisly details. The number of shots. The position of the body. It was impossible not to picture the horror of my aunt's final moments. She had been shot through the heart.

I called my friend Larry Lonergan. To him, as a medium, death is very matter-of-fact, and I found that he all but overlooked the shocking circumstances of her demise, simply telling me that she was now fine. I needed to hear that, but it did not really help me with my own trauma. Try as I did not to dwell on it, I replayed the death scene over and over. My siblings and cousins told me they did the same. My sister Libby was badly shaken. She e-mailed me updates as they occurred. The news was never good.

I needed my friends and I needed them badly, but some of them were missing in action. I could not find my literary agent, Susan Schulman. She was coping with family emergencies of her own. My friends Dori and Rhonda, normally stalwarts, were also preoccupied with their own life events. Functioning both as a producer

and teacher, Nave was busy setting up creativity camp, and when I
needed to simply vent, he needed to discuss business. Everywhere
I turned, people seemed to have their own agendas. Feeling alienated and alone, I began to complain to Emma that I wasn't sleeping well. In fact, I was sleeping very little. Then I started to have
mysterious stomach pains. They seemed to strike at night, when
they were most frightening. My section of the house was far away
from Emma's. I would wake up in pain and then pace and write
until morning. Exhausted, I would sleep a few hours.

The pain became chronic. Now I really couldn't sleep, even in
the mornings. My fears mounted, some grounded in reality and
others founded on my impression that people seemed quite indifferent to my plight. Emma exhausted herself trying to wrest help
from the dysfunctional Taos medical establishment. Was it appendicitis? I wondered. We saw three doctors in a row to no avail. My
diagnosis was elusive to them. My condition wasn't acting like appendicitis. Whatever it was, my pain was nightly and real. For the
better part of a month, I slept sketchily, and then, just as it had before, my appetite disappeared.

By then, Emma was talking to Christopher Barley, our New
York doctor. She told him about the stomach pains and the sleep-
lessness and the fact that the Taos doctors had ruled out appendicitis. Dr. Barley listened with mounting alarm. My condition
was clearly worsening.

Once more I was afraid of electricity. I begged to be put in a
silent, dark room. I wanted to eat only oatmeal. Then I didn't want
to eat at all. I wrapped myself in blankets, turning the kitchen oven
to five hundred degrees, claiming I was "cold, cold" and that my
heart was going to stop. I started counting my heartbeats. Emma
was terrified. Dr. Barley told her I was not about to die of heart

failure, that it was mental not physical illness that was the threat. Every day, for no apparent reason, I deteriorated further.

"I don't know what to do," Emma would tell Dr. Barley, Gerard, my sister Connie, and my loyal friends Lynnie Lane and Judy Collins—all long distance. They didn't know what to advise her either, except the impossible: "Try to stay calm." All I was clinging to was "just don't drink." That seemed the one positive I could be assured of. Domenica called me, but I didn't return her calls. I was afraid of sounding too crazy. My radio silence set off her alarms. She phoned Gerard and she phoned Dr. Barley, both of whom told her to stand by in New York. Anxiously, she waited for news—none was forthcoming.

Emma was reduced to a bodyguard and nurse. Once I escaped her vigilance and ran naked down the drive. She caught up with me and threw a sheet over me. Hysterical now herself, she one more time called Dr. Barley, who said I was having delusions and that it was time to take me to the emergency room. By then he knew how rudimentary Taos health care was and he promised Emma that he would not let them admit me unless they listened to his counsel. Emma called Nave, and together they drove me to the emergency room. I vomited all the way there.

True to his word, Dr. Barley was on the phone to the emergency room staff. They listened—but only up to a point. What they saw was someone delusional, "crazy," and needing restraints. They tied down my arms and legs. I screamed for help. Emma, hearing my cries, one more time phoned Dr. Barley. He was able to convince the staff to put me in a private room, take off the restraints, and give me some calming Benadryl. Delusional as I was, I was still afraid of drugs. I knew I needed them, but I still fought them. Dr. Barley's long-distance advice was the only thing I would listen to.

With his consent I was transferred to an ambulance and driven the seventy-five miles to a hospital in Santa Fe. I remember Emma sitting by my side as the ambulance made its twisting and turning way along the mountain roads.

Calmer from the Benadryl, but weeping now, I was led into a locked ward. I didn't want to be there, but I knew I had no choice. With the help of the Benadryl, I fell into an exhausted sleep, and while I slept, Emma figured out to call my old and trusted doctor, Arnold Jones. She reached him at six A.M. He was retired but agreed to come out of retirement to supervise my case. What I needed, he said, was a dose of Navane. That would quickly bring me around. I trusted Dr. Jones and took the drug. Within hours my consciousness had steadied. I began to sleep in great quantities. My appetite returned. By the end of a week I was writing and meeting with Emma daily, always asking to hear her progress on *Magellan*. I was finally able to talk to Domenica on the phone.

The time had come for creativity camp, but I was clearly unable to participate. Nave shouldered the camp himself while Emma made arrangements for me to visit with my cousin Terry and his wife, Peg, who had planned to attend camp with our aunt Bernice. Theirs was a welcome and calming presence. Emma remembers "talking Terry's ear off"—it had been three months since she had had a sympathetic listener. With the help of my family, it was arranged that I would fly back to New York, where I would be met by Gerard. Gerard would stay with me at the Riverside Drive apartment until Emma and her brother Ben could drive the dogs back across country and rejoin me. More like a package than a person, I was loaded on a plane and shipped east. Gerard met my plane.

Safely back in New York, I tried to reconstruct what had happened to me. It was frightening to think that a breakdown, a severe breakdown, could come on me out of nowhere. Looking back, I could see that the breakdown had been building for a very long time—as far back as my frantic peripatetic geographic "cures." Surely it had been madness moving from place to place to place, New York to Los Angeles to Taos. Without Emma I'd have been hospitalized long before. Even with Emma, even with our portable routine, my stability was illusory. It was frightening to think that Navane was all that stood between me and another "psychotic episode," as my breakdown was now being called.

I do not remember much of Gerard's stay except for his perennial optimism and insistence on normalcy. Just as he had in London, Gerard tried to cheer me up by drawing my attention to the small things, the beauty all around us. "Look at that bird, will you?" He would direct my attention to a bold grackle on the window ledge. Or "Look at that tug. It's got all it can handle." I think that bird watching and boat watching were how I spent my days until Emma's return. I probably wrote—I always write and I was working on *Prayers from a Nonbeliever*, a novella about faith in the modern world—but I do not remember working. My journals from those days are lost. I sometimes think it is just as well.

Emma and her brother Ben were back just a few days, when the phone rang early one morning. It was Domenica, who was in New York, and she was panicked. "Mom. They've attacked the World Trade Center," she blurted out. "Turn on your TV. It's awful."

I did turn on the TV and saw the images of the planes piercing the sides of the towers. There was a hallucinogenic quality to the sights. "Domenica," I told my daughter, "put on some loose clothing, take some water with you, and walk to your father's house. Call me when you are safely there." Martin's house was halfway between Domenica's apartment and my own.

Now Emma needed some reassurance. Her brother Ben was at that moment on his way to Newark airport. He had left our apartment moments before the attack. "We'll just have to wait until he calls," I told her. But no call came from Ben. Finally Domenica called back to say she was safely at her father's house, where she would remain for the next week. At eight P.M. Ben came walking home to us. He had been stranded on the New Jersey side of the George Washington Bridge until he decided to walk back into Manhattan.

For the next few days Emma and Ben were glued to the television, watching the same horrifying images over and over again. I was in constant phone communication with Domenica, who was badly shaken. Her neighborhood south of Fourteenth Street had been evacuated. She couldn't go home. She remained at her father's for safe haven. The television made the attack a constant presence. Her stepmother, Helen Morris, carefully monitored the news: more terrorist threats, an anthrax scare.

"Mommy, I am scared," Domenica would call to tell me.

"Of course you're scared. Try watching less of the TV. Try praying. I love you."

Up on Riverside Drive, we seemed a world removed from the crisis. We walked the dogs, we went for groceries, and we prayed. It seemed to us that praying was the single most useful thing we could do. Finally the airports began to function again and Ben flew home to Colorado. Like all of New York, Emma and I were poised for a second attack of some kind. Our friends from across the country phoned us repeatedly to see that we were well.

"We're okay," we told them—and we were okay. In some ways, it was easier to be in New York than to be watching New York on the news. Like Londoners during the blitz, New Yorkers rallied in the face of the crisis. Money was raised and clothes donated. Shrines appeared on sidewalks. Under a constant barrage of frightening media, the days passed in a blur. Rather than feeling grief, I felt numb, due to medication and perhaps shock.

What I do remember is that when Emma arrived in New York, my chronic stomach pain seemed to come back. I would wake in the night, cramped and in agony, trying to talk or pray or write myself back into slumber. Each night the pain seemed to be worsening, but since the doctors in Taos had ruled out appendicitis, I tried to simply bear with it. It was not too terrible—and then one night it was.

"Emma, I think I need some help." I went into her room and woke her. "That stomach pain is back and it's really bad."

Emma insisted that we call Dr. Barley even though it was the middle of the night. He arranged for me to have a CAT scan at six A.M. The results came back swiftly. I had a rare and unusual type of appendicitis. Dr. Barley hospitalized me immediately and put me on heavy antibiotics to stabilize what was a slowly leaking infection. At that point my appendix had been leaking and miraculously healing itself for about two months—ever since I first went to the doctor in Taos.

"You're very lucky," the surgeon told me. (I later learned my condition had been life-threatening.) The plan was to stabilize my appendix with medication and then remove it when it was safe.

And so I was placed on a strong drug called Cipro, at a premium because of an anthrax scare for which it was the recommended treatment. Dr. Barley, who often worked in Third World countries, got a taste of practicing Third World medicine right in New York. I remained in the hospital for about a week, frightened the whole time that the nursing staff would miss a Navane dose and I would one more time find myself skidding toward psychosis.

Home from the hospital, I faced a rigorous drug regime. The antibiotics had to be administered carefully and regularly. I began to write down every time I took a pill. I couldn't shake the idea that if I missed even a single dose of Navane I would one more time slide toward madness. It did not help that my diagnosis was a "psychotic episode." The more I read about such episodes, the more they seemed to sweep in out of nowhere, as savage and unpredictable as a tropical storm. Although it wasn't rational, I resented being dependent on a drug. I felt shamed by my condition, embarrassed by my frailty. Perhaps, I told myself grimly, I had inherited my parents' fragility after all. This thought made me frightened for Domenica.

If Emma and I had a job during this period, it was to keep our spirits up creatively. It was all too easy for me to be the identified patient and Emma to become my caretaker. These were roles we did not want. The way out of them seemed to lie with music. Emma began to orchestrate and arrange the vast skeleton that was *Magellan*. I started work on yet another show, this one about Hollywood. I called it *Tinseltown*, and into it I poured my locked-up feelings. The heroine of *Tinseltown* endures a locked ward and lives to tell the tale. I, too, hoped to survive and prevail.

"Take it one day at a time," I told myself. I met faithfully with other sober alcoholics who warned me about the dual dangers of self-pity and self-dramatization. What I was going through was difficult. It was scary, but it was not so difficult or as scary as a drink would make it. "Just don't drink," I repeated to myself like a mantra. "Just don't drink."

Now it was time to return to the hospital for what they promised me would be a routine appendectomy. When you are the patient, nothing feels very routine. I was slated to be operated on the day before Thanksgiving. All holiday festivities were put on hold. As promised, the operation did turn out to be routine, even minimal in feeling. They were able to operate laproscopically. I had very little pain, a few stitches. One day out of the hospital I went jogging in Riverside Park. "Safe"—I thought I was bionic.

Thanks to my sober friends, I now had the help of an addictions specialist, a distinguished psychopharmacologist. Under her tutelage, taking a carefully monitored dose of Navane, I became more stable and able to focus on my writing. My book *Walking in This World* was proving demanding. I was trying to articulate difficult creative issues. For the first time, I did not have Jeremy Tarcher as a sounding board. I wanted the rigor of another disciplined mind. Talking to my friend Natalie Goldberg, I discovered that she had worked successfully with an editor named Linda Kahn, rumored to be both tough and smart. She sounded like the ticket to me. Left to my own devices, my book was becoming too cumbersome. Once more, as I had with *The Vein of Gold*, I was trying to shoehorn everything into a single volume. Clearly, I needed help.

"This book is going to eat me alive," I complained to Emma, who was grappling with her own Goliath in the form of *Magellan*.

"Just focus on today's writing," Emma would advise me. "Let yourself get a rough draft. It can be trimmed and shaped later."

"Trimming" and "shaping" seem like modest words for the overhaul I had in mind. The book was one and a half times as long as it needed to be. I wanted Linda to tell me where I was repetitious. I stood prepared to slash and burn. I wanted a tightly written book.

Walking in This World was to be round two of *The Artist's Way* work. I started out with eighteen weeks, but with Linda's tough-minded assistance, I was able to boil it down to twelve weeks. That felt more doable to me. I wanted to challenge my readers, not overwhelm them. In retrospect, I felt that *The Vein of Gold* had been too dense a book, too demanding for many people to work through successfully. (Although those who had reported glorious results.) This time, I resolved, I would do it right. With this in mind, I enlisted a small corps of readers, including such hardheaded people as Ed Towle, Bob McDonald, and, as always, Gerard. Their job was to spot softheadedness and redundancy. I wanted the book to be smart and lean—or as lean as I could make it, trying to distill a decade's worth of teaching.

"Emma! Listen to this!" I found myself caroling out many mornings. Melody once more seemed to flood the house. *Magellan* was on the move again.

"I am listening!" Emma would carol back. She was excited by the beauty of what was unfolding. *Magellan*, large to begin with, seemed to be getting larger and larger still.

"I don't know if we'll ever be finished with it," I would fret. *Magellan* felt as unwieldy and unmanageable as my life.

"What does it matter when we finish it?" Emma would ask gaily. She loved arranging and found herself far more happy writing music than she ever had been merely playing it.

Playing the piano as I did—badly—I found myself wondering what it might be like to really feel comfortable with the instrument. Perhaps the time had come to take real piano lessons. There were worse things to do with your fifties, I told myself. And so I set out to find a teacher. Bob McDonald taught piano but only to advanced students, and I was a novice. My friend Cyril Brosnan suggested that I try calling the Lucy Moses School for gifted children, which had a small adult program that might suit me. Looking in their catalogue, I saw that one teacher, Chaim Freiberg, advertised himself as loving Broadway as well as Beethoven. "He's for me," I thought.

And so I began what I promised myself would be a decade of piano lessons. Every Monday at noon, I entered my teacher's studio. To my delight, Mr. Freiberg was both playful and inspirational. He didn't like many of the beginner's piano books available and so he simply wrote his own. I learned to play on his own compositions, often written out by hand just for me. Who could resist the clumsy, childlike notes in Mr. Freiberg's hand? Certainly not I.

"Do you like this? Does it interest you?" Mr. Freiberg would cajole me, sniffing out the faintest scent of boredom. I began to feel spoiled, having my piano lessons shaped so carefully to my own needs and desires. Sometimes I would balk altogether at trying another piece of classical music, and it was then that the show tunes came out. "Try this one. It's wonderful," Mr. Freiberg might introduce a Rodgers and Hammerstein number. He could play most of their work by ear and he encouraged me to do the same.

"You see? You have a wonderful ear," he would tell me. Who could resist such encouragement?

A beginning pianist, I still hesitated to think of myself as a real musician despite the amount of melody that seemed to flow through me.

"You're a composer," Emma would say firmly. "You write beautiful melodies."

"I'm a something," I would tell her.

I was very lucky to be surrounded by musicians who were not competitive or judgmental. Bob McDonald, Bruce Pomahac, and

Emma's classical friends were all encouraging. My late-blooming gift for melody struck them as miraculous, but they knew stories of other composers who knew nothing of music except how to write it. Time and again, by way of encouragement, people invoked the legends of Irving Berlin. All that he was ever able to do was pick out a melody line, and yet look how that gift had served him! All that was required, I told myself when I despaired of my lack of skills, was the humility to be a musical beginner. Beautiful melodies came to me, and that was a mystery that did not need to be solved, only enjoyed. When Emma played *Magellan* back to me, I often was unable to believe that I was the source of its melodies. It seemed far grander than anything I could devise. Yet it knocked on my door near daily.

With *Magellan* unfolding at the living room piano, the dining room became the work site for *Walking in This World*. Linda would arrive laden with pages. She would have a list of inserts needing to be written. I set up an IBM Selectric typewriter on the dining room table and methodically typed out what Linda felt was required. "It's all your years of training as a journalist," Linda would tease me. Grateful for her help, I was eager to do just what she required. Writer's block was a luxury we could ill afford.

Shaped by both of our sensibilities, the book began to take form. Its essays were more dense than those of *The Artist's Way*. Its issues were those encountered by artists further down the trail. Often I felt I was reporting straight from the front. I was trying to clarify the very issues I was grappling with myself in my work on *Magellan* and *The Medium at Large*.

"Just tell the truth. Just be accurate," I would lecture myself. A page at a time, a week at a time, the essays unfolded. "Try to say how it is. Exactly," I would chide myself. My team of readers chimed in their considerations. I wrote some more. After three grueling months, we had a book.

Perched as we were on Riverside Drive, it was all too easy for Emma and me to feel we were floating in a world of our own, a world made up of books and music. New York was right at our doorstep, but it seemed far away. It fell to our friend Bruce Pomahac to entice us out into the flow of life. It was Richard Rodgers's centennial year, and there were many special events all throughout the city to which Pomahac invited me and Emma. Finished with my "big" creativity book, I found myself still eager to write, and so I began a "small" creativity book, *The Sound of Paper*.

Focusing on life in our little neighborhood and on our adventures out with Pomahac, the little book took shape quickly. It was exciting to be writing about real life and not about creative theory. But, of course, real life for me was studded with thoughts about creativity. Outside the window, Riverside Park was turning from winter into spring. I myself felt a sense of hope and renewal. My medication seemed to be working to keep me stable. It seemed miraculous that a tiny dose of Navane could bring me such safety and relief, but it seemed to. So far, I appeared not to suffer from side effects. It didn't impede my writing, and for that I was doubly grateful.

May brought a festive fullness to the trees in Riverside Park. One more time Emma and I packed the car and set off with our dogs on the drive cross-country to Taos. For Emma it was a reluctant pilgrimage. For me it was a stubborn obsession. This time we went Residence Inn to Residence Inn, grateful that they were dog friendly and clean. I was eager to reach Taos and to resume what I still obstinately thought of as my life there. I missed my friends

Larry and Rhonda, but above all I missed the beauty of Taos, which seemed to me to be a friend in itself.

"We're in Ohio," "We're in Nebraska," "We're in Colorado," I would nightly report in to Domenica, who was now splitting her time between coasts, going west for pilot season and east for work in the theater. Playwright-director Richard Nelson cast her as one of his leads in *Franny's Way*, a play which was put on both off-Broadway and at Los Angeles's Geffen Theater. Domenica seemed to live on JetBlue. We spoke to each other from airport lounges and cabs.

"Let me know when you get there, Mom. Are the dogs okay?" Domenica asked.

"They're fine. They love the drive." And they did, lounging atop sheepskin throws, staring out at the scenery.

This year the old adobe house seemed less welcoming—as if it resented our long absence. It took us the better part of a week to put the house in order. My aging neighbor, Bessie Ortega, stopped by to warn us that Taos was suffering from an extended drought and that we should use our water sparingly. We soon learned that the drought was an omnipresent fact of life. The valley's very air seemed dry and lifeless. A constant low wind was an added irritant.

After our initial flurry of housekeeping shores, Emma and I found ourselves restless, irritable, and discontent. We began to take long daily drives. I would dictate impressions to Emma as I drove. These impressions, sharp as a paper's edge, became the second half of *The Sound of Paper*. The long drought spoke to me eloquently of the artist's creative difficulties. I tried to write of the courage and stamina—the sheer grit—that it took for an artist to sustain an artist's life.

One more time Bob McDonald was summering at the Taos School of Music. Many starry nights Emma and I drove up the winding canyon to the Taos Ski Valley. There, in the Alpine coziness of the Hotel St. Bernard, we would enjoy a gourmet meal cooked by Jean Meyer and an after-dinner concert provided by McDonald and his students. More and more, the music school seemed to be our habitat. Less and less often, we found ourselves a part of the year-round Taos community. We were becoming summer people.

The first week of August marked the end of the Taos School of Music. Unexpectedly, I began to feel shaky. My restlessness became a nameless apprehension. Sleep was difficult, then elusive. I called back to New York to talk with my psychopharmacologist. She suggested that I increase my Navane dose. My friend Larry abruptly suggested that I get out of Taos, that I make the drive back to New York early.

"New York seems to be good for your stability," he said correctly.

"Get back to New York and more structure," Sonia chimed in.

And so Emma and I packed the car and the dogs and set out on the long drive back. Once again we went Residence Inn to Residence Inn, grateful for familiar surroundings. True to Larry's guess, I did feel better heading back to New York and a more structured life than I had in Taos. Secretly I was afraid of one more time having a breakdown, and I wanted to be near as much help as I could muster.

If I was coming back to New York for security, that is not what I found there. Instead, I discovered that my New York landlady wanted to move back early and that we would need to find a new place in which to nest. Shaky to begin with, I found this prospect frightening. I was worried we wouldn't find a building that would allow our dogs. I was worried, period. Emma, ever more optimistic than I, thought that the chance to move was an ideal opportunity to fine-tune how we were living.

"Let's move farther downtown, more in the midst of things," she suggested. "Let's see if we can get city views instead of country views so that we really know that we are living in New York."

"Don't remind me," I moaned. If Emma loved New York and thrived in it, I was still scared by the city. Still, Emma's enthusiasm for the move was contagious.

I called Renee Chase, the broker who had found us the place on Riverside Drive. I must have sounded panicked, because she went immediately into a calming mode. "Don't worry. There are apartments to be had, and some of those apartments, some very nice ones, take dogs. I'll get right on it."

And she did get right on it, phoning us back almost instantly. "I think I have found a place you should look at," she said. "It needs some fixing up, but they'll do that if you commit to it. It's worth a look."

I had made a list: "Large, bright, and sunny; city views, dog friendly, separate living wings for Julia and for Emma; convenient to Central Park, room enough for an arranging room and a writing room, good kitchen space, high enough ceilings, close to public transportation; quiet, doorman." My list seemed unobtainable to me. I simply wanted too many things, some of them contradictory and expensive. I was, for example, asking to be right in the thick of things and yet still have quiet.

"Let's look at what Renee has," Emma cajoled me.

"All right." What I wanted to do was hide under the covers. Instead, I let Emma lure me into a cab. The address was twenty-five blocks south.

The lobby of the building looked shabby. The elevator lacked charm. The door to our prospective home was chipped and dented. Inside, the fixtures were hanging by bare wires and the walls were scuffed dark gray with wear and tear.

"I don't think so," I told Emma in the claustrophobic elevator.

"No way," Emma exclaimed.

"Give it a chance," said Renee Chase. "It has potential."

"Wait a minute," I said, mentally replacing the fixtures and painting the walls. The kitchen would need a complete overhaul, but it was more spacious than most New York kitchens. There were large windows and wonderful views. The dingy rooms were actually light and airy. The bedrooms were, as I had wished, in two separate wings, necessary if either Emma or myself acquired a boyfriend. The apartment was half a block off Central Park and located at the building's rear, far more quiet than the front.

"Emma, this place has possibilities," I said, already thinking to myself, "We'll take it."

Now it was Emma's turn to imagine the place transformed by our possessions. Walking through the apartment a room at a time, we began to arrange the furniture. While less formal than our Riverside Drive digs, the apartment had everything we needed and everything I had asked for. I could practically hear my sober mentors chuckling about "let go and let God."

"I think we should take it," Emma said.

We took it and our lives immediately changed for the better. On our very first morning in our new home, an eagle landed on the fire escape outside my window.

"Emma, Benny! Come look!" I called out, and together the three of us peered out our eleventh-floor window at the magnificent bird. It perched calmly, turning its majestic head from side to side, as if taking in the view. My years in Taos had been filled with eagles, but spotting one in New York felt like a magical good omen—even when I learned that the Park Service routinely released the birds into nearby Central Park.

Emma now lived nearly next door to her closest friend. They met for coffee almost daily. As for me, an old friend and very gifted director suddenly surfaced in New York. As associate creative director at the Denver Center twenty years earlier, Randy Myler knew me as a playwright as well as an author. Like John Newland, he liked my alcoholism play, *Four Roses*. He quickly staged an excellent reading. That reading convinced me and Emma that he might be the man we were looking for to work on our musical *The Medium at Large*. We had a reading slated for March at the York Theatre—another introduction courtesy of Max—and we needed a good director.

Once he agreed to work with us, Myler was a stern taskmaster. Tony-nominated himself, he knew what it took to make a solid script—and what it took was a lot of work. We met once a week at the Big Cup, a coffee shop near his home in Chelsea. There, amid booming music and loud conversations, we hammered out our script.

"Why do you need this scene change?" Myler would say. "I think you could just cross-fade." A veteran dramaturg from his years at the Denver Center for the Performing Arts, Myler knew exactly how to make a script both lean and playable. Under his hand, our script lost twenty pages and gained a sense of momentum and velocity. As a playwright, I was relieved to be out of the realm of the imagination and into the realm of the actual. Emma and I had talent, but Myler had experience. For us it was a shift away from "this could play" into "this does play." We were elated.

Myler's expertise was just what we needed. Our creative idyll was soon interrupted, however. It was time for another book tour, this one for *Walking in This World.*

"Will you be okay, Mom?" Domenica wondered.

"I hope so," I told her, and I did hope that while we were on the road my Navane would "hold." I thought of the drug as a sort of wall between me and madness. Sometimes, especially when I was overtired or overstimulated—two regular features of a book tour—I feared that wall would not hold. We would soon find out.

The tour opened in Los Angeles, and that is where Emma took a catastrophic fall. It was our second day out, and she went on an errand to a market, where she slipped on a pool of water, shattering her kneecap. The injury was far more serious than we at first thought. Armed with a cane, Emma continued to hobble through the book tour. She took Tylenol for the pain and was determined to carry on. I have a very clear memory of her dressed to the nines in a silver silk floor-length dress for an awards presentation. *Science of Mind* magazine had chosen me Person of the Year, but it was Emma who deserved a citation as she limped gamely to her place. This she continued through twenty days and ten cities. For once she was the identified patient and I the helper.

For my part, I was seized by an idea and began, longhand, to write a novel I would call *Mozart's Ghost.* A romantic comedy set in New York, the novel became a joyous obsession. I wrote it in hotel rooms, in airport lounges, in the back of limousines. One notebook grew to two and then three. I read it aloud to Emma as I went. The novel was lighthearted, and I am sure that undertaking it helped us to relieve the psychic pain of Emma's injury.

"Then what happens?" she would ask and, like Scheherazade, I would continue the story.

"And then what happens?"

"I'll have to write some more!"

Arriving back in New York, I had the rough draft of a novel. Emma, on the other hand, was faced squarely with the seriousness of her injury. Dr. Barley one more time swung into action, referring her to a specialist, who broke the bad news. It was no mere fall. Her leg was severely damaged. Her knee would require multiple surgeries and lengthy rehabilitation. They needed to operate as soon as possible, early in December.

Waiting for her hospitalization, Emma focused obsessively on both *Magellan* and *Tinseltown*. Tragedies felt cathartic to her at the time. She arranged piece after piece. Like me, she blocked anxiety with overwork. Writing flat-out, I finished a second draft of *Mozart's Ghost*. I was ready to show it to readers Gerard, Ed Towle, Bob McDonald, and Linda Kahn. I yearned for a little romantic comedy in my own life, and I thoroughly enjoyed putting some of it onto the page, but would readers take to it?

"I love it," said Gerard.

"This is good," said Ed Towle.

"I enjoyed it," said Bob McDonald.

"I don't get it," said Linda Kahn.

What Linda Kahn didn't get was the basic premise of the novel, that two shy people could meet, fall in love and drunkenly into bed, and then have reservations about commitment. Was I crazy to have concocted such a scenario?

"Maybe she's never had a dysfunctional relationship?" joked Ed Towle.

"Maybe she's never had a drink," joked Gerard.

"How old is she?" asked Bob McDonald.

Still, I knew Linda's braininess too well to simply shrug off her comments. Instead, I dug back into the book, working to shape my characters more clearly. Drafts three, four, and five followed in fast succession. When I got to draft six, I was ready to show Linda again.

"Now I get it!" she shot back.

I gave the book to my agent to put up for sale. I gave it to Domenica to adapt to screenplay form. She had optioned a novel, *Saturn's Return to New York*, and I had to wait for her to finish that script before she could begin on mine. While I was proud that she was initiating work of her own, I waited impatiently.

Emma was scheduled for surgery December 2. Her brother Ben came to stay with us again to oversee her operation and help her in the days that followed. A jazz violinist, Ben was a welcome presence in our house. He hadn't been there two days before I was on fire again with yet another book idea, *Letters to a Young Artist*, for which he was indisputably the muse.

It was tonic to me having a young artist in the house. He was full of questions, and I found that I had some answers I wanted to share with him and other young artists. The book quickly took on form and size. With Emma bedridden and on pain medication, Ben's company was reassuring. He gave Emma a sense of safety and he gave me a sense of hope. As a threesome, we were an oddly workable household. Perhaps because I had grown up in a large, creative family, I enjoyed having a house full of life.

At Christmas, with Emma still on crutches, we all traveled to Maine to visit with their parents. They greeted us with open arms, plying us with candies and holiday treats. Rob Lively is a theologian. Martha Lively is a computer scientist. Conversations with them are always spirited and interesting. We stayed through the New Year. My bedroom was upstairs under the snowy eaves. Outside my window, birch trees glistened with ice. Although I said nothing of this to anyone, I was quietly auditioning Maine versus Taos.

Back in New York again, it was time to prepare for our upcoming reading at the York. Now we redoubled our meetings with Randy Myler. Seated around our dining room table, we read the script aloud.

"That's not a good enough button," Myler would say, pointing out a weakness in closing a scene.

"I like it," I might protest.

"Well, it doesn't work." He would win the argument.

A director with years of experience under his belt, Myler was for us a stubbornly sure-footed guide. Under his hand, the script became crisper and more fast-paced. We hired Kim Grigsby, a veteran Broadway conductor, to be our musical director, and that allowed us to listen to our score with fresh ears. Now all we needed was actors—but that proved to be a cliffhanger. Myler wanted to use Broadway pros, who always seemed to be in high demand. No one would commit until the last minute. Emma and I were nervous but excited. "Hold out for the best," Myler would tell us. This was good but difficult advice. Over a long weekend, with the reading nearly upon us, the casting came together. Myler's stubbornness was vindicated. Our cast was strong.

The York Theatre is dedicated to developing new musicals, and they had a ready audience for ours. Emma and I sat in the very back row. The show whirled by nearly in a blur. Our jokes got laughs. Our songs got applause. The audience seemed to be with us moment by moment. Then it was over. Emma and I stood in the theater lobby receiving comments and compliments. Max's friend James Morgan, the York's creative director, was pleased, and so were we.

"Now what?" some people asked, and we asked ourselves the same thing. The answer was that it was time for a backer's audition. A backer's audition was a major jump and not one that we could take immediately. "No one" was in town over the summer, we were told. With spring upon us, it was time to head back west to Taos, where we would have more than enough thinking time to consider our options.

This time Taos welcomed us like a spurned lover. The old adobe house felt unmanageable. We had plumbing problems, heating problems, and, worst of all, bugs. The earwig is the cockroach of the West. A succession of expensive experts passed through the property. We decided to rehab an old outbuilding. Our absentee landlordship was clearly taking its toll. As much as I hated to face it, I no longer really lived in Taos. That fact made it feel all the more beautiful. Stubbornly I clung to my past. I reached out to cherished friends: Larry Lonergan, James Nave, Crawford Tall, and Peter Ziminsky.

My closest girlfriend, Rhonda Flemming, had one month earlier suffered the loss of her longtime lover. His death by heart attack was sudden and unexpected. She was catapulted deeply into grief. There was little that I felt I could do for her except take long daily walks with her. I hoped that the land itself could prove to be a healer. There were no easy answers, and in attempting to alleviate Rhonda's despair, I found myself writing to her. Every day I would sit down and write Rhonda a prayer. She would read them and say that they gave her solace. Gathered together, those prayers became a slender volume, *Answered Prayers.* I had written a book behind my own back.

Meanwhile, my own prayers felt unheard. I loved Taos but again found myself frightened and uncomfortable there. Except when actually walking or writing, I was apprehensive, and it was a feeling

I now knew all too well. My Navane defense seemed like a very weak one.

"Mom, are you okay?" Domenica one more time asked me. Not wanting to scare her, I steered the conversation back toward her adventures.

"I am afraid I am getting sick again," I told Emma.

This announcement frightened but did not surprise her. She got on the phone to New York. It was suggested that I increase my medication. I did this with reluctance. I hated the fragility that the medicine implied. Then, too, there was the fact that Navane could cause dangerous side effects and that the larger the dose, the graver the risk.

"Be careful," Peter warned me.

"Watch yourself," echoed Crawford.

Beset by depression, which the Navane did not really address, I turned my hand to some of the darker passages of *Magellan*. Emma, too, found herself drawn to melancholic melodies. She wrote a harrowing song where Magellan is lost at sea. The metaphor was not lost on us.

"I think we should go back to New York early," Emma proposed.

"I hate to give up," I answered.

"You can't afford another breakdown," Emma countered. "Especially out here." To Emma, New York meant safety and good doctors. I listened to her reluctantly. Then I decided to go to Larry Lonergan for a reading.

"Go back to New York," Larry advised me, just as he had the summer before. "Pack your things and get out while you still have your health. You've got good doctors in New York and the structure back there seems to suit you. Go."

"Larry says I should go," I told Emma, who heard the news with clear relief.

"Let's pack the house so we can rent it out," I suggested. I hated the thought of renting the house, but it seemed only sensible. Emma set to packing with her friend Kathy Walsh, who came in from Texas to help us out. I stayed out of the way, trying to write and work on *Magellan*, but despite my medication my apprehension kept growing. Daily, I became more distressed. Domenica worried. So did my sister Libby and my childhood friend Lynnie Lane. Everyone feared another breakdown. I listened reluctantly to their fears. I did not want to leave, yet knew I had to. Emma and Kathy put our personal belongings into storage. Stripped of our oil paintings and bric-a-brac, the house stood ready for rental.

"It's time," Emma told me.

"It's time," I agreed.

Once more we packed the little SUV with our work, our clothes, and the sheepskin throws for our dogs. We pulled across the little wooden bridge that marked our property. It was a long drive back to New York. We anticipated difficulty but quickly found the opposite. By the time we reached Colorado, we were laughing, telling each other jokes, giddy at our timely departure.

"Maybe there is something bad about Taos for me," I reluctantly admitted to Emma.

"Give me New York," Emma answered. We headed east.

11.

The drive cross-country did seem a drive back to sanity. I decreased my medication as we drove. When we arrived back in the verdant East, I found myself feeling more grounded. Precarious as I might have felt, it was hard not to be excited. An old college friend had resurfaced just as we left for Taos. His name was Jack Hofsiss, and he was a distinguished director. Our show *Magellan* was of interest to him. We were thrilled to have his support. Again, New York seemed to offer us exactly what we really needed. Larry phoned us to say he had detected a "natural resonance" with a new player. We told him about Jack. "That's him," Larry snapped. "He wants a challenge."

Magellan was nothing if not a challenge. It was a larger-than-life undertaking. Divided into seven sections, the story unfolded through sixty-five distinct pieces of music. There were sailors, sailors' wives, storms at sea, mutinies, starvation, and eventually triumph. Magellan was a man obsessed, a visionary who struck out to wrest his destiny from the gods. At no point could he pause to consider the odds against him. He had to stomach his fears and simply sail on.

Working on *Magellan*, there could be no looking back. Piece by piece, like a great boat, the work had to be built. I would hear heroic melodies. Emma would supply harmonies. Sometimes the story was so harrowing that it was difficult to write. Two hundred fifty-seven men began the voyage. Seventeen survived. Scurvy and mutiny beset the ships. They suffered starvation crossing the Pacific. Writing music to match these events was an emotional challenge—and one I often felt too fragile to accomplish.

This was when I would follow Max's advice, sending up a prayer to Oscar Hammerstein II. He had written *Show Boat*, an outsize piece of work. He was no stranger to gargantuan tasks. "Just keep on," I seemed to hear. One more day I would go to the piano, picking out the melodies that came to my ear.

"What are you writing?" friends would routinely ask me. I hesitated to say, "An opera." Who was I, an untrained musician, to be trying such a grandiose project? And yet the project itself seemed to call to me inexorably. Like Magellan's wife, I was obsessed with his voyage. I picked out more and more melodies.

As fall turned to winter, Emma and I kept our shoulders to the grindstone. The vast skeleton of *Magellan* was beginning to take on flesh and sinew. For the first time, we dared play it all the way through for Jack Hofsiss. His enthusiasm was heartening and contagious. "I love it," he would say—followed by a list of changes he thought we might want to consider. Hofsiss's changes were often challenging. He picked at lyrics, insisting on accuracy and specificity. He demanded that we etch a clear picture of each character.

What did they want? Would they get it? Under his hand, the story took on shape and symmetry. "I'm a bit of a task-driver," he would comment mildly—only to set a further set of tasks. Emma and I felt lucky to have his direction. I prayed to Oscar Hammerstein II and to John Newland to have the creativity necessary to execute them.

Magellan took up the mornings. In the afternoons I found myself writing about the lessons it was teaching me, lessons of endurance and patience. *Faith and Will*, I titled the book I found myself shaping. It had to do with finding courage in the face of doubt. As for myself, I felt I needed to find courage. I had long known that the medication I was taking could cause serious side effects. Now it was causing them. I began experiencing an involuntary tic.

"You're doing it again," Emma would tell me. Trying to make light of it, we nicknamed the tic Tah-dah, as in, "You're doing Tah-dah."

"If we don't change drugs, the tic could become permanent," warned my psychopharmacologist.

"I am afraid to change drugs," I told her. I trusted Navane to keep me out of the locked ward.

"I am afraid you have to," she insisted.

I sought a second opinion and met with even tougher news. I learned that I had already remained on Navane far too long. Even my lowest dosage was dangerous. Reluctantly I decided to change doctors. I would have to change drugs or risk a permanent and disfiguring disability.

"But how do we do it?" I nervously asked my new doctor.

"We do it slowly and carefully," came the answer.

My drug withdrawal from Navane was handled by crisscrossing me over onto the new drug. Every week I took a little less Navane and a little more of something called Risperdal. My sanity seemed stable enough, but my weight zoomed up by twenty pounds. I found the sudden weight gain terrifying.

"Oh, yes. That can happen," said my doctor. Focused on my psyche and not on my physique, he was unconcerned. I, for my part, was very concerned. My clothes were tight. I found it embarrassing to stand up and teach in public. I felt frumpy.

"You look fine," Gerard told me reassuringly. "You have a beautiful face."

"I don't feel fine," I answered him.

And I didn't feel fine. In addition to the extra physical weight I was carrying, I began to carry a psychic weight. For no apparent reason I felt cut off from spiritual contact. Faith became a concept instead of an experience. Writing about faith, I found myself writing about the dark night of the soul. I seemed to have stumbled into difficult country.

"Just don't drink," I reminded myself as my depression deepened. Liquor stores were starting to glow. Bars winked at me. I could taste scotch on my tongue. "There's nothing going on that a drink is going to make better," I told myself. At night I would crave sugar, a craving I medicated with fruit. It was better than drinking, but I became awfully sick of strawberries.

"I'm high-strung," I complained to Emma. "I feel like drinking."

"But you're not drinking," she would point out.

I sought out the counsel of someone sober fifteen years longer than I. I explained my discomfort and met with some sharp reality.

"No one ever said it would be comfortable to be sober," my mentor pointed out. "It's great when it is comfortable, but that doesn't really mean we should expect it. Life is stressful. Anyone who tells you that it's not is a fool—or living a life I don't understand. Just stay sober. Don't take your emotional temperature so often. Work with another alcoholic. Get out of yourself a little. That always helps. Some times are simply not comfortable."

It wasn't difficult to find another alcoholic to work with. My long years of sobriety were impressive to people. My experience, strength, and hope were valued. Listening to another's problems, I found myself less focused on mine. I was able to finish *Faith and Will* and to begin writing new essays, this time based in New York rather than Taos. I was still fighting with depression and I still craved a drink. Both of these factors emerged in my writing. My essays seemed to be about how to keep on keeping on, the power of persistence, which all artists sorely need. Writing daily, I myself searched for stamina. Everything felt uphill. What I needed, I thought, was a dose of good news. That isn't what I got. Instead, I got a solid round of artist's blues.

"An editor was crazy about your *Mozart's Ghost*," my agent told me, "but she wasn't able to get it through committee."

I had heard of this phenomenon from other writers. Increasingly, decisions about what to publish are being made not only on literary merit but on market potential as well. If a book doesn't look like a big seller—in other words, if it doesn't look a lot like something that has been done before—a writer may have a hard time placing it.

"Another editor loved your novel," my agent phoned me again to say. "Now we have to wait to see if he can get it through his editorial board."

And so we waited, and when the news came, again it wasn't good. "It didn't make it past marketing," I was told.

Two more times my agent phoned with "good" but tentative

news. Despite myself, I began to feel the odds were stacked against me. Maybe my book was too quirky, maybe it didn't bear a strong enough resemblance to previous winners. Discouraged, my agent threw up her hands. "Maybe you need to look at the book one more time," she told me. "We keep getting so close!"

So I took my novel back and read it. I still liked the characters. I still liked the plot. Surely there must be something to be fleshed out or altered? I couldn't figure out what. I sent the book back to Ed Towle, back to Gerard, and back to Linda Kahn. The notes that came back from them were minimal. "We think it's fine," came the consensus. Frustrated, I sent the book to Domenica, who was working on her screenplay. To my rue and delight, she came back with detailed notes, notes that seemed right to me.

I decided to execute Domenica's notes. Ever since she was a child, she had the knack of seeing what was wrong with a piece of art. I had often joked to Martin that by crossing a director and a writer, we had emerged with a critic. We had certainly emerged with someone with fine critical faculties. I found Domenica's notes picky—"Virgo notes," she called them—nearly microscopic in their focus. They were probably just what I needed. Reading the book after implementing them, I had to admit I thought it was subtly better. My agent thought so too. We put the book back on the market, hoping again for the best.

Emma and I were hoping for the best on another front as well. It was time to put up our backer's audition for *The Medium at Large*. We had planned it for mid-January but found casting difficult, as people took extended winter breaks. On Myler's advice, we re-scheduled for February, planning to use our "extra" time to keep on tinkering. We were at a dangerous point, however, the point where we would be changing things just for the sake of change, not improvement. An artist needs to know when to stop, and so, restless as we were, we forced ourselves to stop tinkering. The show we had in hand was the show we had.

One more time we hired Kim Grigsby to be our musical director. One more time Myler swung into action on casting. Emma made lists and more lists. We cast a wide net of invitations. A backer's audition costs about fifteen thousand dollars, and we wanted to do only one. At Myler's suggestion we hired a woman whose sole job was to ensure that backers actually attend. I was teaching a weekly class at the New York Open Center, and I extended an invitation to all of my students to come and see our work—wanting to be an example of my creative tool kit.

This time we put on two performances, not one. On both occasions the theater was jammed. To our delight we had an even stronger cast than we had before. The audience laughed and clapped, sometimes interrupting the show with its applause. Emma and I sat in the back row again, trying to be objective but finding it hard.

"They really like it!" I hissed to Emma.

"Yes, I think so," she whispered back.

Standing in the lobby after the performances, Emma and I received our compliments and encouragement. Only one person voiced a sour note. "Too much music!" Talking among ourselves, we didn't really see how the show could have gone any better. Exiting the theater, Jack Hofsiss told us, "I didn't like it. I loved it. I want to direct it, but I don't want to step on Myler's toes."

This was more than we had hoped for. Earlier, Myler, who was busy writing his own shows, had said to us, "I will take the show as far as I can, but then someone will come along who is perfect for it and then you should go with him." When we told Myler about Hofsiss, he was excited for us, even exuberant. "I admire Jack," he told us. "He's perfect for your show. If Jack will direct it, he absolutely has my blessing to take over from here. This is an opportunity you can't afford to miss."

To Myler's eye, we had scored exactly the win we needed. To our own way of thinking, we were still missing the backing of a real producer or theater. In the days following our reading, we kept waiting for the phone to ring. It didn't ring. Emma fell into a depression. I quickly followed suit. So much work! So much money! So little feedback! At two weeks and counting, our friend Bruce Pomahac took mercy on us and invited us to a celebratory lunch. Once he had us seated across from him, he said, "This is the hard part, the waiting-for-something-to-happen part. Now you have joined the club. Stephen Sondheim and everyone else is in the same boat you are."

Pomahac's words snapped us out of our self-pity. Musical theater was simply tough. We determined to be tough enough to take it. But what should we do?

"You're lucky you have multiple projects," Bruce told us. "Just go back to work."

For the moment there was nothing more to be done on *The Medium*, but there was a lot of work left on *Magellan*, and that is where we focused our efforts. Once a week we met with Hofsiss. He continued to suggest dramatic changes. Under his guidance the drama in *Magellan* became ever sharper. But we still needed the backing of a producer or a theater.

"We need a miracle," I told Emma. "We've had our share but we need more."

In the meanwhile, I wrote and taught. Emma orchestrated and

arranged. As my sober mentors adjured me, I tried to put first things first, taking life one day at a time. It was difficult. "Don't drink five minutes before the miracle," one elder chivvied me.

I finished teaching my twelve-week class at the New York Open Center, and on the last night a tall, beautiful blonde, Barbara Roberts, approached me. She handed me an envelope, saying, "I thought this might be of interest to you." Enclosed I found her very impressive résumé and a letter offering to help with *The Medium at Large.* She didn't really want to be a theatrical producer, her letter said, but she didn't mind acting like one on our behalf. She thought we might be a good match with the Vineyard Theatre, origin of the hot Tony Award–winning show *Avenue Q.*

Emma and I pinched ourselves. We were delighted to have help with our show, and so we said yes to Barbara Roberts. She knew Jack Hofsiss's work and she thought that he, too, might be of interest to the Vineyard. Talking with Hofsiss, we discovered that he thought the Vineyard was a perfect venue for *The Medium.* All that remained now was for them to like the show. We waited on pins and needles while they read. Just as we were at our wit's end, Barbara phoned: they liked the show. In fact, they loved it. While they couldn't offer us a production, they could offer us their backing for a full-scale reading. They wanted to support us in any way they could. This included networking for us and matching us up with a proper agent. We were thrilled. As I glanced at Emma in our first meeting with them, my eyes smarted with tears of relief.

Accustomed to life as outsiders, we now found ourselves on an inside track. The Vineyard was a name to be conjured with. At Hofsiss's suggestion, we switched gears from *Magellan* to *The Medium.* He had some tinkering in mind, and we began to work with him as we had with Myler to fine-tune our script and score. We soon found that if his opinions on *Magellan* had seemed helpful, his opinions on *The Medium* were even more so.

"Now, girls," he lectured us. "I don't ever want you to change anything or go along with anything that you feel violates the show in any way. Having said that, I do have my thoughts."

His thoughts included a new opening number and a new romantic duet. Emma and I happily set to work writing the tunes. Hofsiss believed in the music part of musical comedy. "Give me a little more. Make it a little longer," he would say. Or "This song needs to be funny. Find me a word that rhymes with 'crusader,' means 'nadir,' but is funnier."

The score wasn't all that came under his scrutiny. The book took some surprising new twists at his suggestion. I had written one spinsterish sister and one repentant floozie. "Repentance isn't funny," Hofsiss scolded me. He wanted his characters stubbornly willful, sinners to the very end, and he was right. That made them far funnier. "Think of Ado Annie from *Oklahoma!*" he urged me. "She never repents."

It was a relief to be funny. Our work sessions with Hofsiss felt like play, and yet the show was shaping up nicely. We wrote an overture. We wrote a new duet. When I spoke with Bernice, she would chuckle with delight at how everything was unfolding. She thoroughly approved of anything having to do with music, and with both *Magellan* and *The Medium at Large* on the boil, she hoped that my temperament would lighten up a little—and not a moment too soon.

Rickety and beset by mood swings as I altered my medication, I suffered from repeated bouts of depression. Everything was fine—but I wasn't. Each day was a steep uphill climb. I had no patience for my own temperament. My dark moods angered me. One day I pressed my hand to my forehead and sighed dramatically, "Darkness!" Unfortunately for me—or fortunately—Emma overheard my exclamation and she found it hilarious.

"Darkness?" she teased me.

"I know. Everything is really going well, isn't it?" I asked.

"I think it is!"

After that, "darkness" became a household joke, and I needed jokes more than ever now. Once more it was time to accept the things I cannot change; change the things I can. The new medication caused the same involuntary tic as the old. We would need to change a third time, my psychopharmacologist said. The tic was simply too dangerous to ignore.

"What would happen if I tried going without medication again?" I asked him.

"Not a good idea. You might last about two months, but then it would be bad—and we know what bad means."

I did know what bad meant, and I didn't want to go through it again—or put Emma and Domenica through it again. Carefully monitored and medicated, my biochemistry was bearable—and far better than another breakdown. By using Morning Pages, Artist Dates, and Walks, I often could keep my depression at bay. It would lie in wait for me each morning as I woke, but I could—and did—dig my way out. If I wasn't happy, if I still suffered from "darkness," at least I was functional, and that went a long way toward making things better. Functional, I could write prose. I could teach. Functional, I could show up at the piano and meet my melodies there. Beautiful music seemed to be born despite my temperament. "Good enough," I told myself. "One day at a time." Blessedly, my obsession to drink was lifting.

So, once more we tinkered with my medicine. Now I was given

two differing drugs to take, Abilify in the morning and a low dose of Risperdal in the afternoon, soon to be discontinued. "Try to be grateful we have the medicines," my psychopharmacologist cajoled me. "Think of how it was before we had them." I thought of my parents and their recurrent breakdowns.

"I don't want to think about that," I told him. I took the resented medicines.

I hated the regime but had to admit that within a week I felt subtly better. Evidently my malaise had been biochemical after all. That was certainly what my doctor thought. I thought perhaps it was also the stress of long-postponed decisions. To wit: I lived in New York but still yearned for Taos.

"I think Taos is just a dream for you," Domenica weighed in. "It's never delivered what it promised. "

"You were never happy in Taos," my closest sober mentor crisply informed me.

"I think you're romancing a drink." This time the warning brought me up short.

"How can you even think about Taos?" Emma wanted to know. "That place nearly killed you. It's not safe there for you. You need doctors. You need medicine. You need structure. It's a matter of life and death."

"It's the beauty. I miss the beauty," I explained.

"There's beauty in New York," Emma lectured me. "There's beauty in Central Park, and you can go there every day."

"I can," I admitted. I began to pray for guidance.

One morning I woke with the answer: let go of Taos. Accept the fact that my time there was over. Keep my friends. Keep my memories, but move on. I held this answer to the light. I expected to feel a wince of pain as I thought of giving up my home. Instead, I felt oddly at peace. Maybe there really was safety for me in New York.

"Bloom where you are planted," the sober elders advised.

I understood suddenly that by relinquishing Taos, I was placing myself squarely in the hands of God. "Build with me and do with me what you will," I had prayed—and this was evidently God's will for me.

In New York I had many students to teach. I was an artist among other artists, one more soul striving to make my way in the great sea of souls. And further, in New York I was one more sober alcoholic in a great river of sober alcoholics. My story was one more story amid many. And that story wasn't over. I wasn't at an end. Instead, I was at a beginning. I could add my voice to a choir of voices. I could try.

"Just try. That's all you need to do," I repeat to myself as I grab for a jacket. Tiger Lily, my cocker spaniel, runs to get her leash. Her enthusiasm is contagious. I catch myself grinning. We are headed out to Central Park, where the flowering trees are at the height of their bloom: crimson, ivory, fuchsia. We will walk along the cinder bridle paths amid the elders and the lovers.

About the Author

Julia Cameron has been an active artist for more than thirty years. She is the author of twenty-two books, fiction and nonfiction, including *The Artist's Way, Walking in This World, The Vein of Gold, The Right to Write,* and *The Sound of Paper,* her best-selling works on the creative process. A novelist, playwright, songwriter, and poet, she has multiple credits in theater, film, and television.